MagicImage Filmbooks
Presents

THE WOLF MAN

(The Original 1941 Shooting Script)

Edited & Compiled
by
Philip Riley

Foreword by Evelyn Ankers
Introduction by Curt Siodmak

Production Background
by
Gregory Wm. Mank
Philip Riley
George Turner

MagicImage
FILMBOOKS

UNIVERSAL FILMSCRIPTS SERIES
CLASSIC HORROR FILMS - VOLUME 12

THE WOLF MAN

FIRST EDITION

Published by MagicImage Filmbooks, 740 S. 6th Avenue, Absecon NJ 08201

Library of Congress Cataloging-in Publication Data:

MagicImage Filmbooks presents The wolf man : (the original 1941
    shooting script) / edited & compiled by Philip Riley ; forward by
    Evelyn Ankers ; introduction by Curt Siodmak ; character make-up by
    Jack Pierce ; commentary by Lon Chaney Jr. ; production background
    by Gregory Wm. Mank, Philip Riley & George Turner.
        p. cm. -- (universal filmscripts series. Classic horror
films ; v. 12)
   ISBN 1-882127-21-8 : $19.95
    1. Wolf man (Motion picture) I. Riley, Philip J., 1948-
II. MagicImage Filmbooks (Firm) III. Title: MagicImage Filmbooks
presents The wolf man. IV. Title: Wolf man. V. Series.
PN1997.W5983M35 1993
791.43'72--dc20   93-32968
                                CIP

This edition published in the USA by:
BearManor Media • 1317 Edgewater Drive #110 • Orlando, Florida 32804
www.bearmanormedia.com

Hardcover: ISBN 978-1-62933-599-5
Paperback: ISBN 978-1-62933-598-8

The purpose of this series is the preservation of the art of writing for the screen. Rare books have long been a source of enjoyment and an investment for the serious collector, and even in limited printings there usually were a few thousand produced. Scripts however, numbered only 50 at the most, and we are proud to present them in their original form. Some will be final shooting scripts and some earlier drafts, so that students, libraries, archives and film-lovers might, for the first time, study them in their original form. In producing these volumes, we hope that the unique art of screenplay writing will be preserved for future generations.

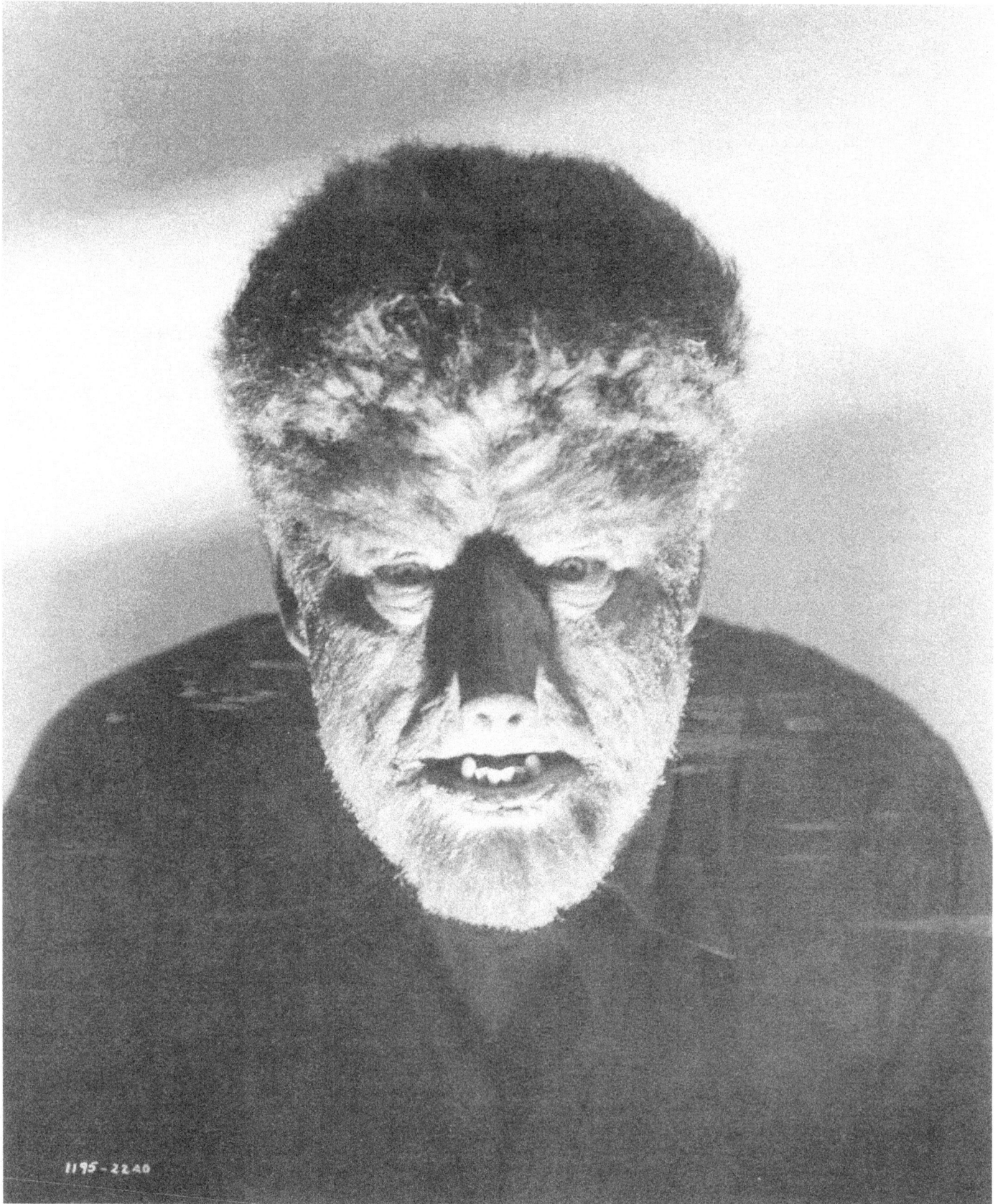

MAGICIMAGE PRODUCTIONS

Publisher
Michael D. Stein
Chief Editor
Philip Riley
Production Manager
Christopher Mock
Art Director
Marisa Donato
Artists
Robert Semler A.S.I.
Marisa Donato
Paul Spatola
Creative Consultant
Andrew Lee, Retired Head of Research, Universal Studios
Music History Consultant
Joseph Marcello

CREDITS AND ACKNOWLEDGMENTS

Pressbook - MagicImage Archives
Richard Bojarski Collection
The author wishes to thank the following individuals and institutions for their generous assistance:

Donald Fowle	Margaret Ross
Ned Comstock	Linda Mehr
Nancy Cushing-Jones	Dorothy Swerdlove
Ernest B. Goodman	Sue Dwiggins
Michael Voss	Rita Duenas
Judd Funk	Maria Jochsberger
Richard Bojarski	Douglas Norwine
Armondo Ponce	John D. DelMargio
Sharron Williams	Ernest Ricci

THE BILLY ROSE THEATER COLLECTION
New York Library at Lincoln Center, NYC
THE MARGARET HERRICK LIBRARY
Academy of Motion Picture Arts and Sciences
USC CINEMA & TELEVISION LIBRARY - Ned Comstock
UCLA FILM AND TELEVISION ARCHIVES, Robert Gitt
THE UNIVERSITY OF THE STATE OF NEW YORK
Office of Cultural Education - State Archives, Albany, NY
THE BISON ARCHIVES - Marc Wanamaker
MURPHY'S LOFT BOOKS - Mullica Hill, NJ

Grateful acknowledgment is given by the editor for permission to present advance photographs and text from Douglas Norwine's upcoming definitive book on the life and films of Jack Pierce, which will include photographs from Pierce's personal scrapbooks along with an in-depth scholarly history of film history's first great makeup artist.

Also to Preston Jones for permission to quote from his research on the music of Universal films and his interviews with Hans Salter - for Joseph Marcello's music chapter.

Manufactured in the United States of America
Typesetting by Computer House, Absecon, New Jersey

Printed and Bound by
McNaughton & Gunn Lithographers

ABOUT THE AUTHORS

Gregory Wm. Mank - Author, actor and teacher, has written the background material for MagicImage's *Frankenstein* and *Mummy* volumes. He is the author of *It's Alive! The Classic Cinema Saga of Frankenstein*, *The Hollywood Hissables*, *Karloff and Lugosi* and, his new book, *Hollywood Cauldron*, as well as many features for such magazines as *Films in Review*, *Cinefantastique*, and *Scarlet Street*. Greg has received the *Fanex* Award for "Excellence in Genre Film Literature." He lives with his wife Barbara and children Jessica and Christopher in a hilltop home near Delta, PA, and presently is at work on a book about Horror film heroines.

Philip Riley - Author & Film Historian. Series editor for MagicImage Filmbooks' Universal Filmscript Series - Classic Monster Film & Studio History Consultant for Universal City Studios. His work at MGM and Universal during the 60s and 70s brought him in contact with the stars and technicians who made the pioneering monster films of the 20s, 30s and 40s, thus making him one of the last living historians to have the personal, first-hand information that appears in the MagicImage volumes.

For 25 years he has been active in the preservation of film history and lost silent films. His book restorations of lost films include *London After Midnight* (1927), *A Blind Bargain* (1922), The *Hunchback of Notre Dame* (1923) and *Phantom of the Opera* (1925). In recent years he has acted as consultant for several major film remakes, MCA Universal Home Video releases, and has contributed to numerous academic books on Monster films. Member of the Horror Hall of Fame, winner of the Count Dracula Society Award, he received honors from The Museum of Modern Art and the Italian Government for his accomplishments. He is married and has two children and lives on a farm somewhere between Philadelphia and Transylvania.

George Turner - Editor, artist, author is the former editor of *American Cinematographer* magazine. Author and editor of *The Making of King Kong*, *Forgotten Horrors* (with Michael Price) *Murders in Palo Duro*, *Secrets of Billy the Kid*. *The Cinema of Adventure, Romance & Terror*, *ASC Treasury of Visual Effects*.

He has worked as a production illustrator, special effects artist and animator in films and television. Credits include: *Ray Bradbury's Infinite Horizons*, *One From the Heart*, *Outland*, *Zorro*, *Dead Men Don't Wear Plaid* and *Creature*. Retired from *American Cinematographer* in 1992, he is currently an extremely-in-demand matte artist in Hollywood. He and his wife Jean live in Pasadena. They have four sons.

Information in this volume has been compiled from the following sources:

"Werewolves" by Montigue Summers
Universal Central Files
Estate of the late Milton Cohen, Esq.
Interviews with: Lon Chaney Jr., Abe Haberman,
Evelyn Ankers, Robert Florey, Curt Siodmak
Hollywood Publishing Archives
MagicImage Archives
The Jack Pierce Scrapbooks
Other sources noted in text.

For other reading about Werewolves in fiction and folklore we recommend:

Cycle of the Werewolf by Steven King
The Werewolf by Clemmence Housman
The Werewolf in Western Culture by Charlotte F. Otten
The Werewolf of Paris by Guy Endore
The Wolf Man by Art Bourgeau
Night Walker by Thomas Tessier
Shiny Narrow Grin by Jane Gaskill
Saint Peter's Wolf by Michael Cadnum

Dedicated to Creighton Tull Chaney

... The woods are lovely, dark and deep.
But I have promises to keep,
And miles to go before I sleep,
And miles to go before I sleep.

Robert Frost

"Eena" by Manly Banister - as illustrated by Boris Dolgov - Weird Tales September 1947

Foreword
by
Evelyn Ankers

"I'm glad to see that you're not just another pretty scream." How do you like that for the first words to come out of Ralph Bellamy's mouth when we met way back in 1941 for the film *The Wolf Man*?

My introduction to Universal Studios was worse than pledging for a college sorority. It was an Abbott and Costello picture entitled *Hold That Ghost.* In looking, back I cannot, for the life of me, figure out how they ever got a picture finished. Once Lou Costello found out that I was English, from the English "Theatre", I spent most of my time checking my purse for mice and making sure that I had a solid wall behind me so that I wasn't squirted with a hose or swatted in a most uncomfortable spot though a canvas. They must have kept the local bakers very busy, for a typical vaudeville pie fight was soon a weekly event! They probably had pies written into their contract. At least the antics on *The Wolf Man* set were better than the "vaudeville slapstick through the canvas" trick of Lou Costello. Did I say better? Let's say different!

Lon Chaney Jr. and I did not get off to a very good start. That scream of mine, which Ralph Bellamy so fondly joked about, had gotten me a new dressing room. I was to share it with Anne Gwynne, who also was to make a few scary pictures for Universal. The problem was that it was *Lon's* dressing room that they were giving me. He was not pleased about it at all! This was around the time that he was just making a name of his own and exposed to the star treatment. People were always comparing him to his father, who had died only about 10 years previous. I think he was very defensive about that. Still, I tried to assure him that I had nothing to do with the dressing room incident. I went to talk to Clifford Work, the studio head at the time, and he assured me that he would handle things. It appeared that Lon and his friends, Andy Devine and Broderick Crawford, and a few others, were imbibing a bit too much and getting into wrestling matches, which usually destroyed the dressing room trailers. Lon eventually got the word from the front office. I believe he honestly tried to behave, and I apparently ceased to be a threat to him. But I don't know which was worse. Friend or Foe?

Now that we were a bit social, he began a series of practical jokes that almost topped Abbott and Costello. With Bud and Lou it was either the pies or a mouse in my purse, OR when their friend Jack Pierce, the makeup genius who made all the monsters in his magic laboratory, and his assistants would come down to the set for lunch there would inevitably be a food fight, OR Lou would have Pierce make up something disgusting - which I won't go into detail on - and place it in my sandwich. Lon's attempts at humor, while they probably would have gone over big in a fraternity house, were sometimes not pleasant. He seemed to have a need to be liked by people. When he wasn't drinking he was the sweetest. Sometimes he hid it [the drinking] so well, that one couldn't be sure. But, if a dress were destroyed or a hair-do by the Pierce crew, then he heard from the front office; for they were afraid production would be held up and that meant money lost. Besides they had their hands full with Abbott and Costello.

I would tell the Studio that the ruined dress was my own and that no time was lost. Vera West was a very talented lady. She ran the Wardrobe department at Universal and could come up with a costume in practically no time.

Some things just do not change with time I suppose. The enigma of the "dumb blonde" was just as strong then as it was when I left Hollywood far behind. My singing and vocal training, combined with my natural accent might have presented a confusing contrast to both Lon and Abbott and Costello. I sounded educated but fit the stereotype.

Not all of my memories are full of affectionate frustration. I remember David Bruce as a wonderful man. I haven't seen him in any films lately, but he was quite a good looking man, not as good looking as my husband Richard Denning, naturally, whom I married in the fall of 1942 and who is still active in acting in the television show *Hawaii 5-0.*

Bela Lugosi was a gentleman of the "old world." I think *he* admired my "British accent," being a famous actor from the Hungarian Theatre.

I didn't recognize Bela when I met him out of makeup! We had been talking about this or that for quite some time when he ended the conversation by him saying how much he enjoyed working with me on *Ghost of Frankenstein.* It hit me right then that the snaggle-toothed, horrifying character that he played in the film was the same man. Quite a testament to the talents of Jack Pierce!

In *The Wolf Man* he had a bushy wig and a gypsy moustache - but a year in-between pictures is a long time to one in the profession. During that time you do not come into much personal contact with your fellow cast members (on a certain film). In the theatre you see each other in and out of makeup everyday for the run of the play. But Mr. Lugosi was quite the opposite from his screen characters, he was refined, cultivated and charming. This transition is not an easy thing to do as an actor. I learned from first hand experience when I made *Weird Woman* a few years later, again with Lon Chaney Jr.. The studio made *me* the villain in that

film! Every time I would try to work myself up to look evil, especially in the scenes with Anne Gwynne, I would scrunch my eyebrows, try for a mean look. When I turned to Anne [Gwynne] we would both become hysterical with laughter. The director, Reginald LeBorg, was very patient. I was never cast as the "bad guy" again! So much the credit to Mr. Lugosi's acting ability. He could get "into character" instantly - the meaner the better!

George Waggner had a man's man type personality. Perhaps it could be best described as John Wayne's action packed screen personality in a suit. He was patient, yet demanding, experimental, yet always conscious that we were all in the motion picture business and time was money. He took such pride in his work that even a monster film was treated as if he were making *The Ten Commandments.*

I only saw the special effects man on the set, John Fulton, briefly. The scenes involved Lon Chaney and his transformations. There were always technicians and cameramen with measuring tapes and light meters running around. Since there weren't many scenes that I *wasn't* in with Lon, I needed a break - for he did not appear to be in good humor with all of them fussing about him - with the lighting and makeup changes.

We used to wait quite a bit for the technical part of motion picture making. Was the fog just right? Were the lights in the proper position? While Lon was being made up into the Wolf Man, they would take advantage of the time and have me scream my close-ups - or take publicity pictures. I remember the first time I saw Lon in makeup. Very clearly - I'm afraid! I also remember that my reaction was a form of attention that he enjoyed and he insisted on doing it over and over again until it became exasperating.

I was standing on the set, occupied with learning lines or something like that when I felt a tap on my shoulder. Turning around, expecting to see Ralph Bellamy or one of the other production members, I found myself inches away from a snarling beast! He bared his fangs and grabbed me with these hairy claws. I almost jumped right out of my skin. He would always break into chuckles. It was good that he was so big and didn't let go as he tried to quiet my screams- for he did anchor me down preventing me from knocking over the prop trees or running headlong into a wall giving myself a bump on the head. But once was enough for me - not him though.

There were two other things that I remember about *The Wolf Man.* One was the horrible fumes from the constant fog on the sets and the other involved a huge bear.

At the end of the picture the werewolf is chasing me. I turn and see him for the first time and faint in his arms. Claude Rains comes out of the fog and Lon, the werewolf, drops me on the ground and attacks him instead. If I remember the sequence properly, after I am dropped into this chemical fog, I was to lie still for a few seconds until I heard "Cut!" I didn't hear cut. They started to prepare for Lon to finish the fight scene with Claude Rains. Well, they forgot me in all the hustle and bustle of changing camera setups. I had been overcome by the fumes and passed out. Fortunately someone in the crew nearly tripped over me and I was saved.

Lon didn't make out so well either, for in the next scene, Claude took a wild swing with the walking stick, which had a very heavy head - made from metal with the wolf's head and it hit Lon in the face. Lon took pain very well, but poor Mr. Rains was almost overcome with the thought that he had actually done some violence to another person. Either that or maybe he used his exceptional acting talents and was getting even with Lon for something that Lon might have pulled on *him,* too!

Then there was the bear. The studio brought in a special animal trainer with an animal that weighed as much as three men. It was very old and quite smelly. The script called for Lon and I to enter the gypsy camp while the trainer and his bear were just part of the scene. Later Lon was to wrestle the bear when the werewolf personality began to overcome his human side. The music was playing, the stage was crowded with all the principals and the gypsy extras. Lon and I walked past the bear and all of a sudden everyone started to panic and run. Lon looked back, grabbed my sleeve to pull me away, but kept going when I broke free (Thinking he was about to pull one of his practical jokes). I turn and I am greeted by this great beast, standing on his hind legs, almost seven feet tall! The bear had apparently taken a liking to me and was heading straight for me. As I began to run, the bear dragged the poor trainer after him and broke loose - heading right for me! The next thing I knew, I was being pulled up to the lighting scaffolds by the electricians and the bear was temporarily blinded by the grips shining the stage lights in his eyes. The trainer came up and quickly took control of the situation. Getting down those wooden scaffolds was a lot harder than it was going up them. Especially when your knees will not stop shaking.

I can tell you that it was not Lon who was fighting that bear in those scenes. Aside from the studio, not wanting to risk him getting hurt, he wouldn't get within 20 feet of the old bear while it was on the set.

The rest of the memories have faded a bit in time. I had my fortune told by a real fortune teller, who was a player in the film, too. It was the usual, "fall in love with a tall dark stranger," type future in my palm. I thought she meant the bear at first, but when I met my future husband shortly after, ... maybe there are things that exist that can't be explained - I know it almost made a believer out of me, for Mr. Denning and I have been happily married ever since.

Evelyn Ankers,
Hawaii, 1974

Et facet omnies pusillos er magnos
diu. er paupites libres. r sanos liu auiite
icm in drea manu. aut iswaribs sius.r uegs
pisit cuse auc nende. nisi qui baler caraut

icu bsthe. aut numeium nominis eius
lj sapiencia e. & lir mrelliccu. compurit
numeium testie. Numerus caum biise
er numeius ci e seraturu seraguca sic.

Even a man
who is pure in
heart, and says
his prayers by
night,

May become a
wolf when the
wolfbane blooms,
and the Autumn
moon is bright

Introduction to My Screenplay, *The Wolf Man*

by
Curt Siodmak

'Habent sua fata libelli.' Books have their fate, so have motion pictures.

When I was working for Universal Pictures, turning out screen plays for Susanna Foster and Ginnie Sims, my producer George Waggner asked me to write a Gothic tale. We didn't consider the Frankenstein pictures horror pictures,. they were Gothic tales, which has a refined connotation.

"We have a title," George said.

"The title comes from a story written for Boris Karloff, ten years earlier but he can not play in that picture, since he is busy on another one. The title is *The Wolf Man*. We have Claude Rains under contract for one more picture. Also Lon Chaney Jr., Madame Ouspenskaya, Evelyn Ankers, who is gifted with a terrifying scream, Ralph Bellamy, Warren William, and Bela Lugosi. Of course Bela would like to play the Wolf Man. His Hungarian accent is right for Dracula, but not for the Wolf Man. Since we have Claude, the tale might play in England. We are limited in funds, as usual, and I will get from the front office $180,000 for the production. That's why you can't have a raise. Confidentially, get your raise at another studio, and we'll match it. We shoot in ten weeks. And don't talk to me until you've finished the screenplay. I want your ideas, and not mine. Good-bye."

I started working on the film at Universal - I got $400 a week in those days - and wrote the picture in about seven weeks, from scratch. I did research on the legends, of course - all my books and scripts are based on research - but much of the film was made up.

That's how pictures were made in the forties. They had their financial limitations. Not the big ones with Clark Gable, but the inexpensive companion 'B' pictures. It was the time of block booking, a kind of studio blackmail directed toward the distributors. And it was the time of the double features, to fill three hours of entertainment; which the public expected to buy with a ticket. If the theater owner wanted to show a Clark Gable, or Deanna Durbin, he also had to buy the companion feature. I wrote 38 of them for Universal and other studios. I was the king of the "B's".

Looking back and evaluating that time, those pictures contained literary freedom for a writer. He could express himself without much interference from the producer. It had also to be a disciplined story, and even could be experimental. When I was through with the screenplay, always delivering it close to the production deadline, the front office and the producer or director didn't have time or money to engage another writer or mess up the original screenplay themselves. That's why among my "originals" many have survived, while the big ones disappeared in the mist of time.

I must pat myself on the shoulder, since nobody has the inclination of doing this. I am the creator of research for the background, and history of stories. In researching, a writer finds many "original" ideas without being forced to think himself. I studied many books about Lycanthropy, or wolf madness, a mental delusion in a human being, believing himself to be a wolf. There was ample material about this in books about psychiatry. Even Sigmund Freud wrote about it. Then I made up a ditty:

Even a man who is pure in heart, and says his prayers by night, may become a wolf when the wolfbane blooms and the autumn moon is bright.

I passed that four liner off as part of an old German saga about werewolves, and even today, after almost half a century since I wrote those lines, aficionados of horror stories ask me to write the verse down for them, if possible on parchment, to have it framed. I gave the Wolf Man a name, LARRY TALBOT, and it stuck to him. My original story was that of an American mechanic who is sent to Scotland by Bausch and Lomb to install a telescope in a Scottish castle. I couldn't visualize Lon Chaney Jr. with his broad American accent, to play an Englishman. Besides, for an American, innocent, and certainly not a mystic, to be afflicted with wolf madness was more horrifying to me than the change George Waggner made: making him the son of a Scottish nobleman; who was played in style by Claude Rains. I also didn't want ever to show the Wolf Man's gruesome face except when Lon Chaney looked at his own image in a mirror or in a pool of water. But George changed all that, maybe rightly so. The public doesn't like mysticism, especially since there are no ghosts in America. They all live in Europe, preferably in England.

The shooting began. George didn't change the screenplay and accepting that I knew more about Lycanthropy than he, the director consulted me before any line was changed. Against my will I extended Madame Ouspenskaya's speech, holding the dying Larry in her lap; though the addition made the monologue a little gooey for me.

The way you walk is thorny, through not fault of your own. For as the rain enters the soil and evil enters the sea, so tears run to their predestined end. Your suffering is over. Now find peace for eternity, my son.

That speech was based on HARMATIA. In ancient Greek tragedies HARMATIA means that a person must suffer by the whim of the gods, though he has not committed a crime. That notion was the pivot of my idea for *The Wolf Man*. We all have HARMATIA in us, and suffer in life's mishaps and pain, without

Chaney's pathos gave life to Siodmak's words as seen above - Here he realizes his good deed in saving Jenny has turned against him as he and Maleva the Gypsy watch Bela's Funeral.

having been guilty of any misdeed. The world as we saw it was being drawn into wars. Life itself contains the curse of the Wolf Man: sufferings without having been guilty, being subjected to fates, which are decided by the pleasure of the gods.

By chance the Larry Talbot story parallels the story lines of Greek tragedies, as Aristotle has defined them in his book POETICS, written 2000 years ago. It is a criticism of Greek plays. The laws of those plays are still valid. That's why the Wolf Man, now, after running for over a half a century, has not lost its impact on the emotions. The only shortcoming, in my opinion, is that I got paid a skimpy salary; while by now the studio, for whom I wrote that "B" picture must have collected many millions. But when I look at the credits, which name George Waggner, Lon Chaney Jr., Claude Rains, Madame Ouspenskaya: they all have died by now. So that's why I am better off, I guess, still being alive and writing. As I said to the editor, Phil Riley, "Take care of your health, you can buy everything else!"

But I'm convinced that *The Wolf Man* will survive me.

Curt Siodmak
Three Rivers, California, 1991

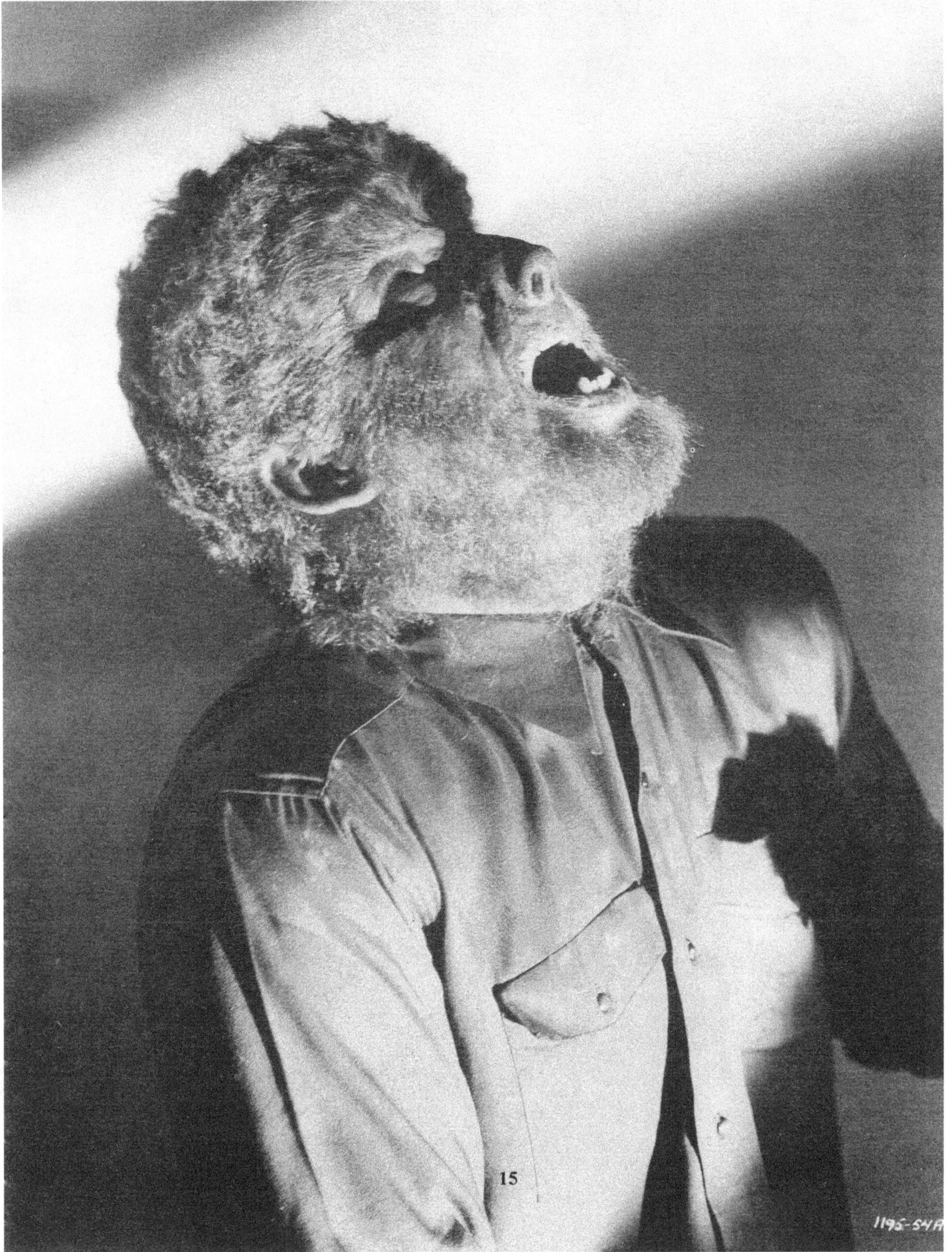

15

The Werewolf from Ancient Myths and Legends to Literature & the Silver Screen

Lycaon is turned into a wolf by Jupiter - illustrating the Romanized version of the Greek legend.

"Of ye Wolf and his nature... ther ben some that eten chyldren & men and eteth noon other flesh from that tyme that thei be a charmed with mannys flesh, ffor rather thei wolde be deed. And thei be cleped Werewolfes ffor men shulde be war him."

Bodley Manuscript, from The Booke of huntynge or Master of game. (c. 1400)

The metamorphosis of the werewolf legend reflects the moral standards and beliefs of each period of civilization through which it passed.

Egyptian tombs are covered with stories and pictures of their gods. Most of them were depicted as having human bodies with the heads of various animals. It was an honor to be depicted in this transitory state. The priests of Egypt practiced magic, fortune telling, palm reading and tarot cards. One sect was banished by an ancient Pharaoh, whose name is lost in time. Their crime had been using magic to transform men into animals. They were driven out to sea and landed near Turkey, where they continued their practice. Eventually they travelled all over what was to become Europe and as the legends of Werewolves grew the name of the Egyptians was Anglicized into the word Gypsies.

As the Egyptian civilization faded the Greek and Roman periods brought about a new belief.

Transformation into a lower life-form was, at first, the punishment of the gods of ancient Greece and Rome. As magicians and sorcerers learned the knowledge of the gods, they too could transform humans into beasts as in the story of the travels of Ulysses. Circe a sorceress, turned Ulysses' [Odysseus'] men into pigs; The Roman legend held that Romulus and Remus, the founders of Rome, were raised and nurtured by a wolf mother.

As each civilization assimilated the previous one, the legends and myths survived in various forms. The Greek gods were given Roman names, Zeus became Jupiter, Aphrodite became Venus, etc., and the modern medical name for transformation into a wolf originated.

In Ovid's poem "Metamorphosis", which reflects the Roman viewpoint of the Greek moral standards, Jupiter called the gods together and told them that they had a problem. It seemed that the nymphs, satyrs and fauns, along with all the guardians of nature were doing a fine job. The problem was with their creation of man. Certain men represented the highest ideals of the gods and were supposed to set examples for the rest of mankind. One of these men was King Lycaon of Arcadia.

Jupiter revealed that he had heard rumors of the extreme cruelty of the people to one another on earth. The most vicious and unacceptable was the common practice of cannibalism. To see for himself, Jupiter left Mount Olympus and descended to earth. He crossed the ridge of Maenalus, where wild beasts, still untamed by the nature guardians left him unharmed and journeyed into the pinewoods of Lycaeus.

At nightfall he finally reached the castle of Lycaon. When he entered the Castle he announced his true nature and the people began to pay homage to the god. Lycaon was jealous of this and plotted to expose Jupiter as a hoax. When all of his plots failed he announced a banquet for Jupiter.

While Jupiter sat at the table, slaves were brought in, their throats slit and their blood drained into a boiling pot. The slaves were then cut up, cooked and served to the guests.

Jupiter responded, in Mary Innes' translation of the poem:

"No sooner had he done so, [served the human flesh to the guests], than I with my avenging flames brought the house crashing down upon its household gods, gods worthy of such a master. Lycaon fled, terrified, until he reached the safety of the silent countryside. There he uttered howling noises, and his attempts to speak were all in vain. His clothes changed into bristling hairs, his arms to legs, and he became a wolf. His own savage nature showed in his rabid jaws, and he now directed against the flocks his innate lust for killing. He had a mania, even yet, for shedding blood. But, though he was a wolf, he retained some traces of his original shape. The greyness of his hair was the same, his face showed the same violence, his eyes gleamed as before, and he, presented the same picture of ferocity."

Jupiter then told the gods that all men who continued the practice of eating other humans would suffer the same fate and if it meant that *all* humans must die or be transformed, so be it.

The gods were panic stricken. If Jupiter were to destroy all men, who would bring offerings of incense to their altars, who would be there to honor them? Were not men created for the sole purpose of worshiping the gods?

Jupiter assured them that he would take care of everything. For it appeared that not only had mankind a problem of consuming itself, maybe the gods themselves were a bit self indulgent. He would create a new race of beings on earth, ones who would not only be of higher awareness of their divine origins, but also not as dependent on their gods for protection and providers.

This Roman tale was written a long after the Greek legend had originated, but its message was clear enough. Man was now to leave his beast nature behind and grow into his destiny.

Nice thought, but mankind was not very cooperative. The ancients began to realize that it wasn't good to eat your neighbor, but as far as any spiritual growth, man is usually dragged kicking and screaming into any form of new enlightenment.

The medical term given to anyone who reverts back to their beast nature is Lycanthropy after Lycaon, the first werewolf.

As the Roman empire began to expand and eventually convert the world to the Holy Roman Church, each country had its own form of werewolves as reflected in the languages of each people. In German the prefix; *Wer*, in Latin *vir*, in Sanskrit, *vira* in ancient Gaelic, *fear*, all combined with the corresponding word for "man" meant werewolf.

In Montague Summers, "The Vampire, His Kith and Kin" Kegan Paul, London 1929, he traces the word origin back to a Greek derivation of the word for hobgoblin (Mormo). "This word *volkodlak, vukodlak, vulkodlak,* is a compound form of which the first half means "wolf", whilst the second half has been identified, although the actual relation is not quite demonstrable, with *blaka*, which in Old Slavonic, New Slavonic and Serbian signifies the "hair" of a cow or a horse or a horse's mane. Yet whatsoever the analytical signification of the compound may precisely be, the synthesis in the actual employment of all Slavonic tongues, save one, is the equivalent of the English "werewolf"; Scots "warwulf"; German "Werwolf" and French "loup-garou". The one language in which this word does not bear this interpretation is the Serbian, for here it signifies "a vampire".

Summers goes on to explain the legends of Transylvania in which a man who had been a werewolf in life would become a vampire after death. It was also believed that a person who ate the flesh of a sheep killed by a wolf might become a vampire after death. Although the vampire and werewolf are closely related, a werewolf must have a living body, where the vampire is precisely defined as an incorrupt and re-animated dead body. In Summers second Vampire book "The Vampire in Europe" (1929) he discusses the Greek version of the Lycanthropy origins. He quotes from Plato's *Republic* as to the happenings at the temple of Lycaean Zeus in Arcadia, Greece. In conversation with Pliny Plato says:

According to it, the worshipper who tasted the one human entrail, which was minced up with the other entrails of other victims, was inevitably metamorphosed into a wolf.

Then, in like form, Pliny, himself, speaks of werewolves in his *Historia Natualis XXXIV, 22 Vol II pp. 186-7*

Agriopas, the author of a work upon the victors in the Olympic games, tells how Demaenetus an Arcadian, transformed himself into a wolf, by partaking of the entrails of a boy who had been sacrificed at Mount Lycaeus since the Arcadians used to offer human victims to Lycaean Zeus, but that after a space of ten years, he recovered his original form and overcoming all others in boxing, was crowned a victor at the Olympic games.

To the Greeks this transformation was not evil, but a sign of strength and virility. In a sense the word also had an erotic connotation. Often the same word used for werewolf could also mean "an older male athlete's younger male lover" (which was quite acceptable in that society).

Medieval German wood cut of a werewolf carrying off his victim -- in Serbian dress unhampered by her rosary beads which carry the Lutheran German cross instead of the crucifix

Reverend Montigue Summers - compiler and author of the definitive works on Vampires, Werewolves and Witches published from 1925-1933

Again, the meaning behind the word itself had changed with the times. Only the Romans considered the affliction punishment by the gods. But the Greeks eventually came around.

Eventually Roman empire began to fail and each country went back into its own way of life. The only tie that was to remain was the centralized Church in Rome. The Dark Ages was mankind's decent into the old superstitions, who now had adapted themselves to the new Christian beliefs.

The ancient myths of werewolves were a powerful warning for man to abstain from its lower nature and from obeying the powers of the mind. Now the warning was more of a spiritual warning to avoid being trapped by the Devil. Jupiter's desire that men become responsible for their own actions had a demonizing effect. If you did something wrong and became a werewolf you could blame it on Satan.

Medieval tales of becoming a werewolf evoked pity and sympathy for the victim. He would be banished from the Church, by his fellow man and forever would be forbidden the companionship of his family and love of God until he was either destroyed or found some way to repent.

Time passed. The control of the Church began to bring about a sense of community life. Spiritual well-being, mental health and strength against evil were the mental and moral foundation of cities.

Then science and common law began to bring Europe out of the Dark ages into the Renaissance. Common man was now allowed to read and the legends of the werewolves began to appear in writing.

In *Ancient Laws and Institutes of England* edited by B. Thorpe, published in 1840, he notes that the word "werewolf" first appeared in the English language in the Ecclesiastical Order of King Cnut who reigned in England from 1017-1035.

Thonne moton tha hydras beon swydhe wacore and geornlice clypigende, the widh thonne theodsceadhan folce sceolan scyldan, thaet syndon bisopas and maessepreostas, the godcunde heorda bewarian and bewarian sceolan, mid wisican laran, thaet se wodfreca werewulf to swidhe ne slyth ne to fela ne abite of godcundse heorde.

Translation: Therefore must the shepherds be very watchful and diligently crying out, for they must shield the people against the spoiler, such are Bishops and Priests who perform the Mass, are to preserve and defend their spiritual flocks with wise warnings that the mad were-wolf do not too widely devastate nor bite too many of the spiritual flock.

Apparently it was all right for a few of the spiritual flock to get bitten, but it wasn't the sort of thing that the Church wanted as common Friday night occurrences.

The words *lycanthrophia* and *lycanthopus* made their first appearance in English in Reginald Scot's *The Discoverie of Witchcraft* published in 1584. From this point the two words began to have the same meaning in literature.

It is curious, that words, being a body for our thoughts, reflect the accepted "norm" of any given society. In the 14th and 15th centuries tales such as *Le Morte D' Arthur* (1470) one of Arthur's knights was betrayed by his wife and turned into a werewolf. In *The Book of William of Palerne*, translated in the mid 14th Century and reprinted in the Early English Text's Society volume in 1867, William is a Spanish Prince turned into a werewolf by his wicked stepmother. Around the same time that tales of witchcraft were a popular source of entertainment, tragic for the victims of the real life drama, it appears that society felt that women were a better target for the Devil and thus the cause of most transformations into werewolves were blamed on the ladies. Marital infidelity then was added to the lists of "How to become a Werewolf."

Another source in tracing the history of werewolves comes to us in the form of 17th and 16th century trial transcripts. By this time the hidden form of the werewolf was one who went against the social order. The community laws were separating themselves from the old order of the central church. Behavior in public was to be controlled at all times.

In 1589, Europe's most sensational werewolf trial took place in Cologne, where a Peter Stube claimed to have made love to a succubus for 28 years, receiving from the female demon a magic belt - which could transform him into a giant wolf. Stube had devoured and mutilated many victims (two of his own daughters-in-law testified that they had survived his cannibalistic attacks). He remained in "human form" in court, claiming to do so only because he had hidden the magic belt in a valley. Stube's sadistic ravings inspired many search parties to seek this magic belt, which never was found.

Stube's sentence for being a self-proclaimed werewolf? His flesh was yanked off with red-hot pincers, his bones were smashed by a hatchet - and he was decapitated. [See Appendix for the complete original transcript of this trial.]

The fate of Peter Stubbe and his family as described in the trial transcript

France has a similar tale, the story of Jean Grenier which was published in *Book of Were-Wolves* Smith Elder & Co London 1865.

A group of village girls were tending sheep when they came upon a boy of 13. "His hair was of a tawny red and thickly matted, falling over his shoulders and completely covering his narrow brow. His small pale-grey eyes twinkled with an expression of horrible ferocity and cunning, from deep sunken hollows. The complexion was of a dark olive colour; the teeth were strong and white, and the canine teeth protruded over the lower lip when the mouth was closed. The boy's hands were large and powerful, the nails black and pointed like bird's talons."

He tells the girls of a man named Pierre Labournat, who lives in a place of gloom and fire with an iron chain about his neck. Around him are companions who are seated on burning hot iron chairs and others who cast men upon blazing coal while others roast men in fierce flames and then into caldrons of liquid fire. When the girls asked him why he kept himself so impoverish and dirty he replied that it was because he was given a wolf's skin by Pierre Labournat. Every Monday, Friday and Sunday for about an hour before dusk he becomes a werewolf when he puts on the skin. The girls fled in terror when he began to cackle like a maniac.

Not long after a young girl who tended her flocks with Grenier in normal form came home and told her parents that she could no longer go into the fields with Grenier for he was scaring her with tales of selling his soul to the Devil and that while in the form of a werewolf he had killed and eaten several dogs and several little girls.

With apprehension, she went out the next day and found that Grenier was not there. As she returned home she heard a rustle in the bushes and a wild beast leaped on her, tearing her clothes with its fangs. As the creature turned she took her heavy shepherds staff and hit it several times. The beast retreated a few paces and sat on its haunches. She described the animal as "resembling a wolf, but as being shorter and stouter, its hair was red, its tail stumpy and the head smaller than that of a genuine wolf."

Grenier was brought to trial and admitted to many atrocities. "When I was ten or eleven years old, my neighbor, Duthillaire, introduced me, in the depths of the forest, to a M. de la Forest, a black man, who signed me with his nail, and then gave to me and Duthillaire a salve and a wolf-skin. From that time have I run about the country as a wolf."

The towns lawyer asked the court to set aside all thoughts of witchcraft and lycanthropy and pointed out that the court had only to look at the dull and idiotic expression of Grenier's face. He stated that Lycanthropy was a state of hallucination and the change of shape existed only in the disorganized brain of the insane, therefore, not a crime for which he should be held accountable.

The Judge agreed and although the guilt of murder was well established as well as cannibalism, Grenier was sentenced to be imprisoned in the monastery of Bordeaux, where he would be instructed in his Christian and moral obligations, under penalty of death if he attempted an escape.

The monks at the abbey reported that as soon as he was released in the grounds he began to run around on all fours, eating scraps of garbage off the ground.

French Loup Garou appears more like a madman than a Lycanthrope

open, and the corpse hideously maltreated. "Every means were taken to discover the criminal; but the only result of the increased surveillance was that the scene of profanation was removed to the cemetery of Mont Parnesse, where the exhumations were carried to such an extent that the authorities were at their wit's ends.

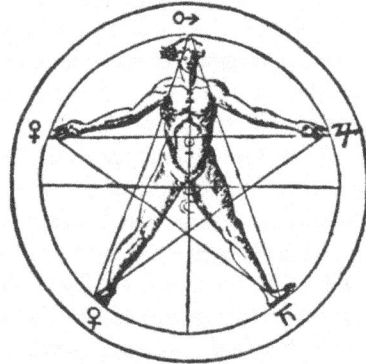

The pentagram as illustrated in Occulta Philosphia by Agrippa of Nettesheim, 1530

Within 7 years he had withdrawn completely from reality and died. Another French military transcript tells of a Sergeant Bertrand, who is remembered more as a vampire, but whose story was said to be the basis of Guy Endore's *Werewolf of Paris*.

On 10th July, 1849, an investigation was held before a council of war presided over by Colonel Manselon. It is remarked that the court was extremely crowded and that many ladies were present. For many months various cemeteries in and around Paris had been scenes of the most frightful profanations. The guardians of Peré la Chaise had noticed, or believed they had noticed, a shadowy figure flitting by night among the graves, but they could never succeed in laying hands on him and some began to suppose it was a phantom. Graves were found fearfully desecrated. The bodies were torn from their resting-places, violated and scored with hideous mutilations. When these events ceased at Pére la Chaise they began in a remote suburban graveyard. The body of a little girl aged seven who had been buried one noon was found on the following morning torn from the earth, the coffin burst

Considering, by the way, that all these cemeteries are surrounded by walls and have iron gates, which are kept closed, it certainly seems very strange that any ghoul or vampyre of solid flesh and blood should have been able to pursue his vocations so long undisturbed. " At length by a trap the guardians of the cemetery were able to surprise the mysterious visitant who none the less escaped with severe wounds, leaving a trail of blood from their shots. A few scraps of military attire were found, and when some sappers of the 74th regiment remarked that shortly after midnight one of their sergeants had returned so injured that he had been conveyed to Val de Grace, the military hospital, it was realized that the culprit was found. At his examination Bertrand avowed that an irresistible impulse drove him to disinter and violate corpses, after which he fell into a sort of trance or coma. The details of the corpses he had outraged were of the most horrible nature, and his mutilations seem to have been wrought in a state of dementia. The doctors, however, judged him responsible, and he was sentenced to a year's imprisonment.

Two illustrations from "Wagner the WehrWolf" 1847

The 19th century machine age brought the werewolf legends into popular literature. One of the earliest followed Thomas Pecket Prest's 1847 pulp story of 868 pages - sold in weekly supplements, "Varney the Vampire". It was called "Wagner the Wehr-Wolf" by G.W.M. Reynolds, published in 1857. Both stories were geared for the general public and could be said to be the Victorian era's version of the soap opera. If nothing else the equally ponderous "Wagner" story told the writers of the day that werewolf stories were lucrative, but to keep your audience one had to keep your distance. That is, to make it captivating and believable you had to retain the "Long - long ago, in a galaxy, far-far away" format. (Even Bram Stoker used this formula 40 years later in Dracula, where the opening chapters in Transylvania outshadow the remaining chapters in London throughout the book - until the last chapter where the group of vampire hunters chase Dracula back to his Transylvanian fortress)

One of the more interesting books of the period is Clemence Housman's *The Were-Wolf* published in London in 1896 by John Lane and in the United States by Way and Williams. Housman keeps within the realms of tradition and folklore. The main character is given some sympathy and pathos.

Another noteworthy tale is Bram Stoker's short story, *Dracula's Guest*, published by Stoker's widow in 1914, two years after his death in 1912. Originally a chapter excised from *Dracula* due to its length, it tells of a side journey that Jonathan Harker takes on his way to Dracula's castle. Lost, he stumbles into an ancient unholy graveyard in the middle of a snowstorm and is about to become the victim of a voluptuous female vampire when he is saved by a giant black wolf. The wolf turns out to be Dracula, who apparently was saving Harker for his own dark purposes and wanted to be assured that Harker reached Castle Dracula. The short story became the basis for Universal's *Dracula's Daughter* in 1936.

Dracula as a werewolf illustrated on the dust jacket of the 1914 First Edition of "Dracula's Guest"

The vampire had a sexual mystique which kept the readers thrilled from the Victorian to the modern era interested in the story line. And why not? The Vampire promised forbidden passion, eternal life, eternal youth and freedom from the conventional restrictions of society. Not so for the werewolf. Few people could find any feelings for a vicious beast who would promise you nothing but having your throat torn out before you were eaten!

The face of Europe was rapidly changing at the turn of the 20th Century; boundaries changed, whole populations moved and America called to many from across the Atlantic Ocean. The werewolf in literature was lost in the shuffle for a short time.

Other than a few mysteries, which *promised* something supernatural, but ended up disappointing the general reader by revealing a real life murderer disguised as a werewolf to scare the other heirs away from the mansion or even cover up for an extra marital affair, there was little in fiction about the werewolf. H.G. Wells, Saki, Alexander Dumas and other classic writers all dabbled in short stories but it wasn't until Guy Endore's *Werewolf of Paris* was published by Farrar & Rinehart in 1933 that a full novel was available. There were serious ventures into the occult; such as Elliot O'Donnell's *Werewolves* published in London in 1912, and Montague Summers history of the subject, *The Were-wolf* published again in London but in 1933. If you wanted to read about werewolves, you had to have an "in" at one of the ancient Monasteries and be able to read Latin, Sanskrit or ancient Gaelic or you had to settle for what you could get. The werewolf came to America along with immigrants from all corners of Europe.

Bison's 1914 The Were Wolf

The natural progression for mythical monsters that survived into the 20th Century was found in the new media of motion pictures. Millions of people arrived in America with little or no possessions. Books were a luxury. The tales were soon replaced by the silent movie. Motion picture pioneers such as Carl Laemmle, realized a perfect market in the newly formed ghetto neighborhoods of the various nationalities. Once you filmed the story, all you had to do was provide titles in the appropriate language. One year before Bram Stoker's werewolf story *Dracula's Guest* was published in England the werewolf made its debut on the silver screen.

Universal City, 1913 - the big stars of the day were Ethel Grandin, Warren Kerrigan, King Baggot (Universal's number one makeup man/character actor), Robert Leonard and Lois Webber.

While one of the new character players on the lot, Lon Chaney, (the father of the man destined for fame as the Wolf Man 30 years later) was busy making a comedy called *An Elephant on His Hands,* the 101 Bison Company dared to make a THREE-REEL picture.

Universal's founder, Carl Laemmle had converted his lease-option of 435 acres in the San Fernando Valley, north of Hollywood and bought the land. He called it Universal City. The main occupation of the citizens of Universal City was making Universal Pictures. Laemmle signed the charter, appointed a mayor, fire chief and got the city planners started and then left for New York City where he could watch over the New Jersey Studio and tend to money matters.

Most of the independent companies operating under the Universal banner were getting away with whatever they could in his absence. One Laemmle rule that was never to be broken without his OK was, ''Moving Pictures are not be longer than 2 reels.'' Most of the products were comedies, melodramas, westerns and borderline sexual, alcohol or narcotic theme pictures disguised as moral dramas.

Writer Ruth Ann Baldwin turned in a drama with the title ''She-Wolf'' and it was approved by the NY office. At the time the Bison company was involved in a battle with Laemmle, along with all the other companies operating on the lot: Powers, Victor, IMP, Nestor, Joker, Rex, Crystal, Eclair, Frontier, and Gold Seal all had separate partners and owners. Laemmle wanted to unite all the small groups into one major company. His partners felt that he was going against all that he had represented in his battle with Edison over the patents of motion picture productions and equipment by independent film makers. Being that Laemmle's concentration was on business affairs it was not noticed that the ''She-Wolf'' production by ''101 Bison'' was changed to ''The Werewolf '' - with two forbidden themes, the occult and reincarnation.

Reproduced below, the synopsis is all that remains of the film, for it was destroyed, (along with all of Universal's films from 1908 to 1917), in a fire at the Fort Lee, NJ film vault in 1924.

Punished for Hundred Year Old Crime

McCrae Directs Wonderful Play, Based on Indian Legend. Wolf Plays Important Part.

"101 Bison" Two-Reel Drama —Released December 13

Ezra Vance, prospector and trail blazer,
                          Clarence F. Burton
Kee-On-Ee . . . . Marie Walcam
Kee-On-Ee, years later . . . . Lule Warrenton
Watuma, her daughter. . . . . .Phyllis Gordon
Stone Eye. . . . . .Sherman Bainbridge
William Clifford, prospector. . . . . . Wm. Clifford
Jack Ford, reincarnation of Wm. Clifford,
                          Wm. Clifford
Ruth Anne Baldwin, one of our most prolific photoplay writers at the Pacific Coast Studio, adapted the story involved in this play from an Indian legend, dealing with the supposed ability of persons who have been turned into wolves, through magic power, to assume human form at will for purposes of vengeance.
Henry McRae, the inimitable director of heavy, spectacular screen plays has staged "The Werewolf" with all the skill at his command. Weird knowledge, gathered in the open West among the early Indians and animal life, have prepared the scenes. The way wolves of the plains have been worked into many of them betoken only the master at conceiving daring and original situations. Mr. McRae was not curtailed for lack of settings and players and properties. Situated in sunny California as he is, he has a wealth of beautiful settings at his command.
Phyllis Gordon and William Clifford, artists of known and acknowledged reputations, enact the lead roles. It is a feature of real merit, distinctive of the "101 Bison" brands and we feel certain that you are gong to be immensely pleased with it.
The play opens in pioneer days. "Kee-On-Ee" an Indian maiden, is married to Ezra Vance, a trail blazer. When her child is five years old, Kee-On-Ee is driven back to her tribe by Ezra's brother who scorns all squaws. Ezra is killed by an old enemy and Kee-On-Ee, thinking his failure to return to her to be indifference, brings up her child, Watuma, to hate all white men.
When the child is grown, Clifford and a party of prospectors appear. Kee-On-Ee, now a hag, sees her way to be revenged. She sends her daughter to Clifford's camp and he is driven nigh mad by her beauty. Clifford finds her in the arms of a young Indian. She taunts him. Enraged beyond control, Clifford shoots the buck. He flees to the mission. Watuma leads the enraged Indians against the Friars. When one of them raises a cross, Watuma slowly dissolves into a slinking wolf.
A hundred years later, Clifford, now reincarnated in the form of Jack Ford, a miner, receives a visit from his sweetheart, Margaret. Hunting with her he comes upon a wolf which he is unable to shoot. The wolf dissolves into the woman of old, and there appears before his puzzled eyes the scene where he slew the Brave. The "Wolf-woman" would caress him, but he throws her off. She returns again as the wolf and kills his sweetheart. Clifford's punishment for the deed of past life is made complete at the death of the one he loved.

The same theme was remade by the Nestor company at Universal in 1914 called *The White Wolf*. This time the plot revolved around an Indian medicine man who, in the form of a wolf, is caught in a trap set by white hunters. In the fall of 1915 Reliance films released *The Wolf Man*. This film was a 4 - reel "masterpiece" as the publicity states. (D. W. Griffith's *Birth of a Nation* had changed the industry and redefined the term "Feature Film". Any film after that, that was less than an hour long, was now considered a short). In the Reliance *The Wolf Man* of 1915, the title referred not to a monster but to "an unscrupulous businessman who will stop at nothing to win." The plot revolved around a scheme to steal a formula that would revolutionize the methods of glazing pottery.

During the early decades of the 20th century the words "vampire" and "werewolf or wolf" again adapted to the society, losing their supernatural connotations in the process. A "vampire" was a seductive woman who used her beauty to gain wealth from older admirers. A "wolf" was a man who had no ethics in business or his sexual conquests.

In 1924 there were two films called *The Wolf Man*. One made by Fox which dealt with a man giving his brother a narcotic which made him insane and the other by Sunset Productions which referred to silent star, John Gilbert's personality change whenever he drank too much.

Toward the end of 1931 the meaning would again return to its supernatural connotations when director/writer, Robert Florey wrote a treatment for possible portrayal by Boris Karloff.

With the success of Dracula and Frankenstein, the Universal lot became a year-round Halloween factory in 1932-33. As *Murders in the Rue Morgue* was released, other titles were in various stages of production. "Cagliostro" later to become *The Mummy*, "Automatron", a science fiction film, *The Invisible Man*, "A Trip to Mars"(unfinished), "The Return of Franken-stein", (*Bride of Frankenstein*), *The Old Dark House*, "The Wandering Jew" (Unmade), a remake of *The Hunchback of Notre Dame* (postponed); *Dracula* was being synchronized into French, *Frankenstein* dubbed in German and an unnamed pro-duction, which prompted the prestigious National Geographic Magazine's reporter Frederick Simpich to describe as "the illusion of prehistoric monsters invading a modern city", was achieved with Texas armadillos. Shot at 20 times normal size, while wadding past the toy buildings of a miniature city, the final effect on the screen was realistically hideous. On December 23, 1931 Robert Florey turned in a short story idea (below) called:

"The Wolf Man."

The wolf has ever been the symbol of the enemy to mankind. In speaking of poverty it is expressed as 'keeping the wolf from the door.' The three little pigs were only afraid of 'the big bad wolf' and the child of four in its nursery is told the story of Little Red Riding Hood and the wolf. You will remember the Wolf-Bane, the herb which Dracula feared because herbs and plant life have a great place in the legends which have been handed down of werewolf and of the undead. We did not see Bela Lugosi turn into the werewolf in Dracula, rather it was implied by the boy, who saw him in wolf form running from Dr. Seward's asylum.

In the book the Invisible Man when he ran across the snow we did not see him but we saw his tracks, and further, were he to swim across a lake we would not see him but the ripple that he made in the water; we find scientific basis for the statement that the werewolf man, when he runs across the newly fallen snow, leaves no tracks; although we can see him, and were he to swim across the lake, he would make no ripple in the water.

Dr. Garnier is a beautiful gentleman who lives on a estate outside of Paris. His gardens are notorious for their beauty. Yet Dr. Garnier, unknown to the people of the countryside, is cursed by God as a werewolf man.

Our first clue that Dr. Garnier is a werewolf man is that he was hirsute. Often he had to shave 6 times a day.

Dr. Garnier is over 400 years old. He was cursed by the mother of a young maiden that he had deflowered and left. The witch's curse caused him to turn into a wolf unless he had a ring of Wolf-bane to tie around his neck during the full moon when the curse struck every month.

Dr. Garnier joined the army and under the cover of battle he would turn into a wolf and kill every man in his path. This went unknown to his men. Now in time of peace he had no protection from the curse nor anywhere to hide. Like Dr. Jekyll he wanted to be good but was changed into the evil Mr. Hyde.

His only hope was to cultivate the little flower that grew on Wolf-bane. Unfortunately the flower will not bloom the entire year. Werewolves must kill each night or forever remain a wolf.

During this time Dr. Garnier is forced into the deep woods near his estate where he must kill in the form of a wolf.

It was soon that his young ward returns from her school in London with her fiancee, a young soldier. The young soldier had heard tales of the doctor when he had been in the Army. When he finds a diary, he connects that the two are one and the same.

Through some type of powerful storm, the scientific means by which Dr. Garnier keeps his Wolf-bane growing is damaged. It is the night of the full moon. He begins the transformation into the werewolf-man. Before he is completely transformed he re-calls that his ward and her fiancee are in the woods on a picnic and he sets out after them.

The story comes to a close in a great chase in which the fiancee leads the local infantry into the forest knowing the danger that the two girls are facing.

✸

Laemmle Jr. liked the idea and told Florey to join with Richard Schayer of the scenario department. On December 30 the story was revised with temporary dialog and it was announced as a 1933 film for Karloff. The property then went to writer Ardel Wray where it was revised and submitted on January 2, 1932.

The story as it exists in incomplete form, along with the holes filled in by Florey himself in an interview in 1973, made it a totally unique and well concocted script.

By this time it was known that Paramount was working on a sound version of *Dr. Jekyll and Mr. Hyde* and also Guy Endore's "Werewolf of Paris" had been published, which was based on a real life werewolf story of Sergeant Bertrand.

To avoid any copyright entanglements, Laemmle Jr. hired an entomologist and biologist, Dr. R. Woodward, to review the story as it presently existed. A rewrite was ordered.

This time the assignment went to Joseph Laren Kelly. By the end of January of 1932 the idea was put on hold. There were so many variations floating around that now no one could find a way to make a cohesive script from the original Florey idea. It turned out to be the *Frankenstein* ordeal all over again for Florey,* so rather than risk more frustration he took the money and after *Murders in the Rue Morgue* Florey left Universal.

Having purchased the story rights from Florey and Schayer for an undisclosed fee, the project was revived again in 1933 with an excellent screenplay written by Edmund Pearson. Pearson kept the wolf-bane theme but changed the original opening location from France to Tibet, where new discoveries had been made by the National Geographic Society expeditions. Stories of the Abominable Snowman, werewolves and demons from Tibet became the fashion topic of the literary groups. The doctor's name was changed to Glendon and the location England. Dr. Glendon finds the nocturnal flower, but is bitten by a werewolf in the valley of demons. The next group of screenwriters tried to make the story seem more scientific and believable by connecting the murders of the real life serial killer Jack the Ripper in the 1890s with the werewolf in the beast form of Dr. Glendon. Glendon would leave his estate/laboratory when the wolf-bane would not bloom and head for the Whitechapel district of London where he would murder prostitutes.

The project, intended for Karloff in 1932 & 1933 became Universal's first sound venture into werewolves as *The Werewolf of London.* (1935) [Guy Endore's book *The Werewolf of Paris* eventually made it to the screen 30 years later as the Universal film, *Curse of the Werewolf* made in England starring Oliver Reed.]

It would be another 5 years before the right people were in the right place, at the right time to produce what was to become the only tale of lycanthropy based on traditional folklore to become part of our own heritage, alongside Dracula, Frankenstein's monster and the resurrected mummies of ancient Egypt.

In 1914, when *Dracula's Guest* was published, there was a 12 year old boy, Kurt Siodmak, in Dresden Germany who would be destined to do for the werewolf what Bram Stoker had done for the vampire.

*Florey to be the orginal director of *Frankenstein*. When James Whale took an interest in directing the project, he let Florey go and hired another writer.

Henry Sandham's illustration for "The Werewolves" by H. Beaugrand-The Century Magazine, *August 1898*

"Loup Garou" by Alan Sullivan - Illustrated by Dudley Tennant for The Windsor Magazine, *July 1905*

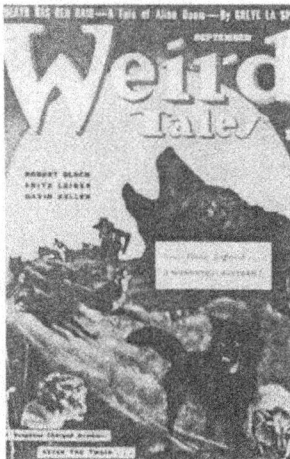

A. R. Tilburnes' Weird Tales *cover for the September 1942 issue which contained "A Werewolf Western"*

"The Werewolf Scourge" illustrated by Harold S. De Lay, January 1944

August 1952 - Famous Fantastic Mysteries' *ALL WEREWOLF ISSUE - cover by Norman Saunders*

1195-84AB

The Making
of
THE WOLF MAN
Universal City, 1941

THE LEGEND OF THE DAMNED

In many a distant
village there exists
the Legend of the
Werewolf or Wolf
Man...A legend of
a strange mortal
man with the hair
and fangs of an
unearthly beast...
his hideous howl
a dirge of death -

- from Universal's coming attraction
for *The Wolf Man*, 1941

Fog. Mysterious, foreboding fog, swirling about twisted, gnarled trees in the forest near 300-year old Talbot Castle, Wales...

An Autumn moon.

The howl of a wolf.

A beautiful blonde runs through the mist in her high heels - and sees, leering at her from behind a tree, the werewolf.

She screams lushly and wildly as the Wolf Man attacks, fondling her and tearing at her....

A small, dynamic man with magnificent eyes and a silver, wolf's-head cane runs to the rescue...With the cane, he wildly beats the beast to death....

Finally, through the fog, there comes a carriage - driven by an old Gypsy woman. She kneels beside the broken beast and recites her quavering prayer:

The way you walked was thorny,
through no fault of your own...

As the torch-bearing hunters approach, the beast transforms slowly, into Larry Talbot, son of Sir John Talbot - the man who had killed him, and who now looks on in anguish.

The blonde girl sees the body of the thing that had attacked her.

''Larry,'' she gasps.

The music swells mournfully, beautifully. The final credits roll, paying tribute to the unforgettable performances of Claude Rains, Evelyn Ankers, Maria Ouspenskaya and - in a portrayal that takes its place in Universal's Horror Mythology with Karloff's Frankenstein Monster and Lugosi's Count Dracula - Lon Chaney Jr.

It is, of course, the finale of Universal's 1941 classic, *The Wolf Man*.

LYCANTHROPY: The transformation of a human being into an animal. The term is derived from the Greek words, LUKOS a wolf, and ANTHROPOS a man, but it is employed regarding a transformation into any animal shape. It is chiefly in these countries where wolves are numerous that we find such tales concerning them...But in India, and some parts of Asia, the tiger takes the place of the wolf; In Russia and elsewhere the bear, and in Africa, the leopard...

- from THE ENCYCLOPEDIA OF
OCCULTISM AND PARAPSYCHOLOGY
(Gale Research Company, 1978)

Since ancient days (and nights), the belief that a man can transform physically into a beast has proven one of the most potent and perennial of supernatural fears. It is a terror that has haunted centuries of people, from soldiers of early Rome, to Gypsies of the Balkans, to the farmers of China - where, on nights of the full moon, peasants of some remote valleys are said still to keep vigil for were-cats, were-tigers, and even were-crocodiles.

The most infamous of the man-to-beast creatures, of course, is the LOUP-GAROU, or Lycanthrope. Its roots can be traced to Sociology (the wolf being the most feared predator of medieval Europe), Sexuality (the "liberated" carnal appetites of the wolf fascinating to the religious peasants), Literature (as described in such works as Bram Stoker's 1897 *Dracula*) - and even to History as well.

As early as 1932, Universal had announced a vehicle for Boris Karloff entitled *The Wolf Man*. It sat on the production shelf as the Monster of *Frankenstein* enjoyed new triumphs in *The Old Dark House*, *The Mummy* and *The Black Cat*.

Then, as Karloff, Elsa Lanchester and Colin Clive were starring in *Bride of Frankenstein*, Universal began shooting *Werewolf of London*. Scripted by John Colton, *Werewolf of London* originally was set to team Karloff as Lycanthrope as Dr. Wilfred Glendon, battling fellow werewolf Bela Lugosi as Dr. Yogami.

However, when shooting began January 28, 1935, under the direction of Stuart Walker, *Werewolf of London* starred Henry Hull as the tragic Glendon and Warner Oland as the cursed Yogami. Hull's Glendon is bitten by Oland's werewolf in a valley in Tibet while seeking the MARIPHASA LUPINO LUMINO flower (an antidote to Lycanthropy) on the night of a full moon. Back in London, Glendon becomes a werewolf himself, battling Yogami for the plant. Come the climax, Glendon's beast attacks his wife Lisa (Valerie Hobson, "Elizabeth" of *Bride of Frankenstein*), because as Yogami had ominously warned:

"The werewolf instinctively seeks to kill the thing it loves best."

Completed February 23, 1935, at a cost of $195,393.01, and released in May of 1935, *Werewolf of London* is a far better chiller than usually credited. Henry Hull (1894 - 1977), a marvelous, barnstorming character player who had created the role of Jeeter Lester in *Tobacco Road*, gave a controversial portrayal of the Werewolf. Many cinema reference books report that Hull refused to endure the heavy makeup concept of Jack P. Pierce, rejecting the long hours of application; Hull himself claimed late in life that he preferred the bat-like, almost satanic makeup because he felt

it necessary there be a resemblance between Glendon and the beast to accent the tragedy. Hull's Glendon is rather cold - although he does manage to evoke sympathy in his death scene, invoking one the great lines of the genre:

"In a few moments now, I shall know why all this had to be."

Even after *Werewolf of London*, the title *The Wolf Man* remained in the Universal files. Come 1941, after 1939's *Son of Frankenstein* had introduced gloriously Universal's Second Wave of Horror, the studio decided to unleash a new Lycanthrope...

And engaged a celebrated Hollywood fantasist to provide the script.

Yah, the old horror films hold up. They were classic tales; the violence was implied, the menace was implied. It wasn't like today, where you cut people open and see blood flying all over the floor. We only had the menace - which was much more tempting and frightening.

- Curt Siodmak

In 1937, Mrs. Curt Siodmak, fearful of the war brewing in Europe, persuaded her writer husband to flee to the sanctuary of America - and Hollywood. After success in Germany (1933's *F.P.I Antwortet Nicht* for UFa Studios), France (1935's *La Crise Est Finie*) and England (where he wrote the 1935 classic *Transatlantic Tunnel*), Siodmak arrived in Hollywood - and began work at Paramount, concocting the Dorothy Lamour escapism, *Her Jungle Love* (1938).

However, Curt Siodmak truly began making his mark on Hollywood folklore after reporting to Universal City, and scripting *The Invisible Man Returns* (1940), starring Vincent Price. There followed the Karloff and Lugosi *Black Friday* (1940), and the John Barrymore and Virginia Bruce *The Invisible Woman* (1941). Then came the day when Director George Waggner approached Siodmak with his next project - *The Wolf Man*.

On the set of Beast with Five Fingers - Wolf Man *author Curt Siodmak (seated on stairs) jokes with director Robert Florey who had written the unfilmed Karloff version 10 years earlier.*

*George Waggner and Jane Farrar (*Phantom of the Opera *1943)*

George Waggner - Producer & Director

The man most responsible for putting *The Wolf Man* on the screen was producer-director George Waggner. Waggner was never considered a ''pantheon'' director in the sense of a John Ford or Michael Curtiz. He was not recognized as a stylist or even a specialist, but he possessed a high degree of versatility -- a trait considered admirable among movie people but which seems to be equated with ''hack'' in the minds of most critics and historians. While it would not be possible to say that Waggner's pictures were comparable artistically to those of some of his predecessors at Universal, most particularly James Whale and Karl Freund, he sometimes gave them a close run in terms of pictorial virtuosity. This is eloquently demonstrated in visuals of *The Wolf Man*, the 1943 *Phantom of the Opera* (which he produced but did not direct) and the unsuccessful but even more elegant looking *The Climax*.

Another strength of Waggner's horror films is that in the male romantic roles he usually gave us virile characters who invited considerably more audience response than could be summoned up for the ''tennis anyone?'' juveniles who decorated so many horror films. ''Dynamo Dan'' (Lon Chaney Jr.), the tragic hero of *Man Made Monster*, is a burly carnival drifter, and the juvenile lead (Frank Albertson) is an ace newspaperman. Dick Foran, a former football star, is a seagoing adventurer in

Horror Island. In *The Wolf Man* Chaney is an engineer and his romantic rival, Patric Knowles, is a gamekeeper. Ralph Bellamy is a dashing policeman in both *The Wolf Man* and *Ghost of Frankenstein*, Patric Knowles a grimly determined medico in *Frankenstein Meets the Wolf Man*, Jon Hall a courageous spy in *Invisible Agent.* The romantic rivals of *Phantom of the Opera*, Nelson Eddy and Edgar Barrier, face the dangers of the opera house with bravado. The one exception is the love-sick youth played by Turhan Bey in *The Climax.*

Waggner himself was a man of action. He was born in New York City on September 7, 1894, and grew up in Philadelphia, where he was a pre-med student at the Philadelphia College of Pharmacy. Tall and sturdily built, with piercing blue eyes, square jaws and an Irish temperament, he seemed more the athlete and outdoorsman than a medical man. With the outbreak of World War I in 1916, he served with the Pennsylvania National Guard patrolling the Mexican border, later continuing this duty as a cavalry officer in the U. S. Army. During this time he gained notoriety as a trick rider and also won several division champion-ships as a heavyweight boxer. Mustering out in 1920, he went directly to Hollywood, hoping to get work at a movie studio. He had to settle for a medley of part-time jobs: teaching horseback riding, singing in a trio in cafes and vaudeville houses, and playing occasional supporting parts in plays and movies.

Waggner teamed up with a pal, J. Russel Robinson, a young jazz musician who had sold several songs. One of their collabo-rations was ''Mary Lou'', which was published and became an instant hit. It sold over one million copies and was recorded by 29 leading orchestras, but no money came to the composers because of a copyright suit which lasted for two years. A judge at last ruled for the authors, but the publisher declared bankruptcy the next day and the royalties were never paid. (The song is still a standard with jazz groups and provided the title and theme song of a Columbia picture in 1948.)

Meantime, Waggner's movie work was beginning to pay off. The earliest role in which he received screen billing was Paramount's 1921 hit, *The Sheik*, in which he played Youssef, sidekick to star Rudolph Valentino. He portrayed a slicker named Bradley Carstairs in American's *The Great Alone* (1922), a lead in the independent *Branded Man* (1922); the chief heavy in Robertson-Cole's *Desert Driven* (1923), a good Harry Carey Western; ''Buffalo Bill'' Cody in John Ford's Fox special, *The Iron Horse* (1924); the tough Sascha Basmonoff in Metro-Goldwyn's *His Hour* (1924); and Isaacson in MGM's *Love's Blindness* (1926).

In the early Thirties -- in the depths of the Great Depression -- Waggner also became established as a writer of scripts, originals and songs, mostly for independent producers. Poverty Row prices were low, but seemed opulent in those hard times. His screenplays and originals in 1932-33 included Mayfair's *The Gorilla Ship* and Monogram's *Sweetheart of Sigma Chi*. His impressive writing output in 1934 consisted of three for Mono-gram: *Girl of My Dreams, He Couldn't Take It* and *City Limits*; Liberty's *Once to Every Bachelor*, and a step up to Columbia for *The Line Up* and *Among the Missing*. In 1935 his output of scripts and originals was prodigious, with Fox's *Cowboy Millionaire* and *Spring Tonic*, Liberty's *Dizzy Dames*, Monogram's *Cheers of the Crowd, The Nut Farm, The Healer*, and *Keeper of the Bees*,

Republic's *Cappy Ricks Returns*, and Columbia's *Champagne for Breakfast*.

A long association with Universal began in 1936 with the screen play for a romantic comedy, *Don't Get Personal*. At this time Consolidated Film Industries, Mascot and Monogram had joined with other independent studios in creating Republic Pictures. The former head of Monogram, Trem Carr, became a production executive at Universal and signed Waggner to write two John Wayne non-Western action pictures, *Sea Spoilers* (1936) and *I Cover the War* (1937). Carr was also in charge of Universal's Western features and hired Waggner as associate producer. In this capacity Waggner delivered some of the best "B" Westerns of the period. Under the pseudonym of Joseph West he wrote the scripts of some of these projects, which starred singing cowboy Bob Baker. During 1938 he directed *Outlaw Express* and *Western Trails* and both wrote and directed *The Black Bandit, Guilty Trails, Prairie Justice, Ghost Town Riders, Honor of the West*, and a 1939 entry in the series, *The Phantom Stage*.

After Monogram was reorganized, Waggner returned in 1939 to direct *Mystery Plane* and *Stunt Pilot*, based on the "Tailspin Tommy" cartoon strip, with John Trent, Marjorie Reynolds and Milburn Stone. Also for Monogram he directed the interesting Indian drama, *Wolf Call*, with Movita and John Carroll. In 1940 he wrote a comedy-mystery series with Frankie Darro and Mantan Moreland (titles: *On the Spot, Laughing at Danger*), plus *Son of the Navy* and the last picture in the James Lee Wong detective series, *Phantom of Chinatown*. After directing *Drums of the Desert*, a foreign legion comedy-adventure with Ralph Byrd and Mantan Moreland, he signed another contract with Universal as a writer, director and associate producer.

Waggner also continued his life-long sideline as a song writer, librettist and music publisher, collaborating with Gus Kahn, Ted Fio Rito, and Edward Ward and others. During his lifetime he authored more than a hundred songs, including such palpable hits as "If I Had My Way" (for Bing Crosby), "Neath a Blanket of Stars", "Sweet Someone", and "Love Me To-night". He became a member of ASCAP in 1941.

Nothing in Waggner's work prior to his return to Universal suggested that he would achieve his greatest fame as a maker of horror films. His songs were as sentimental as those of any Tin Pan Alley tunesmith; his scripts and directorial efforts all emphasized romance, comedy and adventure. A few light chills were evident in the Darro-Moreland films, the Wong picture and a couple of Westerns, but nothing that suggested an interest in inspiring spectral fear. His first 1941 directorial assignment at Universal -- *Man Made Monster* -- was something else.

In 1935 Universal had bought a story called "The Electric Man" for their successful horror team, Boris Karloff and Bela Lugosi. It was written by two New York *Daily Mirror* newspaper reporters, Harry J. Essex and Sid Schwartz, and a press agent, Len Golos. After being scheduled as *The Man in the Cab*, it was shelved by the new regime that purchased Universal early in 1936. As Joseph West, Waggner wrote a final script which he retitled *The Human Robot*. The studio announced it as *The Mysterious Dr. R* and gave Waggner the opportunity to direct it for associate producer Jack Bernhard. They were given a three weeks shooting schedule and a budget of only $86,000, although some elaborate special effects brought the costs up a bit.

Most of the advance publicity was built around the fact that Lon Chaney Jr., son of the great character actor, would appear as the title character. Chaney Jr. had recently earned great acclaim in stage and screen versions of *Of Mice and Men* as Lennie, a feeble-minded giant who is both fearsome and lovable. His role as Dan, "the electric man", in *Man Made Monster* exploited these attributes to great effect with the aid of a fine Jack Pierce makeup and an ingenious optical effect which made him appear to glow with pulsing electricity. The basic plot is a standard mad scientist yarn, but there are some inspired touches that lift it out of the mundane.

The studio didn't complain about the extra costs. Waggner and Bernhard had delivered an inexpensive picture that would surmount its origins. It had a lot going for it: the best mad scientist of all, Lionel Atwill; some solid support from Anne Nagel, Samuel S. Hinds and Frank Albertson; a superb photographic job by the up-and coming Woody Bredell, ASC, a fine and mostly original score by Hans J. Salter, and big-time special effects by the hard-boiled genius, John P. Fulton, ASC. Instead of relegating it to a supporting feature slot for double-bill bookings (the fate of other pictures of its financial caste), Universal elected to send it out as a bill-topper.

Accordingly, Bernhard, Waggner, Bredell and Salter were assigned to rush through a lower-half running mate under supervision of the notoriously penurious Ben Pivar. In the cast of *Horror Island* were the leads from Pivar's highly successful *The Mummy's Hand*, Dick Foran and Peggy Moran, plus Leo Carrillo, Fuzzy Knight and Walter Catlett.

Horror Island was shot in two weeks, cast and crew working almost around the clock. Another week was allowed for editing and scoring. It's a mystery-comedy about a treasure hunting expedition to an island with a pirate castle. There are murders, a mysterious phantom, and the big Tower of London sets to provide an impressive atmosphere. Most of the action moves briskly and it's a generally entertaining show.

The double bill release paid off handsomely. Waggner was handed a seven year contract and promoted to larger budget pictures, first as associate producer of an extravagant Western, *Badlands of Dakota* (1941), with Robert Stack, Ann Rutherford, Richard Dix, Frances Farmer and Broderick Crawford. Next he was associate producer and director of a parodic South Seas picture, *South of Tahiti* (1941), which starred Brian Donlevy and introduced Maria Montez in the prototype of her future sarong and sand epics.

Then Waggner produced and directed *The Wolf Man*.

Siodmak faced the challenge not only of creating a moving, frightening and powerful horror story (one he molded along the lines of ancient Greek Tragedy, with Man vs Fate) - he had the task of tailoring the characters to the actors Universal had engaged for the project.

Llansileffraillerchymair!

This is the name of our town in Wales. A train, pulled by a small aged engine, comes to a screeching stop.

''Llans! ...'' The conductor calls out, pronouncing the impossible name in his own private way.

In a small first-class compartment at the end of the train, Donald Hill stretches his 6' 3" frame and sticks his huge head out the window; but he cannot see the long name of the station any more.

Hill is described as a plain-spoken, jovial Texan, primitive but of native cunning. He is met by Professor Talbot, an eminent astro-physicist and they drive on to Wolfendon, the professor's manor house. ''The atmosphere of a century-old sleep has settled over the medieval roofs.''

Don sees the beautiful girl (named Daphne Stokes in this draft) in the professor's telescope and goes to meet her in the antique shop.

The professor in the original draft is aristocratic and impatient. When Hill returns and is reprimanded by the professor, Siodmak has him say to himself, ''The hurry these scientist are in! As if the world wouldn't go on for billions of years! They squeeze a man's time of leisure and make him work. The universe has time to wait, but not his date with Daphne!''

Jenny is introduced as a ''dried-out spinster, at an age when women become less attractive to pleasure-seeking young men. She talks incessantly and flirts in a way that is completely wasted on Don.''

The remaining draft is basically the same as the finished product only more literate. It makes the reader wish that Siodmak had novelized his screenplay for publication.

The only differences that appear, take place at the end.

As Don begins to realize that he too is a werewolf, he tries to leave town by the train, but a violent lightning and wind storm knocks out the crossing bridge and his train is delayed.

Frank, Daphne's fiancee, is introduced and a love rivalry begins. In the end, Don almost convinces Frank that he is a werewolf. Daphne gives back Don's gift of a silver amulet, in the shape of a pentagram with a wolf in the center, to prevent a fight between him and Frank. Don melts down the amulet and makes a silver bullet which he gives to Frank with instructions to use it when he finally meets the werewolf.

❀ In the next treatment, the Wolf Man is not Don Hill but Larry Gill - an American engineer who visits Wales to adjust the new telescope of Sir John Talbot in the observatory of his ancient castle.

❀ When Larry accidentally zooms the telescope into the boudoir of Gwen Conliffe, the unsuspecting heroine begins undressing; Sir John interrupts Larry's voyeurism.

❀ As Larry and Gwen observe the Gypsies arriving in the village, Bela the Fortune Teller gives them a smile - and ''shows his big white teeth.''

❀ Bela's funeral, as conceived by Siodmak, was a tour de force of horror. Larry was to peer into the coffin, and see the Lycanthrope he had ''killed'' in the forest with a bandage wrapped around his head like a turban. ''The dead man's eyes are open; he seems to be looking at Larry with a malevolent grin, as

First page of the first treatment for The Wolf Man

Script Development

Curt Siodmak threw himself into the job of writing *The Wolf Man* script with a passion. He produced a 69-page story outline, dated June 1, 1941, followed by a treatment and then the first draft 142-page script, dated July 1, 1941. At least three revisions followed on August 1, October 9th, and the final shooting script dated October 22, 1941. The script included in this volume is the October 9th version which contains the scenes ordered excised by the censor's office.

A perusal of Siodmak's original treatment (known as *The Wolf Man,* then *Destiny* then back to *The Wolf Man*) reveals a very different concept - and one which, in many ways, was a far more avant-garde approach than ultimately filmed:

May of 1941 - Not long after being given the assignment, Kurt Siodmak turned in the first 44 page treatment on May 28th. (In the written drafts Mr. Siodmak's first name had been mistakenly spelled with the ''K'') Although the title had been owned by Universal since 1931, and all of the treatments and various versions from the Florey version to the final rejected screenplay were still available in the vaults, the multilingual Siodmak did not even need to review the old scripts. Starting from scratch, he researched the old legends from the original sources and decided that the Gaelic version of werewolves legends held the best dramatic possibilities.

The first treatment begins:

if he were not dead at all. The pentagram on his forehead stands out like a dark imprint."

"The impression will be given that Bela is alive - but unable to move," wrote Siodmak, even calling for the camera to be in the coffin as Bela is borne to his grave on the undertakers' shoulders, looking up at the church yard trees and the bell tower - all from the "dead" werewolf's point of view. And when Larry follows the coffin to the crypt, and again bends over the coffin, "Bela seems to stare at Larry with a fiendish smile."

Maleva then arrived, recited her "The way you walked was thorny" prayer - and touched a flower against Bela's mouth - the grin disappeared. She touched the pentagram - and it faded away. And, after this spiritual cleansing, "Bela lies there, a happy smile on his face, as if he had found peace at last."

Indeed, this episode, which wonderfully showcases Siodmak's imagination for chills, is one of the best (and, as will be seen, was designed as one of the most profound) ingredients of the original script.

✪ In the carnival sequence, as the Gypsies come to the village to celebrate Bela's entrance to "a much better world", there was an episode fated for notoriety - a Gypsy with a bear. "Who will dare to wrestle with the bear...?" hawks the Gypsy, seeking a man to fight his gentle bear who takes bows and "throws kisses to the public." Larry, feeling the bestial urges swelling up in him, agrees to the contest. "Come on, you brown beggar!" taunts Larry. As the crowd "howls in delight," Larry cruelly and sadistically beats the bear (Larry's "eyes wild with the lust to kill"); and the poor bear ("too plump to move fast, and seeming to be strangely frightened too...") finally "topples" over after Larry beats him. Even after the bear is down, Larry seems hell-bent on killing the beast, and Gwen rushes to stop the battle. "...Larry stares at Gwen, glassy-eyed, as if about to hit her too."

✪ When Larry goes to church with Sir John, a dog "runs away, yelping, its tail between its legs," and chickens "cackle excitedly in fright, as if a fox had invaded their coops."

✪ As Larry enters the church, a sun beam "throws the shadow of the high cross toward the door. The shadow ends at Larry's feet, as if barring his way." (This actually appeared in the final release print, although in far more subtle manner than suggested in the early script.)

✪ Larry pours out his fears to the Rev. Norman, who takes him to the altar to pray. Larry looks up at a stained glass window, which Siodmak wrote, "depicts 'The Temptation of St. Anthony.' The Saint is kneeling, about to be attacked by fiendish creatures with dragon tails and animal heads. In front of the helpless Saint, a huge wolf rears its head, about to sink its teeth into Anthony's chest. The wolf's head is crowned with a pentagram." As Larry stares at the window, "The wolf's fiery tongue seems to move" - and Larry, his hand clutching where the wolf had bitten him, runs out of the church.

✪ Dr. Lloyd adds to the legend of the werewolf with a line paraphrased from *Werewolf of London* - claiming the werewolves "end up - inevitably - by killing what they love most!"

✪ Frank Andrews expresses more jealousy and animosity toward Larry in the early draft, warning Larry that if he hurts Gwen, "I'll shoot you down like a dog...like I'd shoot that wolf - that kills people in the dark!"

✪ Larry moulds his own silver bullet - from the silver charm

he had received from Maleva, and had given to Gwen.

✪ Larry visits Frank at the latter's hunting lodge in the woods - "built in the style of Henry V, overgrown with vines and surrounded by a small garden." Inside is "a picture of Christ." "If the wolf attacks Gwen," Larry tells Frank, "...then shoot him with this" - and he gives Frank the silver bullet.

✪ At no time in the script has the Wolf Man appeared. Come the climax, during the hunt, Larry leans against "A Huge Tree Near a Dark Pool of Water:"

He looks into the pool: Larry's face writhes in agony, his hands are clasped around his throat. And now: his forehead seems to become overgrown with fulvous grey hair - it sprouts on his cheeks - his arms become wolfishly long and thin - his teeth grow pointed and wolfish....

...NOTE: The wolf-man's face is never seen - ONLY IN THE MIRROR OF THE WATER - AS SEEN THROUGH LARRY'S EYES - AS HE IMAGINES HIMSELF.

✪ As the wolf attacks Gwen, "and HOWLS as if in triumph," Frank Andrews shoots the silver bullet into the beast. The Wolf Man limps to the pool, falls under the tree, looks into the water "and stares at his reflection in agony," and dies.

✪ Then came the finale - a moving, brilliantly-imagined episode which (as it had with Bela the Gypsy), sees the action through the eyes of the "dead" Larry...

Dr. Lloyd examines Larry's body... Sir John looks down at him... Gwen's face appears, "desperately unhappy, her eyes overflowing in terror and grief... A hymn is heard, accompanied by angelic voices..."

And now Larry's eyes look up and see Maleva. She murmurs her prayer - "...so tears run to a predestined end..." - and hands the wolfbane to Gwen.

"Touch his heart...Touch his cheeks... His lips... His eyes..."

Gwen does so, and stops the flower where Larry's lips would be. And, as the camera stays focused on Gwen through Larry's eyes, Gwen, "smiling through her tears," speaks what might have been one of the greatest "curtain lines" of the Horror Genre, as the dead werewolf finds peace.

"Look!..." says the weeping Gwen. "He's smiling!"

Gwen moves the wolfbane toward Larry's eyes, blacking out the camera as "THE MUSIC RISES TO A MAJESTIC HYMN - and the scene ENDS."

Perhaps the most significant change in the first draft shooting script was Universal's decision to drop the Siodmak concept of only showing the werewolf in the eyes of Larry. Such an enigmatic approach was perfect for the works of Val Lewton, who would begin his RKO horror films with *Cat People* in 1942, but Universal wanted a new, all-out monster - and Jack P. Pierce, creator of all the Great Universal Monster Makeups, was waiting in the background, ready to perform his alchemy.

On July 2nd, Siodmak revised his treatment. Universal wanted a monster and they would surely get one. To provide a proper perspective of Siodmak's incredibly visual style of writing, the new ending of the script with the "on-screen" werewolf is reproduced on the following page. Mr. Siodmak remarked that perhaps he subconsciously was sending a message to the producer to give him his raise or else!

The noise of the approaching beaters is heard; their sticks clatter on the trees and bushwood, their voices shout through the night. Again the wolf's howl is heard, nearer now -- the fleeing deer and rabbits have disappeared, hiding, trembling, under brushes.

Suddenly a grey animal breaks through the underbrush. The men on the stand see two burning eyes glitter.

Sir John shoots, Chandler's rifle follows. Shots ring out from every tree.

The wolf rears on his hind legs - then he bolts - a grey fast-moving shadow, which disappears as if the earth has opened and swallowed him.

"We missed!" Chandler says in surprise.

"We can't have missed - not all of us!" Sir John retorts angrily. "I didn't - I had him right in my sight - I couldn't possibly have missed him!"

"It's uncanny!" Chandler reloads his gun. "But perhaps he's wounded. Let's get the dogs after him!"

And dejectedly the men begin to climb down from the stand.

At the lodge, Gwen is putting a log on the fire when Peter the dog suddenly jumps up with a low frightened growl. With his fur standing up, he retreats toward the staircase that leads to the upstairs bedroom.

"Peter!" Gwen calls the dog's name, alarmed at his strange behavior.

Suddenly a wolf howls... his wild, ferocious cry echoes through the small building. Gwen stands petrified.

She can see two glaring eyes shining through the window coming closer... the outline of a huge wolf is clear.

"Frank!" Gwen runs toward the staircase, while Peter, fangs bared, stops in front of her to protect her.

The window is shattered under the impact of a heavy body. The curtains, torn off, crash to the floor.

The wolf stands in the living room, crouching, ready to spring.

Gwen runs up the stairs. The wolf jumps to reach the stairs, but the dog attacks him. A second later, wolf and dog are entangled in a life and death struggle. The wolf shakes himself free, and runs up the stairs. The frightened girl stands paralyzed, her eyes fixed on the beast, which suddenly uneasy, turns.

In the doorway stands Frank. Cool and precise, he pulls the trigger of his gun, shooting both barrels squarely between the eyes of the animal, which stares at him, motionless. But the bullets have no effect - the beast jumps toward Frank, who beats it back with the rifle butt. The beast steps back and crouches. Frank, seeing his death staring him in the face, snatches the silver bullet from his pocket, and reloads his gun as fast as his hands can move.

The wolf jumps, the bullet catches him in mid-air.

The impact of the heavy body knocks Frank down. He collapses under the werewolf's weight.

Gwen watches the scene, terror-stricken, then faints away.

Frank staggers to his knees. Before his eyes the wolf lies dead, his fangs bared as if in agony.

Frank gets up, grabs his gun. He hears the dog whining. Running up the stairs, he sees Peter standing in front of the unconscious girl, trembling, but still ready to defend her. Frank bends down and takes Gwen's still face in his hands, calling her name.

He does not see that the form of the wolf has changed: the body is not an animal anymore... It looks like a hideous human monster, half-wolf, half-man, the forehead overgrown with hair, hair on cheeks and arms, hands like wolf claws, teeth long and pointed, its feet bare.

The monster slowly changes into a human being...The hair on the forehead shrinks, the mouth takes a human shape... and Larry's motionless body lies on the floor.

"Frank..." the girl opens her eyes, weakly she supports herself on his shoulder. Looking down into the living room, she sees Larry's body.

The window is broken, the door open...Her memory returns.

"Frank!" she cries out. "What happened to Larry...?"

Frank follows her gaze. Where the wolf had been lying he sees Larry. He pales, his voice forsakes him for a moment. But then he takes the trembling girl into his arms: "Don't be afraid... there's no danger anymore," he says quietly.

He helps the girl down the steps, as voices approach rapidly, dogs bark, and into the room rush the hunters, followed by a score of beaters.

"Mr. Gill...!" Sir John looks at Larry's body in dismay.

"What happened?" Kendall asks.

"I shot the wolf," Frank says quietly, "but the bullet must have hit Larry..."

This was exactly what Universal had wanted, a new monster tailor made specifically for their new horror star.

Waggner set a September 8, 1941 starting date for *The Wolf Man*. Ultimately, the studio pushed production back by 7 weeks to provide for changes asked for by Claude Rains, and many changes *were* made in the script. One dynamic change was Siodmak making Larry Gill now Larry Talbot - long-estranged son of Sir John. Larry has come home following the hunting accident death of his older brother. There was little family resemblance of course, between Rains and Chaney (who was at least 5" taller and 60 lbs. heavier than his screen father!); yet this definitely made for a far more dramatic story.

Indeed, several revisions on *The Wolf Man* greatly improved Rains' role. Siodmak revised a line from an earlier draft ("You policemen are always in such a hurry - as if dead men hadn't all eternity"), which had been spoken by Dr. Lloyd in the early treatment. And, of course, in the revised script, it was now Sir John (and not Frank Andrews) who killed his own son in the forest - a touch reminiscent of classical tragedy. It would be a fortuitous change; the memory of Rains wildly attacking the werewolf with the silver wolf's-head cane, and the anguished look in his eyes as his dead son transforms before him, is one of the most haunting vignettes of Universal horror.

Some of the early script's more avant-garde episodes would be very much revised in the finished film. Many of the religious icons originally called for were cut. The concept of the evil, undead werewolf, as realized in the deaths of Bela and Larry, was eliminated, as Associate Producer/Director George Waggner scrapped the "seeing eye" approach that Siodmak had so cleverly created. This cut the wonderful "Look - he's smiling!" finale, yet the eventual climax, shot in straightforward, full-blooded objective style by the no- nonsense Waggner, would still be powerful.

The project was now in the hands of Jack P. Pierce.

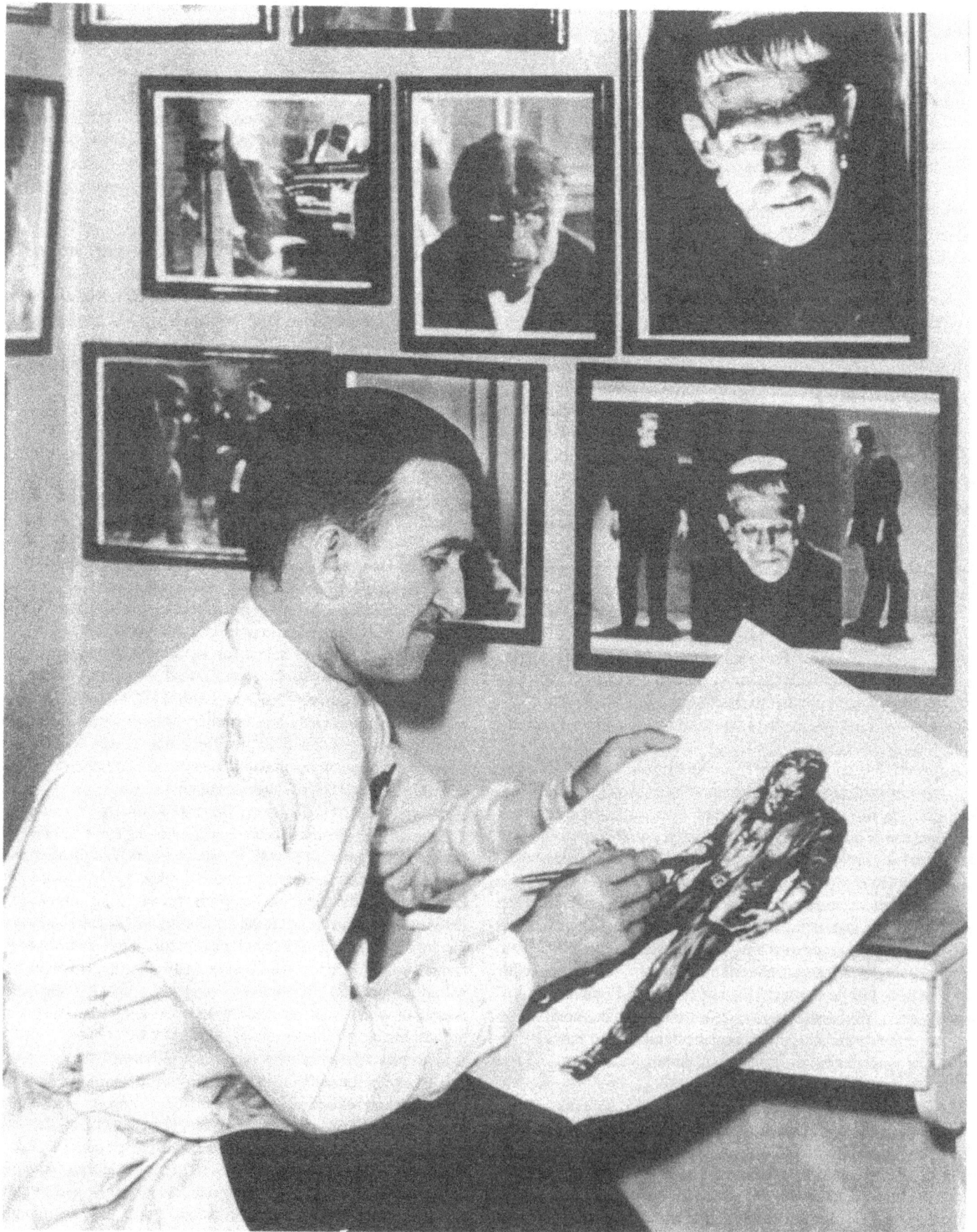

The Wolf Man *(Florey-Schayer version)*, The Hunchback of Notre Dame *and* Bluebeard *were all on the Universal planning board. Here, Jack Pierce sketches a new character for Boris Karloff in his makeup studio 1932.*

Jack P. Pierce
by
Douglas Norwine

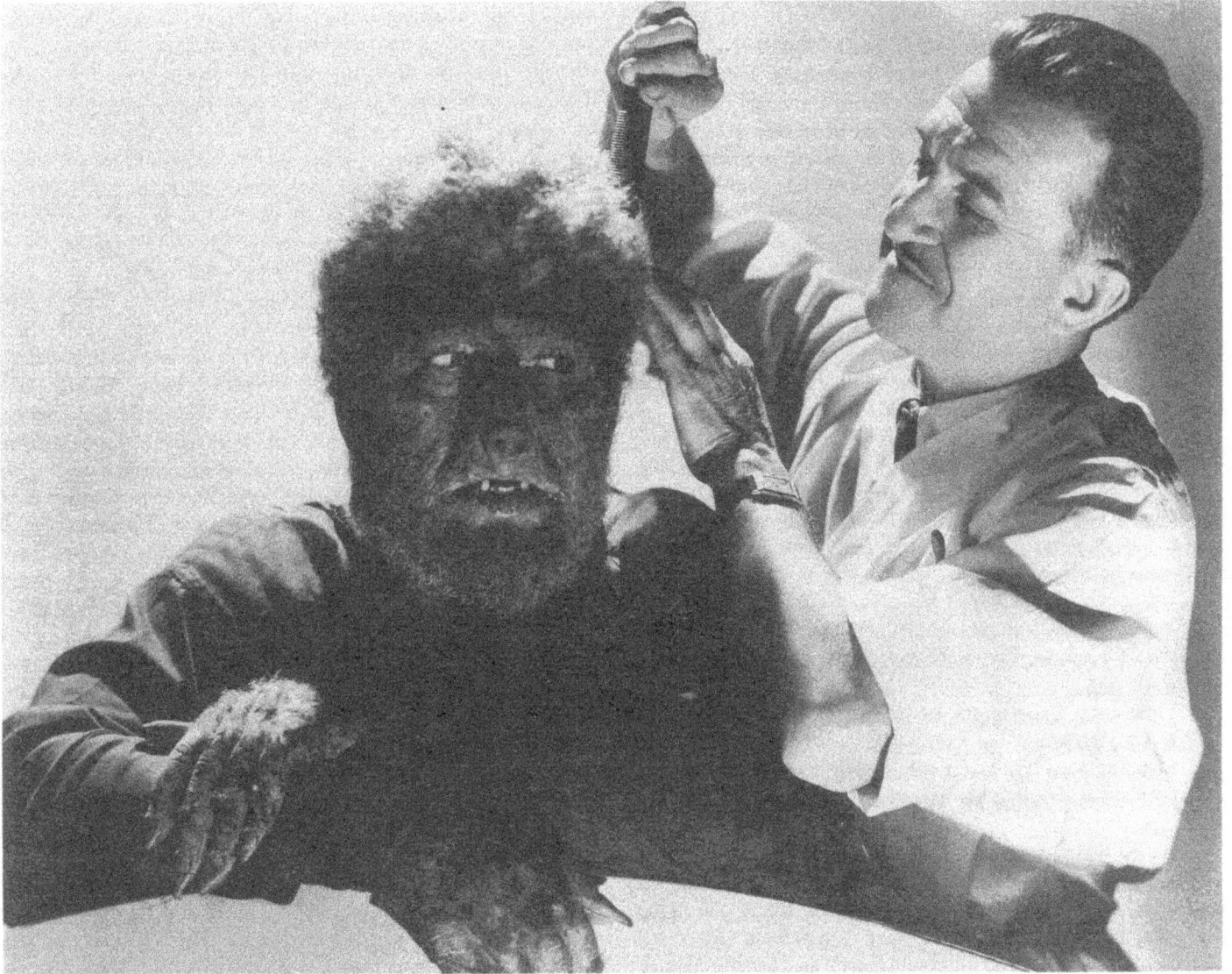

Jack P. Pierce prepares Lon Chaney for his role as the Wolf Man.

Including a tribute to Jack Pierce in this book on *The Wolf Man* is so fitting. It is commonly agreed upon that he was a genius in the field of makeup. His pioneering contributions to the horror genre are undisputed, and his innovative creations will continue to thrill generation after generation. Even with all these impressive credentials, it is really amazing how little is actually known today about our "Modern Prometheus" and how many misconceptions about the man abound.

The Hollywood of 1915 was a paradise. The fragrance of orange blossoms joined with the scent of pepper trees to make the early evenings, the clear skies and the pleasant climate almost unreal compared to the rest of the United States. It was a land where anything was possible. It was a land where dreams came true. It was the land of the moving picture business which gave birth to some of the stories told to millions of European citizens who were contemplating the long expensive journey to the land where sidewalks were made of gold and opportunity for success was unlimited. After all, only 7 years earlier had not Carl Laemmle, the poor boy from Laupheim, Germany gone from a clothing salesman to a motion picture mogul? Now he not only owned a studio, but his own city, too!

Hundreds of thousands of men and women from all over the world flocked to the California dream factory. Carpenters, photographers, fashion models, stage actors, electricians; people from all walks of life sought to cash in on the new Hollywood craze. Many of these people headed over the Hollywood Hills to Laemmle's Universal City, the world's only city devoted exclusively to making motion pictures. It was then that they found out that this process of making these 20 minute adventures into silver shadows projected on a screen, was a little more work than reaching into their pocket and handing the box office girl their five cents admissions. It was a brutal business where one out of a hundred-thousand survived, and those pioneers who did survive all had one common trait: the desire to work hard at what they loved.

It was to this land that a small but powerfully-built Greek immigrant arrived. To him, the wooden sidewalks at Hollywood and Vine *were* golden. To him, the gates at Universal City would be the gates of opportunity that had been spoken about in all corners of Europe. It would take over 13 years of strenuous work, patience, ethics, and the ability to survive the pain of creation that would finally bring to Jack Pierce the title, Head of Makeup for Universal Studios. The opportunity would come about when two important events took place within the politics of the studio. First, the world famous makeup artist and actor Lon Chaney would leave Universal after signing a contract with Metro-*Goldwyn*-Mayer; and second, young Carl Laemmle Junior would become the new Studio Production Manager with the coming of sound pictures.

Janus Piccoulas was born on May 5, 1889, in the small Greek village of Valtetsi, to the North of Tripoli. His father was a nomadic goat-herder, travelling with his flocks at the whims of the Greek seasons. Although this gypsy-style life gave no sense of a permanent home to the small ones of the family, the strength came from the family itself, not the structure in which they lived. As a young boy, Janus helped his father tend the goats as they grazed over the mountainous terrain, and although the Piccoulas family were peasants, they were happy and extremely proud of their work ethic.

Little Janus loved sports. He was a fast runner and loved to tumble down the hills doing somersaults as he chased after a stray goat from the herd. He loved being outdoors, but his favorite pastime became amazing his friends and family with his clever disguises.

As the family lore goes, young Janus would amuse himself and his brothers during the long days of herding by altering his face, using the materials he found in the fields. By the end of the day, when the time was near for the men's return to the village, his mother and sister would be filled with fearful anticipation: not for *when* the men would be returning, but, more like, *what* would be returning. Sometimes Janus would come home with goat horns coming out of the sides of his head, or his nose would be melted away. Sometimes his entire face would be covered with hair, and, even at this young age, he apparently became quite adept at making it all look convincing. Perhaps it was too convincing for some of the simple Orthodox villagers, as, Greece at the turn of the century was still a land full of superstitions. Its borders were near the wild Austria-Hungary Empire, home to the Carpathian Mountains and Transylvania. Werewolves, vampires, and de-mons were not regarded as myths by everyone, and some took these legends literally as the doctrines of the Church. This was a time when men and women were put to the stake for being suspected vampires or werewolves. So Janus and his makeups were not always taken so lightly!

Shortly after the turn of the century, Janus's father received word from a relative who had made the journey to America. There was, it seemed, a world of promise and hope far across the sea, so the Piccoulas family decided to make the move and try their luck in this new land.

Like all immigrants, they arrived in New York Harbor, made their way through Ellis Island, and began to make a permanent home for themselves for the first time... or so they thought. Mr. Piccoulas waisted little time in reverting back to his nomadic life-style and the family soon found themselves in Chicago. It is with all likelihood that the young Jack experienced the Chicago theaters; the same theaters that exposed people like Lon Chaney, Tod Browning, George Loane Tucker, and Wallace Worsley to the world of film during the years of the new century.

Chicago also provided Janus with inspiration for his love of sports. His naturally strong physique gave him the chance to become a physical instructor and a new found love called "base-ball lured Janus to Wrigley Field to see the Cubs.

One thing that became very clear to Janus was that he would never leave the Greek neighborhood of Chicago unless he learned the language of his adopted land. After being the first in his family to speak fluent English, he quickly realized that all the successful innovators and businessmen of the time did not have European-sounding names, even though they were from Europe. Many of these immigrants were the last to be accepted, and a cruel cycle of stereotyping, slang names, and sometimes even beatings were the first American "customs" to greet many of these people. It seemed to Janus that, to be successful in America, one must have an "American" name, so, to the horror of his family, Janus Piccoulas became Jack Pierce. As a tacit acknowledgment of his Greek name, and to appease his family's ire, he added the letter "P" as a middle initial. Jack hoped that this would bring some peace to the family, and it did clam things down for a while but it was never forgotten nor forgiven. The family let this "shame" fester in their hearts, making what was to come in the near future an exaggerated incident that was never to heal.

Just as Jack was becoming accustomed to life in Chicago, the family moved again, this time to California: the golden land of dreams. Unlike the Eastern cities, populated since the 1700s, California was accessible only by train. Even the new giant industries of the early 20th century such as AT&T's telephone service had not yet reached the West Coast with long distance service. Tales of perfect climate, inexpensive land, gold strikes in the Sierra Mountains, and magical seaports such as San Francisco were the talk of the East.

Once again the Piccoulas family and one Pierce pulled up the tent stakes and made their way to the West. They found San Francisco to be all that was promised: a beautiful city by the Bay. It had an Opera House where the great Enrico Caruso would soon be appearing with the Metropolitan Opera's Touring group; and the famous Barbary Coast, Chinatown and Nob Hill were spell-binding.

It was only a few day's before the Piccoulas' discovered that San Francisco had something in common with their native Greece: earthquakes! At 5 o'clock in the morning on Wednesday, April 18, 1906, about the time when the family was rising to begin the day's work, the first wave of the disastrous quake hit. In Greece, earthquakes were confined to the sparsely-populated mountains, but San Francisco was a different story. Thousands of people rushed into the streets and for the next 3 days, aftershocks and fires all but leveled this beautiful city by the bay.

Out came the tent pegs again; this time the destination was Los Angeles. The Greek community in Los Angeles was smaller than in Chicago. Only a few miles away was Hollywood: now the home of the same motion pictures that had fascinated Jack in Chicago.

He spent more and more time away from his family as he was exposed to the fringes of the industry, and at first he survived by selling newspapers and doing odd-jobs. The time away from home caused more strain between himself and his family and eventually, he moved out of the family home altogether.

His people were still having a hard time accepting his Americanized name, but when he married Blanche Craven, a non-Greek woman, that was the final blow. The family wanted nothing more to do with the newlyweds, and Jack and Blanche felt the same toward the Piccoulas clan. It was at this time that Jack turned his back on his Greek past, never to return.

The man credited with giving Jack Pierce his start in the industry was Harry Culver. Culver was a real estate genius who

As the villain in an early Universal film - The handwriting is Pierce's.

spent most of his time developing land between Los Angeles and what was to become Venice, California. Harry Culver loved motion pictures and, like Carl Laemmle in Chicago, was one of the first to begin building theaters for the viewing public. As his business expanded by the exhibition of the newest 2 and 3-reel pictures people swarmed out on Saturdays to stand in line and pay their 5 cents admission, taking in a full day of movies, sing-alongs and vaudeville acts. Culver was in need of staff and trained personnel for these theaters, so he gave Jack Pierce a job as a projectionist. Soon Culver made an astonishing announcement that he was willing to ''give'' 20 acres of land to any producer who would build and develop a moving picture studio on a dry and barren stretch of land between downtown Los Angeles and his new resort, Venice, which he was developing complete with canals.

The man who accepted Culver's offer was Thomas Ince, so Jack quit his job as a projectionist and went to work for Ince, loading film into cameras, helping with the scenery, and finally, taking on stunt jobs that seemed too risky for the stars to perform. Soon Jack got similar work at Carl Laemmle's studio in Hollywood (Universal City in the San Fernando Valley was still under construction) and at J. Stuart Blackton's Vitagraph company in Santa Monica.

Twenty years later, while looking back at this time in his life, Pierce humorously recalled, ''I used to do falls from horses, buildings, and bluffs, at *one dollar* per fall! Occasionally, a real risk, such as a jump through a window, from one building to another, or falls from a fire escape would come along, and I would gladly risk my life for the sum of *ten dollars!*''

By 1914, Blackton had moved his studio to Hollywood and had bought a piece of land on Prospect and Talmadge Avenues, only a trolley ride over the Hill from Universal City.

Gradually, through his built in work-a-holic personality, Jack began to get acting parts in the movies. Having a background in cameras, projectors, stunts and sets made Pierce a very valuable character to have around, since most of the higher-paid directors were new to the motion picture business. Jack was usually cast as the villain, and it was through these parts that his destiny would soon be achieved.

I was a villain, but I was only five-feet five inches in height. I wasn't big enough to scare the hero!

There were no makeup men in those days and Jack's childhood pastime of disguises opened the doors to a totally virgin area in the film industry. Character actors were usually required to come up with their own ''look''. At Universal actors like Lon Chaney, Monroe Salisbury, King Baggott, men with no real box office name or the special exceptional good looks required to be a star, were making a living at character parts by using their own stage makeup techniques. While working at Universal from 1913 to the late teens Jack often came into contact with those actors and, when he did he watched, learned, and experimented. His talents, however did not come from years of stage experience, but by his own experimentation and imagination. Between 1915 and 1925 he acted, directed and did makeup for other actors at Vitagraph, Lasky's Famous Players, Inspiration Pictures and Universal. It was also during those years that Lon Chaney had taken the imagination of theater-goers by storm. So diverse were Chaney's acting abilities and talents in makeup that the public anxiously awaited his next role regardless of the quality of the movie itself. This showed the novice producers the value of having experienced makeup men around.

Jack Pierce's acting prowess was not the talk of the town but his talent in makeup was becoming highly regarded.

Pierce's portfolio shot of his work as an actor and early makeup creations at Universal and Vitagraph from 1913-1924

Jacques Lernier as seen in The Monkey Talks - *Fox 1926*

Pierce, in retrospect, told an interviewer, "I spent two days at the zoo studying the chimpanzees before coming up with my makeup concept."

It was not long after the release of *The Monkey Talks* that events at Universal were to give Jack the opportunity that he deserved.

The Man Who Laughs had been sitting in limbo for almost a year and a half. Carl Laemmle had paid $35,000 for the rights to the film in anticipation of Chaney's contract and, when it didn't pan out, the picture was entrusted to Paul Kohner, who immediately hired two fellow countrymen: Paul Leni to direct; and Conrad Veidt to star in the part originally intended for Chaney. Who but Chaney could devise the sardonic smile carved into the face of Gwynplaine, which would be so pivotal to the film's success? The dilemma was solved when Carl Laemmle Jr., remembered Pierce's wonderful work. The Monkey makeup was the talk of the town. Laemmle Jr., now an associate producer at the age of 20, was fascinated by the past Chaney films, and stories that delved in the supernatural. The acting abilities of Veidt combined with the talents of Pierce would be the answer. The revelation of this talent in Pierce formed a bond between him and young Laemmle that would never be broken." Universal's first synchronized sound macabre film was one of the biggest hits of 1928.

In Pierce, Junior Laemmle had found the sculptor of his dreams and nightmares. He gave the master makeup artist all the latitude he needed, but it would not be easy to convince Laemmle, Sr. that horror films would be box office hits.

In 1926 director, Raoul Walsh had just completed one of his greatest films, *What Price Glory?*, when he announced that he was about to go into production on a bizarre comedy-drama called *The Talking Monkey*, based on the play *Le Singe Qui Parle*, by Renee Franchois. The plot involved a troop of down-and-out carnival players who come up with a scheme to disguise their smallest member, played by Jaques Lernier, as a talking chimpanzee. Walsh went through 3 adaptations of the screenplay and finally gave his approval to the L.G. Rigby version. Key to the success of the film would be finding someone to do a convincing monkey makeup on Lernier, and Walsh chose Pierce for the task. The picture, retitled *The Monkey Talks*, got good reviews when it was released in April of 1937, and Jack's uncredited monkey makeup led one reviewer to comment "the well-trained chimpanzee had almost human qualities."

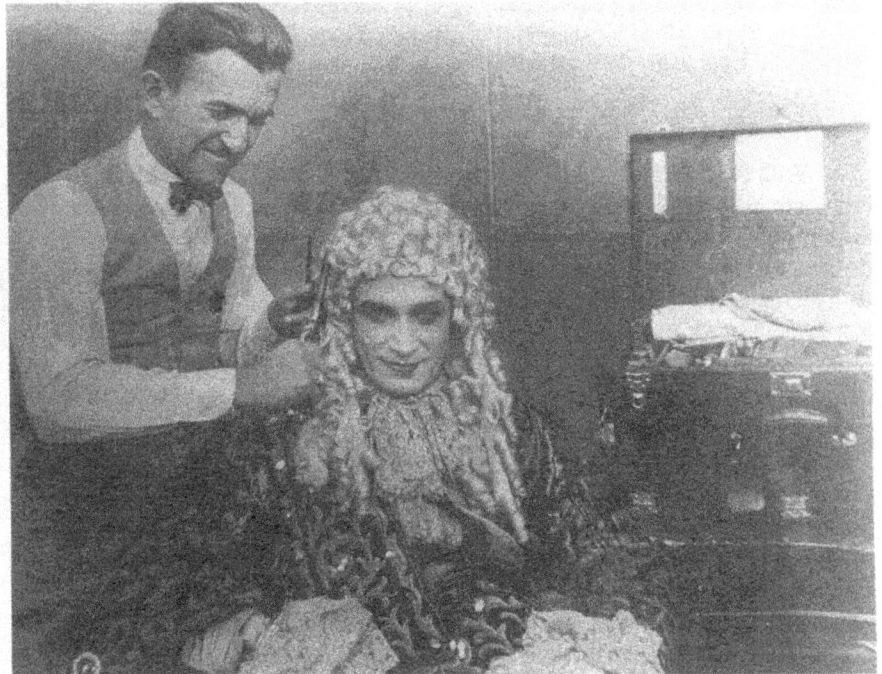

Pierce prepares Conrad Veidt for The Man Who Laughs - *1927*

Veidt in the final screen makeup for The Man Who Laughs - *1927*

Boris Karloff presents Pierce with his Makeup Award for The Mummy *(below).*

With the death of Lon Chaney in 1930, the Industry in general had little faith in investing in morbid themes and less faith that one could be made without Chaney, but it was Junior Laemmle's faith in Pierce's artistry that inspired the first "Golden Age" of Universal horror pictures. Armed with Pierce's conceptions, Laemmle Jr. had the confidence and knowledge that he could pick his own actors, turn them over to Pierce, and anything could be possible.

The results were like nothing the world had ever seen before! The box office results also speak for themselves, as these Pierce creations kept Universal's head above water, while all other Studios suffered heavy financial losses during those early depression years.

Perhaps the best way to provide new insight on Jack Pierce is to let the man speak for himself. After completing the makeup for, not only the character roles, but also for Bela Lugosi and his vampire "brides" in *Dracula* (1931), as well as the brilliant work he did in *Frankenstein* (1931), Pierce was asked to write an article on makeup for *American Cinematographer.*

Character Make-up

by JACK PIERCE

Head of Makeup Dept., Universal Studio

IN SO far as character makeup is concerned, the work of the makeup artist is closely akin to that of the cinematographer. Each is creative art of the most intricate order. Each demands that the artist have, in addition to technical ability of a high order, the imagination wherewith to visualize the effect desired, and a thorough understanding of dramatic values by which to judge the desirability of these effects from a story viewpoint. For, even as the best photography—judged solely as photography—can be out of place if not properly keyed to the story requirements, so can the best individual makeup be worthless if it does not perfectly fit the story.

Character makeup may be divided into two main classes: the common, run-of-production type—such as turning out Chinamen, Indians, and Hindus or building beards to dress a set; and real character-study makeups, in which the makeup artist literally creates a character over the frame-work of some star or featured player, to play a prominent role in a picture. The former is relatively easy, for all that is needed is technique and experience; certain mechanical operations—a dab of paint here, a touch of liner there, a bit of tape somewhere else, and an inch or two of crepe hair will automatically produce the desired result, just as, in camera work, a "broad" here, a rifle there, so much front light, so much back light, and so much top light, will put enough light on a set to assure an exposure.

The latter variety, however—true character makeup—is not so simple. It is pure creative art, just as is getting unusual effect lightings. There are no rules to follow; nothing to guide one except the story requirements and the physical materials at hand. The result must be the outcome of experience and technique guided by artistic sense and imagination.

In creating such a makeup, the makeup artist must first of all know what the story requires. Then he must have time to study the actor in question, and visualize what can be done to make that actor into the desired character. What are the most prominent features of the actor? What does he rely upon most in putting his points over? What should be the most prominent features of the character? Should the actor be concealed by the makeup, or is his normal personality a near enough approximation of the desired character so that the makeup be merely a filling-in of the more sketchy details? And, finally—in such parts as the "Monster" in "Frankenstein" especially—is every detail technically correct?

The creation of such characters requires time. First of all, there must be sufficient time for the makeup artist to familiarize himself with the story requirements. Secondly, there must be time for him to delve into the technical, anatomical and psychological background of the character. Thirdly, there must be an abundance of time for him to study the player, and

Sidney Fox, featured player

Sidney Fox made up as Chinese girl

visualize the exact methods that must be used to make him what is wanted. This last is vitally important, regardless of how well the artist may know the actor already. To cite an instance that is fresh in everyone's memory, let me take Boris Karloff. I have known Boris for a long time, and have the very highest opinion of him both personally and professionally. But this does not by any means obviate the need of studying him anew for each part that he plays. After all, the mere fact that I created his makeup for "Frankenstein" did not greatly help me in creating the one he wore in "The Old Dark House." I was working with the same physical framework, it is true, but in one case I was working for one result, and in the other I was seeking an entirely different effect. Therefore, in each case, I had to spend many days studying Mr. Karloff's physiognomy—not simply as Boris Karloff's face, but as a framework upon which to create the desired character. If you study the illustrations, which show Mr. Karloff as he is, as the Monster, and in his new role in "The Old Dark House," you will see that in each case the character is basically different; in one, the eyes, for instance, are treated one way; in the other, quite differently, and so with every feature.

Boris Karloff, as he appears normally

Boris Karloff, made up as the Monster in "Frankenstein"

Once this study is completed, and I have, either through imagination or research—or a combination of the two—succeeded in visualizing the character, I prepare sketches of my conception of the character, and submit them to the director. His conception of the part, influenced as it is by consideration not alone of the one part, but of the whole picture, may differ slightly from mine. Either of the two may be the better; sometimes a combination of the two will prove better than either individually; sometimes we have to test both makeups photographically in order to decide. But when this decision is finally made, the rest is purely routine. The makeup can be applied identically day after day throughout the picture, with no further reference to anything other than my memory, save where there must be fresh wounds or bloodstains, when, for exactness, I refer to still photographs.

Next to the ability to completely visualize a character makeup, technical research plays the largest part. Sometimes this leads one into strange paths. In "Frankenstein," for instance, I spent months of study on the anatomical possibilities of the monster alone. I studied every operation that would be necessary to create such a body from human "spare parts," as

was related in the story. I studied the physical effect of each, and strove to reproduce them in Mr. Karloff's final character. Every line, every scar, every peculiarity of contour had to be just so for medical reasons; the eyes, for instance, were exact duplicates of the dead eyes of a 2800-year-old Egyptian corpse!

For other parts, this research may be more on the psychological side than the anatomical. In such a picture, for instance, as "Back Street," I studied and visualized the physical result of the emotional and psychological experiences undergone by the leading characters during the course of years. In "Resurrection," I had to study not alone the results of the lapse of years, but of the psychological experiences and environments of the characters played by John Boles and Lupe Velez.

All of these details must be coordinated with the one basic requirement of any good makeup: that it must not look like a makeup. The sole reason for any makeup—and particularly a character makeup—is not to proclaim the skill of the makeup

(Continued on page 43)

Another picture of Karloff in character makeup

Character Make-Up

(Continued from page 9)

artist or the actor, but to help to tell the story. Therefore, the makeup must not be obviously "makeuppy." This in turn demands that the makeup be supervised by a qualified makeup artist, for the actor—no matter how skilled he may be in the technical details of applying his makeup—rarely has the right perspective to enable him to judge the makeup without bias. Some few actors there have been, of course, who have proven themselves artists in makeup as well as in acting: Lon Chaney was one, and Emil Jannings another; but even these frequently erred for lack of the detached, impersonal viewpoint. Therefore, it has always been my policy, for the protection of the actor quite as much as for the protection of the studio and myself, to insist that I supervise all such makeups, regardless of the ability or importance of the player. In practice this has worked out to excellent advantage, for if the player was not skilled in makeup, I have had a free hand; and if he was, I have had a capable and doubly interested fellow-worker. When working with such artists as Jean Hersholt and Lucien Littlefield, I have found that the intelligent cooperation they were able to give was of inestimable value to both of us.

In some studios, it is the policy to assign a makeup man to every company, regardless of the nature of the picture. I regard this as basically wrong. It saddles the company with unnecessary expense, and too frequently gives the actors the feeling that the makeup artist is there merely to serve as a valet or ladies' maid, to fetch and carry powder-puffs at their bidding. Furthermore, any cameraman who is qualified to have charge of the photography of a modern production is certainly familiar enough with makeup to know when a makeup is wrong, or when one needs repairing. Why, then, have two makeup men on the set, as is actually the case when both a first cinematographer and a makeup artist are retained?

As regards the cooperation that must exist between the cinematographer and the makeup artist, I have always found this readily obtainable. For, if the cinematographer is naturally more or less of a makeup artist, so too, from the nature of his work, is the makeup artist something of a cinematographer. Personally, I feel myself rather favored in this connection, for before I became a makeup artist I was a cinematographer, working my way up to a camera through the laboratory and an assistant's job. Therefore, I can not only speak the cameraman's language, and understand his problems and requirements, but view rushes and makeup tests with a cameraman's eye and judgment; if anything is wrong in either photography or processing, I can see it, and make allowances for it in judging my work, without any delays, or asking of questions. Yes, I am convinced that camera and laboratory training are vital for a makeup artist.

Looking forward, the future holds great possibilities. Makeup is only beginning to reach its artistic stride. We have far to go, just as cinematography has. Color, third-dimension, and all the other developments that lie in the future offer us as great possibilities and as great problems as they offer the cinematographer. But if the present close cooperation between the two crafts is maintained and improved, nothing is impossible.

◆

New S.O.S. Catalogue

THE S.O.S. Corporation of 1600 Broadway, New York City, has just issued one of the most comprehensive catalogues dealing with sound equipment that has come to this writer's desk. Of particular interest is a large section devoted to rebuilt and reconditioned sound apparatus covering everything used in the making and showing of pictures. Anyone looking for used equipment would do well to write for this catalogue. It will be gladly mailed if you mention this notice.

By the time this article appeared in *American Cinematographer*, Jack Pierce was the accepted master of character makeup and the envy of his contemporaries. Although at this time there were not many recognized by the general public. Most of the major studios were becoming aware of the importance of a makeup department. Fox listed Charles Dudley, Samuel Goldwyn & United Artists - Robert Stephanoff, MGM had Cecil Holland for men's makeup and Lillian Rosine for women, Paramount had Wally Westmore, RKO had Mel Burns, Pathe listed Bill Knight, Warner Brothers - Perc Westmore. Jack Dawn, Bill Tuttle, George and Gordon Baus, Ben Nye Sr. were all to come to prominence at their prospective studios in the later 30s when the Makeup Artists Union was made a part of the International Alliance of Theatrical Stage Employees Union.

The Westmore family had department heads at many of the larger corporate structures, but all of them had to acknowledge the creative genius of Pierce, and many envied the artistic freedom to create that was given to him by Carl Laemmle Jr. Finally, in 1928, Jack was officially named "Director of Makeup for Universal Studios".

Following his brilliant work in *Dracula* and *Frankenstein*, during the next five years at Universal, Pierce's genius was evident in *The Mummy*, *The Invisible Man*, *The Werewolf of London*, and *The Bride of Frankenstein*.

The original concept for Karloff's Wolf Man, later designed for Henry Hull

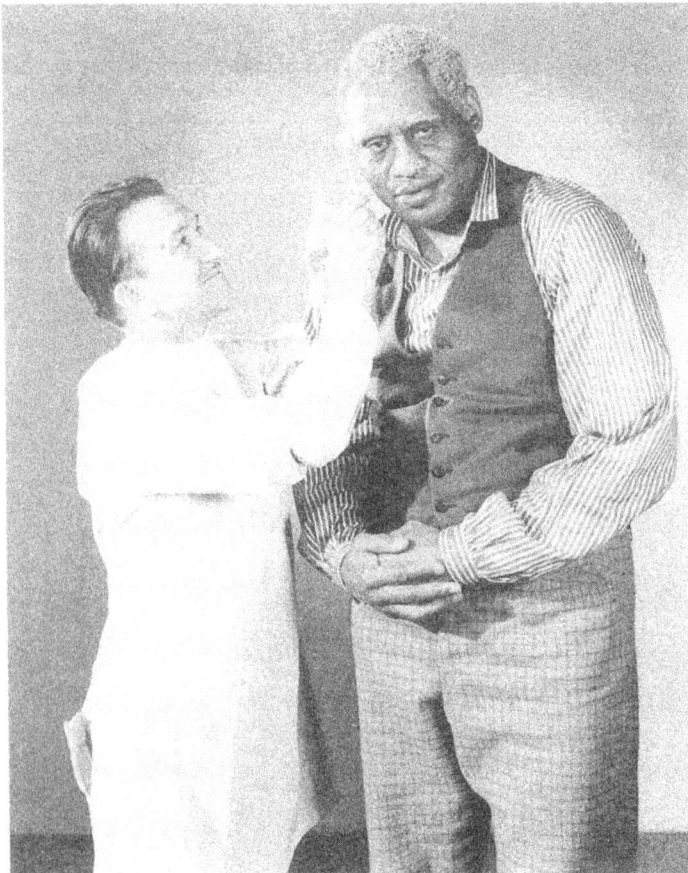

One of Pierce's last assignments with the Laemmles - He prepares Paul Robeson for his role in the 1936 Showboat, directed by James Whale.

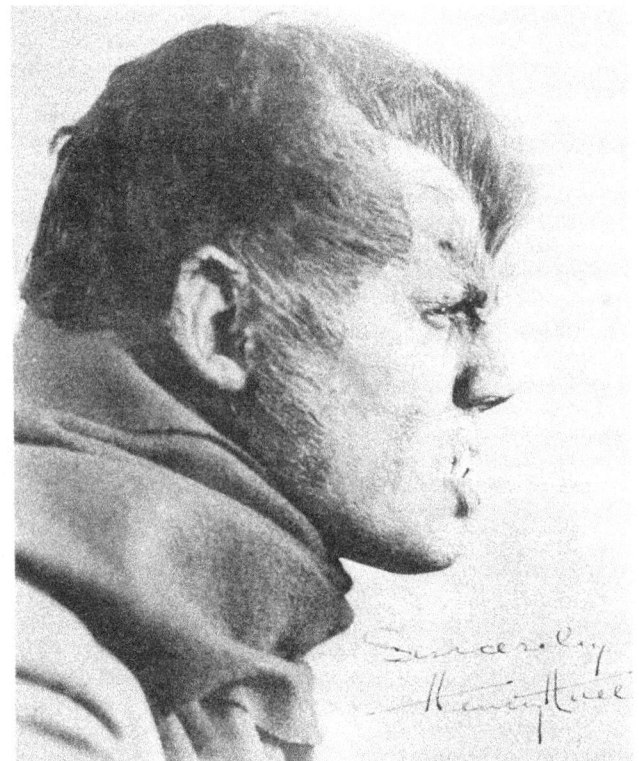

Henry Hull's finished and simplified makeup for Werewolf of London - 1935

Preparing Mary Philbin for her role in Surrender *(Universal - 1927)*

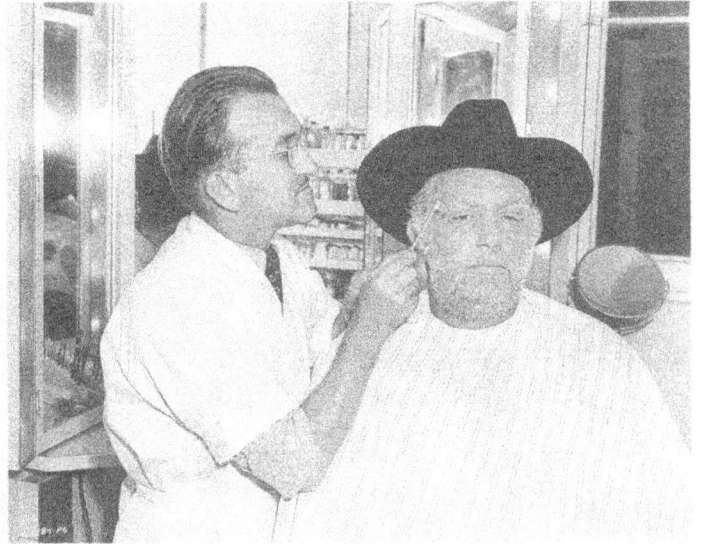

Turning Andy Devine into an 80 year old man for
North to the Klondike - *1941*

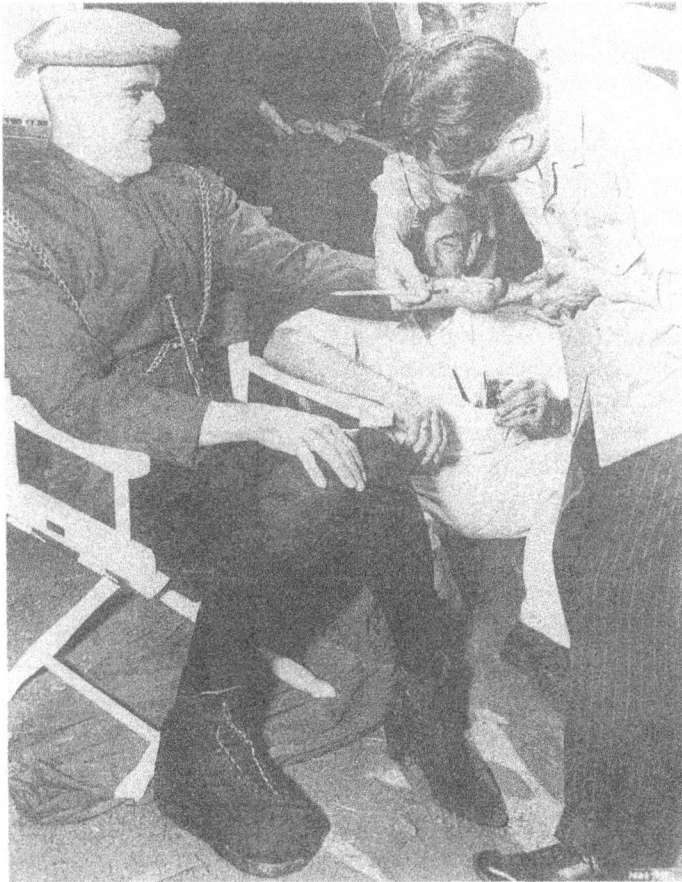

With his old friend Boris Karloff on the set of Tower of London *1939*

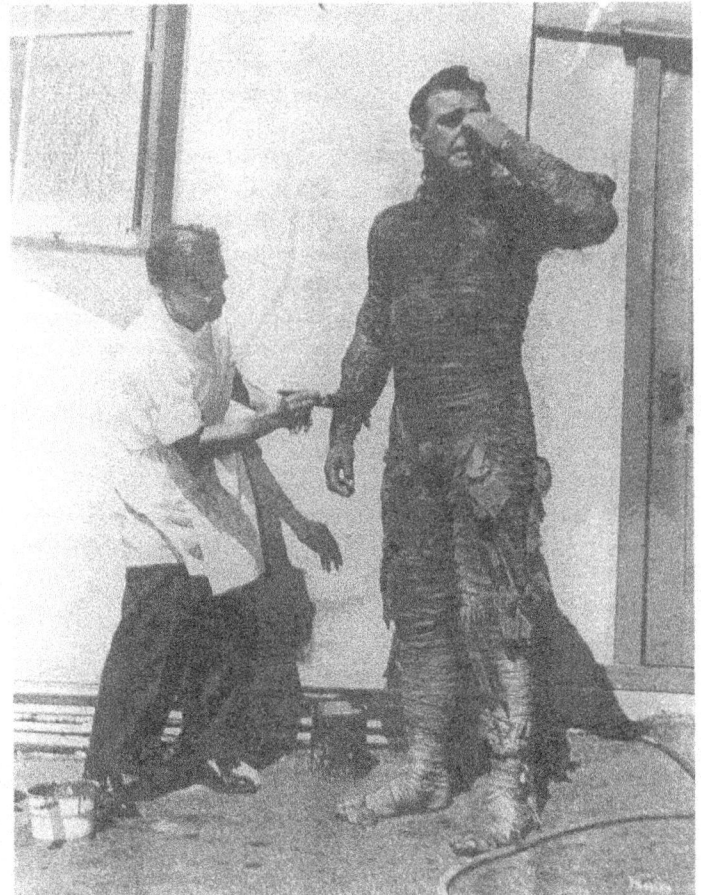

Lon Chaney Jr. expresses it all as he is being prepared for his role in
The Mummy's Ghost.

Sidney Olcott presents to Carl Laemmle Jr. the 1934 Southwest Basketball Championship Award. Pictured with the team from left to right are Al Akst, team manager, Jack Pierce, Laemmle, Olcott and Harry Zehner, assitant to Mr. Laemmle.

The year 1936 was a turning point for Jack Pierce. Even though he achieved makeup triumphs in *The Invisible Ray, Dracula's Daughter,* and *Showboat,* the Laemmles also gave him the chance to devote part of his life to his love of sports. Pierce had been coaching the Universal basketball team, and in 1936, they not only won the National Championship, but also were victorious at the 1936 Berlin Olympiad. He was as full of pride for his "Universal Five" as for any makeup he ever did. About his sporting passion Jack said, "Basketball is the toughest form of athletic competition. It is the one sport that requires perfect coordination of mind and muscle."

His trip to Berlin with the team had a precarious undertone; not only had European boundaries changed with the expansions of Hitler's Germany, but Pierce's mentors, the Laemmles, were deposed of power at Universal through what is known today as "corporate raiding".

J. Cheever Cowdin's Standard Capital Company assumed control of 90% of the stock, and it was announced on March 21, 1936, that Carl Laemmle, Senior would be "retiring", and his lifetime partner R. H. Cochrane would become president. It was also announced that Carl Laemmle Jr. would no longer be Head of Production, but would maintain his own production company with *My Man Godfrey* as his first picture. Then, a month later on April 25th, immediately after the successful premiere of *Show Boat,* Laemmle Jr. announced that he, too, was leaving. Gone were the planned remakes of *The Phantom of the Opera* and *The Hunchback of Notre Dame*, and, one by one, many of the corporate team that gave Jack his freedom were getting axed.

One thing was a sure bet, there would be no more monsters without Junior around. Thoughts of Pierce being "retired" by the new Universal regime were soon put to rest when production assignments piled into his office and he was permitted to hire three new assistants. Pierce not only survived the new administration, but soon put to rest the last remaining gossip that he relied solely on the Laemmle's for his reputation. Following two years of light comedy, musicals, and westerns, the men who replaced the Laemmles, Robert Cochrane and Charles Rogers, resigned and were replaced with a new administration headed by Clifford Work and Martin Murphy. Murphy had been General Production Manager during the days when Junior was in charge; and it was his job to provide Pierce with everything he needed to create. Murphy knew the value of Jack Pierce to Universal's future.

Pierce's reputation had already increased by the beauty creations for stars such as Deanna Durbin and Wendy Barre, along with his handling of melodramas and John Wayne's Universal films. What seemed like no great accomplishment to the general public served to enhance Pierce's trade-mark: that the best makeup was one that you did not notice on-screen.

By the summer of 1938, Pierce was asked to revive an old friend, the Frankenstein Monster, for a film called "After Frankenstein", a property that was written in 1935 by Willis Cooper. When Boris Karloff, at age 51, agreed to return to portray the creature, Pierce's new age of creation was at hand.

"After Frankenstein" was released as *Son of Frankenstein* and Universal's second period of classics monsters was born, aided by Jack's genius.

Tower of London, Black Friday, The Invisible Man Returns, and *The Mummy's Hand* all followed in quick succession. It was also at this time that Universal gave a long-term contract to Lon Chaney Jr., son of Jack Pierce's colleague from the silent days.

With Lon Chaney Jr., Pierce launched a new era of fantasy. Sequels of all his monster creations followed, one after the other, side by side with the Abbott and Costello comedies, dramas and war films.

The starting point of the cycle came in 1941 when Pierce revived the werewolf makeup he had designed for Boris Karloff in 1932. (When Karloff left Universal, the makeup had been abandoned, but was tried again in 1935 on Henry Hull for *The Werewolf of London*. Hull objected to the full facial makeup, so a less restricting design had been used.)

Pierce and his assistants, Ely and Lederer

It was no coincidence that Universal's classic monster films ended with *House of Dracula* in 1945. Once again, rumors of a new administration circulated around the lot. Having survived at Universal for almost 20 years, these rumors just bounced off Jack Pierce and his crew, but in November of 1946, Universal announced that it was merging with International Pictures. With this merger came yet another front office; this time lawyers and administrators, not filmmakers. Leo Spitz, the former president of RKO pictures, and William Goetz, Louis B. Mayer's son-in-law took control of the studio. It was then that Jack Pierce was forced to experience something totally alien to his personality: treachery.

While Pierce continued with the routine Sherlock Holmes and mystery films, the word came down that there would be no more monsters. In addition to this edict, since the entire film industry was now in competition with the ever-expanding popularity of television, Universal let most of the stars of the 40s out of their contracts and began making more independent productions on the lot.

In 1947, to the disbelief of the entire makeup crew, Jack Pierce was fired and replace by a makeup administrator, Bud Westmore, a close friend of William Goetz. Even Edward Muhl, the studio manager who had been with the studio since Jack first worked on *The Man Who Laughs* in 1927, could do nothing for his old friend. Every studio in Hollywood had one of the Westmores as Head of Makeup, so the new Universal-International Pictures

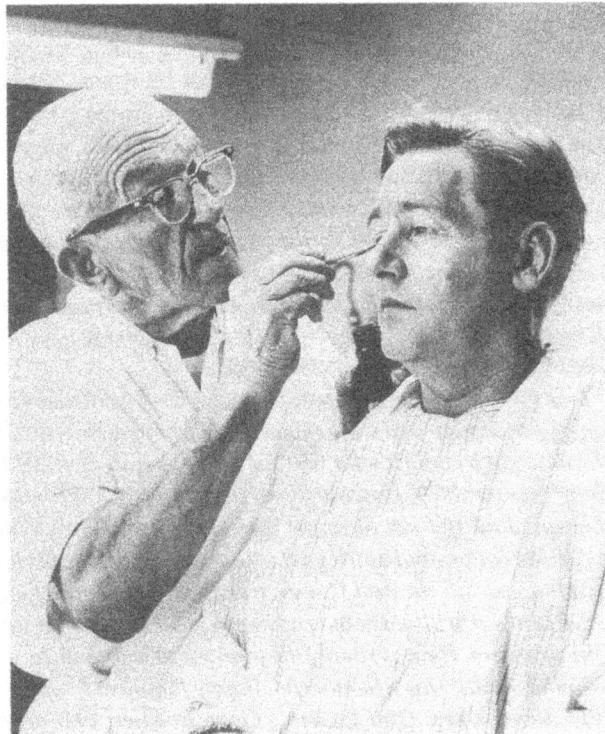

Pierce's last television work for "Mr. Ed" - Here he ages Alan Young - Feb. 1963

had decided to follow suit. (This part of history is not to diminish the contributions of the Westmore family's creative ability. Their accomplishments were amazing and even today a 3rd generation of Westmores keeps up the family tradition with movies such as *Star Trek, the Next Generation* and *Jurassic Park* (Universal 1993); but, it is a fact that Bud Westmore was more of an administrator than an artist, when compared to his brothers. The creations of the Universal makeup department through the 1950s science fiction cycle were largely the result of Jack Kevan's expertise.)

Pierce was now a free-lance artist. Fortunately, many of his former Universal co-workers did not forget his talents, and Pierce joined them in the world of television. Some of his earliest work can be seen on kinescopes of *Fireside Theater* and *You Are There*.

When his friend Edward Muhl, who had saved the near-disasters caused by the Goetz-Spitz administration at Universal, was rewarded by being appointed Head of Production in 1950, here was an opportunity for Jack to return to Universal City, but the same feisty pride that had carried him to the top of his profession, also kept him from asking for a job that he felt he never should have lost. Ever since his youth, once Jack had charted a course of action, he never went back, so he continued in television and low-budget films, like *Meteor Monster* and *The Brain from Planet Arous*.

Director Arthur Lubin, for whom Jack had done a terrific job on Claude Rains in the remake of *Phantom of the Opera* in 1943 (so terrific that the studio ordered the creation toned down to keep patrons from fleeing the theater), gave Jack one of his final assignments by hiring him to do the makeup on the television series *Mr. Ed*, which ran from 1961 until 1965.

On July 19, 1968, Jack P. Pierce died from uremia at St. Joseph's Hospital, in Burbank, California. He was interred at Forest Lawn, Glendale, on July 23. His wife Blanche, ill and bed-ridden by this time, passed away in 1969. They had no children.

Abe Haberman was a member of that Universal Makeup team and was a personal favorite of Jack's. A brilliant makeup artist in his own right, he worked alongside Pierce for ten years and witnessed the difficult transition after Jack was unceremoni-ously fired by Goetz from Universal in 1947. Haberman retired from the makeup profession at age seventy-eight, after moving from film to television and adding his art to such classic shows as *Route 66, The Munsters, The Invisible Man* (the television series) and *Bonanza.* Eighty-three years young and in good health, Abe Haberman had much to say about Pierce.

Jack Pierce was the greatest! He was a kind gentleman and an <u>honest</u> *gentleman, and that set him apart from the rest. He was an absolute perfectionist who worked very hard to develop his creations: researching, sketching, and sculpting each new make-up concept. Jack did not have the materials that are available today, yet his cotton-and-spirit gum technique, as well as his hair application are still the best I've ever seen. Many people forget that Jack also did brilliant beauty makeups in addition to his work with the monsters. He was simply the greatest at whatever he did.*

Under Jack it was a wonderful, happy family at Universal. Bill Ely, Newt Jones, Otto Lederer, Gene Roemer, and myself loved Jack, because he backed his men to the limit. He was like a little bantam rooster and was always on the set, in case any problems arose, and he always insisted that his crew be treated with dignity and respect. He had a wonderful sense of humor, but don't ever cross him, because he was a fighter!

All those stories about Jack hiding his makeup secrets from others and being arrogant are completely false. When I was not on an assignment, I still went in to work so I could be around Jack and learn from him. He was vert humble, he never bragged, and he would show you anything and help you out at the drop of a hat. There were no secrets with Jack at all, and as far as those stories go about his being nasty to stars sitting in his makeup chair, again, completely false. He did resent those few who considered makeup men as mere 'powder boys', but if the actor or actress treated us with respect and dignity, Jack returned the favor. Like I said, he fought hard for his boys, and we loved him dearly for it.

His makeups took hours to do, and Jack usually had to be in deep concentration during the entire process. A lot of idle chatter with the stars would break that concentration. After all, he had to get them done and out onto the sound stage on schedule.

Abe Haberman was a World War II veteran and participated in the D-Day invasion at Normandy Beach. Even during this period away from Universal, he has found memories of the personal side of Pierce and his wife Blanche.

During my time overseas, Blanche would regularly send me news articles about Los Angeles; sometimes caramel corn as well! This kept my spirits up, and, upon my return to Hollywood, Jack and Blanche took my wife and I to the 'Cock and Bull Restaurant' on Sunset Blvd. to celebrate my homecoming. Jack acted like a proud father to me that night, and I'll never forget it as long as I live!

It was devastating when Jack was fired from Universal; the whole makeup team was in shock. It was a difficult time during the transition period.

Abe was one of the three makeup men who attended Pierce's funeral in 1968, and he still shakes his head in disbelief when recalling the poor turnout, but, in defense of his fellow artists he states:

Many of the other guys would have loved to have gone but simply were not notified just when and where the service would be held. The lack of turnout was no reflection on how the other makeup artists regarded Jack, because like I said before, he was truly loved and respected by all his men! I deeply regret that Jack was never awarded an Oscar for his many creations and for his over-all genius. He surely deserved it.

Some of Jack Pierce's memories of his creations:

On the Frankenstein Monster:

"The same makeup Karloff wore in the original film, *Frankenstein,* is adapted to every actor who plays the role. The first step in making up the monster is the application of a flat rubber skullpiece with straight black hair streaked with green. Next, the forehead is built up with cotton and spirit gum. A special putty is applied to the eyelids. Black makeup is applied to the fingertips, nails and lips, and long red scars are placed on the forehead and neck. The facial makeup is finished with a greyish greasepaint. The actor is next clad in padded black garments which broaden the shoulders, fill out the chest, and supply the formless contour of the legs. A heavy black coat and huge boots with soles 2 and 1/2 inches thick finish the costume. Complete, the makeup and costume weigh 64 pounds, of which 12 are in the makeup, 25 in the boots, and the balance in the clothing and padding.

The basic makeup ingredients are amazingly simple -- spirit gum, cotton, powder, greasepaint, and hair. The art is in the application."

On the Mummy:

"First, I make a model, and sometimes I try the makeup on myself. The actor then comes to the makeup department, and I go to work. The Mummy was the toughest of all my creations! To begin with, I obtained photographs of the most nearly-perfect mummy known, Prince Syti, father of Ramses II, from the Cairo Museum. This we carefully duplicated. Bringing our duplicate to life -- in the person of Karloff -- presented the major problem. It started with the simple flicker of an eyelid. Gradually he broke from his '3,500-year-old' wrappings of gauze. Literally hundreds of yards of material had to be painstakingly prepared for this physical awakening. It was treated with acids and flame to give it the semblance of age and to cause it to crack and slough off in powdery fragments. This was extremely delicate work, since, after it was treated and fragile as cobweb, Mr. Karloff had to be wrapped in it."

On his constant experimenting with new products to save time and expenses:

"When I consider the matter, I am reminded that but a few important changes have been made possible in horror inventions in a dozen years. I recall, however, that when we made H.G. Well's *The Invisible Man*, Claude Rains' head had to be wrapped a dozen times a day in gauze. This was slow and tedious. Subsequently, when we made the sequel with Vincent Price, *The Invisible Man Returns*, we seized upon the *new* zipper and zipped the slit wrapping up the back of his head.

About the only other new thing involved in monster creation is rubber. Personally, I don't like it, and use it only under protest. I prefer the simplest items of makeup--natural materials. The 'bone' of the Frankenstein Monster's ponderous forehead is built up with a special type of cotton, for instance.

Keenest disappointment of my career was being refused the privilege of making up the Great Llama in *Lost Horizon* (Columbia 1937). This was done with a rubber mask, contrary to my personal conception, and my conviction is that it was badly achieved."

On The Wolf Man:

"The Wolf Man makeup, though it takes 4 hours to apply, is not as complicated as the Frankenstein Monster's. It consists principally of an artificial nose piece and bristles on the head, face, and neck, which are literally applied yak hair by yak hair. After the application, I singe the hair to give it that 'animal-like' appearance. I also make-up Chaney's feet and I give him claws. It takes about forty-five minutes to remove his makeup at the end of the shooting day."

To conclude this tribute to Jack Pierce on a humorous note, here are Lon Chaney Jr.'s personal thoughts on the makeup removal process by Jack Pierce.

"What gets me," said Lon, " is after work and I'm all hot and itchy and tired, and I've got to sit in that chair for forty-five minutes more while Pierce just about kills me ripping off the stuff he put on in the morning! Sometimes we take an *hour* and he leaves *some* of the skin on my face!"

Douglas Norwine is a professional musician who spends his time performing the saxophone for Lisa Simpson on The Simpsons *and on shows like* Saved by the Bell *and* Seinfeld. *He lives in the Los Angeles area with his wife and son and has a passion for saving the memories of many of the uncredited, forgotten, or overlooked artists in film history.*

From the moment he first saw Frankenstein *as a young boy in Ohio, on television's* Shock Theater, *he became hooked on the classic Universal films. Almost immediately, he began collecting anything and everything on the subject. After long research, extreme luck, and probably naive persistence, Jack has been able to unearth not only much new information about Pierce, both the man and the "Maker of Monsters", but has written the book that film historians and fans thought to be impossible because of the myths about Pierce's reclusive nature and the universal sorrow that his scrapbooks no longer existed.*

Through interviews with Pierce's family members and co-workers, he has filled in this missing chapter in film history. Now with the MagicImage Universal Archives at his disposal with its mountains of documents and studio files as well as Jack Pierce's recently discovered personal scrapbooks, he has created the ultimate book on Universal Studio's classic monster maker.

The photographic treasures alone are stunning. All never before published! From candid photographs such as Kaloff as a pirate to such lost creations as Henry Hull's first Werewolf of London *trial makeup, to beautiful Freulich originals of the classic monsters as they have never been seen! Also, countless details on how the monsters and the madonnas were created with photographs to compliment his unique text.*

Douglas Norwine is currently working on a book about the character actors and actresses from Universal's Classic Monster films, and a book on Horror Autograph Collecting.

Pierce's last resting place at Forrest Lawn, California

The Cast

Each of the carefully selected stars and feature players of *The Wolf Man* would make an indelible impression. They were, in order of *The Wolf Man*'s billing:

Now you ask me if I believe a man can become a wolf. Well, if you mean can he take on the physical characteristics of an animal, no - it's fantastic! However, I do believe that most anything can happen to a man IN HIS OWN MIND!
- Sir John Talbot in *The Wolf Man*, played by Claude Rains (1889-1967)

"Even the moon's frightened of me - frightened to death! The whole world's frightened to death!" raved the bandaged "Invisible One" of Universal's 1933 *The Invisible Man* - directed by James Whale, and starring, in his Hollywood debut, Claude Rains. The small British actor (who, in *The Invisible Man*, played scenes opposite Gloria Stuart standing on a box while she removed her high heels) was a giant talent; a suave, Napoleonic actor with beautiful eyes, a shock of hair that fell above his right eye, and a smoky voice (courtesy of being gassed during World War I). After years on the European and Broadway stage, and a stint as a teacher at the Royal Academy of Dramatic Art, Rains had won international celebrity as *The Invisible Man*, following at Universal with such roles as the insane pacifist writer who beheads his publisher in *The Man Who Reclaimed His Head* 1934 (with Rains reprising his 1932 stage role) and as opium-addicted choir master John Jasper in Dickens' *The Mystery of Edwin Drood* (1935).

In 1936, Rains became the powerhouse character actor of Warner Bros., where he created such roles as the sly, wicked Prince John of 1938's *The Adventures of Robin Hood*. He signed on for *The Wolf Man* with a simple letter of agreement, provided that he receive star billing.

Her jugular vein was severed by the bite of powerful teeth...
- Dr. Lloyd in *The Wolf Man*, played by Warren William (1895 - 1948)

Born Warren Krech, William was a suave, ex-stage matinee-idol who was noted for his resemblance to John Barrymore. His film career dated all the way back to 1914's *The Perils of Pauline*; in the 1930s, he was a workhorse leading man at Warner Bros. William had played Caesar to Claudette Colbert's Princess of the Nile in DeMille's *Cleopatra* (Paramount, 1934) and had also co-starred with Miss Colbert in Universal's powerful soap opera of 1934, *Imitation of Life*. By the advent of the 40s, William had scored as a heavy - such as his "dude" villain of Columbia's western epic *Arizona* (1940), with Jean Arthur.

Let's have a hunt and drive it out! That'll be a valuable addition to anybody's collection of animals! Just imagine having a stuffed werewolf staring at you from the wall!
- Col. Paul Montford in *The Wolf Man*, played by Ralph Bellamy (1904 - 1991)

The Movies had no more likeable or resourceful a leading man than Ralph Bellamy, who matured from playing the "Guy who Always Lost the Girl" (like his Oscar-nominated "Daniel Leeson" in RKO's classic 1937 comedy *The Awful Truth*) to becoming a major Broadway and film star. Born June 17, 1904 in Chicago, his first acting part was in 1922 in Harold Bell Wright's "The Shepherd of the Hills". After many successful and non-successful Broadway plays he was seen in "Roadside" in 1929 and given a four-picture contract. His first film was *The Secret Six* with Clark Gable, Jean Harlow and Wallace Beery. From this point he would make over 100 films and hundreds of television shows. In 1934 he built the Palm Springs Racquet Club with Charles Farrell, causing the town of only 200 residents to become the most popular resort in Southern California.

Oct. 25, 1941 he signed a one-picture contract to make a film called, *Destiny*.

Gwen, be careful, will you?...there's something very tragic about that man. I'm sure that nothing but harm will come to you through him.

- Frank Andrews, warning Gwen Conliffe about Larry Talbot in *The Wolf Man*; Andrews played by Patric Knowles

Born in Horsforth, England on the 11th hour of the 11th month of 1911, Knowles (who dropped the "k" from Patrick after a psychic promised him he'd have better luck without it) had acted with Agnew McMasters's Shakespearean Players at Dublin's Abbey Theatre. Following work in the Irish and British cinema, he came to Hollywood and scored at Warner Bros. in such films as *The Charge of the Light Brigade* (1936) and *The Adventures of Robin Hood* (1938, as Will Scarlet), both with his pal Errol Flynn. After serving in the Royal Canadian Air Force as a flight instructor, and playing in John Ford's *How Green Was My Valley* (1941), the 6' 2" tall Knowles joined Universal, where, beginning with a one picture contract on October 25, 1941, he went on to become a suave, intelligent, leading man in all variety of studio escapism.

I can't tell you anything tonight. Come back tomorrow... Now go away! Go quickly! GO!

- Bela the Gypsy in *The Wolf Man*, played by Bela Lugosi (1882 - 1956)

"Listen to them...Children of the Night...What music they make!" Lugosi as Count Dracula, the role he had created on Broadway, triumphed in Universal's 1931 release. The Transylvania-born star of the European stage and Broadway perpetuated his unholy career at Universal as mad Dr. Mirakle in *Murders of the Rue Morgue* (1932); created a wonderful "trilogy" with Karloff in *The Black Cat* (1934), *The Raven* (1935), and *The Invisible Ray* (1936); and played the unforgettable, bearded, broken-necked old Ygor in *Son of Frankenstein* (1939).

Following the last triumph (played after a career limbo that had cost him his Hollywood Hills house and, perhaps more sadly, a large slice of his sensitive pride), Lugosi had a "come back" at Universal, co-starring with Karloff in *Black Friday* (1940), and playing the "Keeper of the Cats" in the comedy/mystery *The Black Cat* (1941).

Now with 3-year old Bela Jr. at home, the 59-year old Lugosi was anxious to rejuvenate his stardom - and campaigned for the starring role in *The Wolf Man*, perhaps unaware that Siodmak was fashioning the role as a young American. His actual role of Bela the Gypsy, Lycanthrope with the pentagram scar on his forehead, was limited in screen time - yet nevertheless a haunting one, presenting Bela in the togs of his Rumanian ancestors. There was also a poetic touch: Lugosi, whose *Dracula* was the first great Universal "monster" of the 1930s, had in *The Wolf Man* the distinction of gnawing to stardom Universal's Great New Monster of the 1940s. He signed a one-picture deal on October 25, 1941.

The tiny, wizened, dynamo of the Russian Art Theatre had made her Hollywood debut reprising her Broadway role in Goldwyn's *Dodsworth* (1936); an Academy Award nomination had resulted, with a second nomination coming for her role of Charles Boyer's gentle grandmother of RKO's *Love Affair* (1939). Moving her Academy of Dramatic Art to Hollywood, "Madame" Ouspenskaya (as her pupils called her) created one of the Horror Genre's classic characters in *The Wolf Man* - Maleva, mother of Bela the Gypsy, who knows too well the legend and lore of the Werewolf.

Madame Ouspenskaya was born in Tula, Russia on July 29, 1877. She arrived in America in 1923 with the Moscow Art Theater. After the Russian troupe moved on, she remained to act on Broadway and run an acting school.

With her blonde, fairy tale princess beauty and wonderful, full-throated scream, Evelyn Ankers was unforgettably lovely as Gwen Conliffe, heroine of *The Wolf Man* - a performance that at once crowned her as Universal's "Queen of the Horrors". Born in Chile of English parents, Evelyn (pronounced Ee-velyn) came to the U.S. in 1940, following studying at the Royal Academy of Dramatic Art, playing on the London stage, and appearing in a dozen British movies; her Broadway debut was in *Ladies in Retirement* (1940), in which she unleashed a scream that brought down the house. Evelyn made her Universal bow in Abbott & Costello's *Hold That Ghost*; she went on to play everything at Universal from sleek villainess/mistress of disguises, Naomi Drake, in *Sherlock Holmes and the Pearl of Death*, to burlesque queen Bonnie Latour, oomphing an 1890's striptease in *Bowery to Broadway*.

Finally, there would be Special Billing for the actor who would play the title role of *The Wolf Man*. A young contractee at Universal had just achieved success after a decade of misadventures and heartbreak at various studios all over Hollywood.

The Wolf Man would prove to be his career opportunity which would make - or break - the son of Hollywood's "The Man of a Thousand Faces".

Creighton Chaney - a.k.a. Lon Chaney Jr. in 1941

Oklahoma City, Oklahoma, February 10, 1906. Creighton Tull Chaney was born in a cabin - the son of a homely, poor 22-year old actor named Lon F. Chaney (himself the son of deaf-mute parents), and his 16-year old wife, Cleva Creighton. He was stillborn, and his father smashed the ice on Belle Isle Lake, plunging the baby into the bitterly cold water to shock life into him. By age 3, little Creighton performed with his father in an acrobatic act. His mother became addicted to alcohol as the family travelled from town to town in the Midwest, performing wherever they would find an empty hall. Their marriage slowly fell apart, with Chaney leaving several times, being served papers for lack of child support and then coming back. They decided to give it another chance when an offer to perform on the West Coast came in from Chaney's brother John, who managed a theater. They had a new hope and headed to San Francisco.

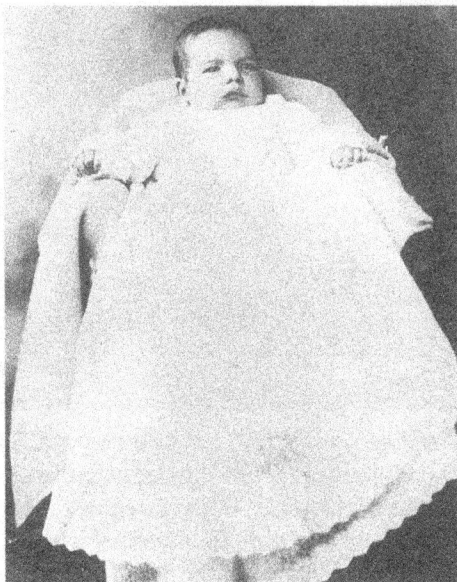

Creighton Chaney's baby picture (Courtesy Carre Chaney-Keyes)

The move only made things worse. Chaney accused Cleva (whose fame as a singer in San Francisco had precluded his fame as an actor) of infidelity and left her and the boy. Again they were reconciled and moved to Los Angeles where he again returned to the stage in a musical comedy review. The demanding Chaney insisted that she stay away from anywhere where alcohol and her lover could be encountered. She responded by sneaking into the theatre where he was performing one evening and poisoning herself. She was committed to an asylum as a psychological alcoholic. Chaney left the theater and began work at Universal as an extra and stagehand. He was given custody of the little boy, who was placed in foster homes when he was not staying with his mother.

[Cleva Creighton Chaney married again, had a daughter Stella, and outlived her first husband, Lon Chaney, by over three decades. She spent most of her last years with her son and his second wife Patricia. She died in a Sierra Madre nursing home on November 21, 1967.]

Cleva Chaney & 7 year old Creighton - taken around the time when his parents were separated. (Courtesy Stella Bush - Creighton's step sister)

Universal City, California, 1913. Chaney received his first screen billing in Universal's *Poor Jake's Demise*. In 1914, he married again, to one Hazel Hastings - chorus girl/ex-wife of a legless man who ran a cigar counter at San Francisco's Princess Theatre. As Chaney progressed in his profession, as a writer, director and actor, who always created his own remarkable makeups, his relationship with his little boy was tragically complex. Curt Siodmak, who came to know Chaney ''Jr.'' well over the decades, says,

...He had a tough time with his father, of whom he spoke to me often. Chaney Sr. was really a sadist. He would tell the boy, ''You go to the shed now, and get the strap, and I'm going to hit you.'' The boy hadn't even done anything, yet he would receive these terrible beatings... Chaney Jr. was changed for all his life because of this terrible youth he suffered.

Carnegie Hall, New York City, August 30, 1923. *The Hunchback of Notre Dame* premiered. Chaney Sr.'s magnificent Quasimodo made him a major star. Creighton Chaney accompanied his dad and step-mother on a publicity tour, but his father was

Left to right - E.T. Fergison, American Legion official, Walter Long, Actor & Post Commander, Creighton Chaney, Committeeman Harold Enfield, Albert Grasso (Chaney's manager - on steps of train), Chaney Sr. & Hazel Chaney, Creighton's stepmother, Walter Smith and Martin Cichy of the American Legion Hollywood Post as Chaney departs for New York City for the Hunchback *premiere in 1923 - Courtesy Wm. R. Hearst Collection*

hell-bent on keeping him out of the spotlight. "In the early days of motion pictures, it was not considered a good thing for a star to be married, much less have a son of my age. Therefore I saw very few of his performances." Chaney Sr. was determined his son would not be spoiled, and Creighton worked as a newsboy, apricot picker, a butcher's boy, a slaughterer, and a poultry dresser. And when Creighton admitted interest in becoming an actor, Chaney pulled him out of Hollywood High School and sent him to Commercial Experts Training Institute to learn the plumbing trade.

The Astor Theatre, New York City, September 6, 1925. Universal's *The Phantom of the Opera* premiered. Chaney Sr.'s Erik, unmasked by Mary Philbin, climaxed his stardom as "The Man of a Thousand Faces". As he prospered as a major MGM star, in such films as 1927's *London After Midnight* and 1928's *Laugh, Clown, Laugh*, Creighton Chaney worked as a boilermaker.

Saint Vincent's Hospital, Los Angeles, August 26, 1930. At 12:55 a.m., Lon Chaney died of throat cancer - weeks after his "Talkie" debut triumph in *The Unholy Three*. On August 28, there was a giant Hollywood funeral, the organ pealed the theme from *Laugh, Clown, Laugh*. Lon Chaney was entombed beside his father in the Great Mausoleum at Forest Lawn, Glendale, later moved to the Sanctuary of Meditation when his wife Hazel died in 1933. The crypt is unmarked to this day.

"Then," said Creighton Chaney bitterly, "Hollywood picked up its newly acquired microphone and forgot."

His father's will was careful to leave his only son sufficient funds to survive, and not enough to give him any thoughts of living on his inheritance, while running the risk becoming an actor.

Hollywood, California, 1930. Creighton Chaney lived at 735 N. Laurel Avenue, with his wife Dorothy Hinckley and baby sons, Lon II and Ronald. He became secretary of a water heater corporation owned by his father-in-law.

RKO Studios, 780 Gower Street, Hollywood, February, 1932. *The Los Angeles Times* reported that Creighton Chaney had signed an actor's contract with RKO-Radio Studios - "a five-year optional contract commencing at a salary of $250 weekly, graduating finally to $3500 weekly..." Chaney joined the male chorus in the musical *Girl Crazy* as his first screen appearance; he had a nice spot in the Dolores del Rio/Joel McCrea success *Bird of Paradise*; He was cut from *The Most Dangerous Game*. He starred as Tom Kirby, action hero of the 12-chapter serial, *The Last Frontier*. RKO toyed with the idea of changing his name to Lon Chaney Jr.; the *L.A. Examiner* reported that MGM expressed "a violent protest" to the idea.

Hollywood, January 24, 1933. Louella Parsons' Entertainment page of the *L.A. Examiner* reported, "May I make a little prophecy? Newcomers in the future will not be given contracts until it's proved that they have box office appeal. Gwili Andre, Creighton Chaney and Julie Haydon, three young players who joined Radio with much ballyhoo, are not having their contracts renewed...Creighton Chaney did not measure up to expectations..."

Creighton Chaney, RKO publicity portrait 1932

Hollywood, January 4, 1935. A desperate Creighton Chaney officially announced he would change his name to Lon Chaney Jr. "They had to starve me to make me take his name," he later revealed bitterly. The name change did little good; he turned to stunt work, claiming he worked during this traumatic time under five different names - for stunts, bits, extra work, parts and leads.

... I knew what Dad meant when he said, "I've taken the bumps." Well I'd taken them. I did every possible tough bit in pictures. I had to do stuntwork to live. I've bulldogged steers, fallen off and gotten knocked off cliffs, ridden horses into rivers, driven prairie schooners up and down hills... everything.

Superior Court, Hollywood, July 25, 1936. Dorothy Chaney got a divorce decree from her husband of 9 years, claiming he stayed away from home "night after night" and "drank to excess." Dorothy received custody of 7-year old Lon and 6-year old Ronald, as well as most of Chaney's personal property. The large inheritance money he received from his father was used to bail out his father-in-law when the hot water business was in trouble [Chaney Jr.'s share of the company - which was worth tens of millions of dollars in the 1970s, was to go to his sons and grandchildren]. Chaney meanwhile grabbed whatever work he could get, such as the role of Captain Hakur in the Republic 1936 serial, *Undersea Kingdom*.

20th Century-Fox Studios, Hollywood, 1937. Lon Chaney Jr. signed a stock contract. It was a humiliating stay as he was wasted time and again in bit roles. An example: *Slave Ship* (1937). The movie opened with laborer Chaney cutting the supports to launch a great sailing ship. The ship slid rapidly down its supports - crushing the screaming Chaney. So much for his role in *Slave Ship*.

The son of "The Man of a Thousand Faces" had become a human prop.

Colton, California, October 1, 1937. Chaney remarried, wedding former model Patsy Beck.

The Ozarks, Missouri, Summer, 1938. Chaney was on location for Fox's Technicolor blockbuster, *Jesse James*, with Tyrone Power, Henry Fonda, Nancy Kelly, Randolph Scott, Brian Donlevy, John Carradine, and former *Werewolf of London* Henry Hull. The film would bill Chaney at the very bottom of the cast list as "One of James Gang". Chaney fell off his horse and injured himself so badly he couldn't remount. Director Henry King blamed the fall on Chaney's drinking and packed him back to Hollywood.

Paramount Studios, Hollywood, December, 1938. Chaney, in full beard, loomed in background shot as "Dollarhide", one of many gamblers in villain Brian Donlevy's saloon, in Cecil B. DeMille's spectacular *Union Pacific*. While he was playing this humble bit in *Union Pacific*, his ex-wife Dorothy charged him with alimony contempt, reporting that Chaney had paid her only $5.37 in alimony since the divorce.

The El Capitan Theatre, Hollywood, April 6, 1939. Lon Chaney Jr. faced the opening night audience of *Of Mice and Men*, carefully coached by Wallace Ford, who had played George to Broderick Crawford's Lennie on Broadway. During rehearsals, the finance company had taken away Chaney's car and furniture. *Of Mice and Men* appeared to be his one last chance.

That night he took 14 curtain calls. He won the role of Lennie in the acclaimed 1939 film of *Of Mice and Men*, directed by Lewis Milestone and co-starring Burgess Meredith and Betty Field. At the age of 33, after a decade of heartbreak, Lon Chaney Jr. was a star.

He played the scarred old caveman in *One Million B.C.* (1940), and the giant "Shorty" in DeMille's *North West Mounted Police* (1940).

Then Universal, where Chaney Sr. made history as the Hunchback and the Phantom, baited Chaney Jr. with a contract. The trial run was *Man Made Monster*, filmed in late 1940 with Chaney as "Dynamo Dan", transformed into a pulsating electrical freak by a wild-eyed Lionel Atwill.

"...Lon Chaney Jr. made a place for himself on the screen in the footsteps of his late great father...," hailed *The Hollywood Reporter*.

Indeed, during the shooting of *Man Made Monster* in December, 1940, Chaney attended a Universal City ceremony which dedicated Universal's Soundstage 28 - "the Phantom Stage" - to his father's memory. A Universal contract followed. Boris Karloff was on Broadway in the smash hit *Arsenic and Old Lace*, Bela Lugosi was nearing 60 and too old (or so Universal thought) to dominate the genre. And Now Lon Chaney (dropping the Jr.) was about to star as *The Wolf Man* - and be billed as "The Screen's Master Character Creator."

Perhaps, at last, Lon Chaney Sr. would have been proud.

Biggest of the Universal horror pictures since Son of Frankenstein, *the new shocker will present Chaney in the role of the monstrous 'wolf-man', around whose inhuman activities the plot revolves...*

- Universal Publicity Release

1940 - Veteran character actor Lionel Atwill shakes the hand of Lon Chaney Jr. in Man Made Monster, *Chaney's first Universal fantasy film.*

Production plans finalized in October. The cinematographer was Joseph Valentine (1900-1949), Universal's ace "Glamour" cameraman, who had shot the Deanna Durbin vehicles.

Left - Joseph Valentine ASC, Right - Arthur Edeson ASC
The man who photographed Frankenstein *and the cinematographer*
of The Wolf Man *at the ASC Clubhouse, 194_.*
courtesy of Frank Tanner

Joseph A. Valentine, ASC

Much of the visual eloquence of *The Wolf Man* can be credited to the director of photography, Joseph A. Valentine, ASC*. At the time *The Wolf Man* was produced Valentine was the highest paid and most prestigious cinematographer at Universal and was assigned only to the studio's top product.

His real name was Giuseppe Valentino and he was born in New York City on July 24, 1903. In 1918, after attending photography classes at New York University he became a still and portrait photographer at Paragon Studios in Fort Lee, New Jersey. He came to Hollywood in 1922 and worked for Selznick for three years.

After working as assistant to many cinematographers, he graduated to first cameraman (what is now called a director of photography) in 1927 on a Shirley Mason starrer, *My Husband's Wives*, at William Fox Studios. He continued as Mason's choice cinematographer on *My Husband's Wives*, *The Star Dust Trail*, *Curly Top*, *Scarlet Honeymoon* and many more. He was with Fox for 11 years and while there joined with Raoul Walsh in making the first test films using the new Movietone sound on film system, which soon replaced the Vitaphone sound on disc method.

In 1931-32 Valentine traveled through England, Scotland, France, Italy, Switzerland and Belgium while photographing exotic backgrounds for Fox's use as projection process plates. He also directed and photographed several Fox Varieties short subjects and Magic Carpet of Movietone travelogues. He then filmed *Man Hunt* for RKO and a number of medium budget pictures for Columbia, including *Night of Terror*, a 1933 Bela Lugosi thriller which was one of Valentine's few genre films prior to *The Wolf Man*.

*American Society of Cinematographers

The attack of the Wolf Man as photographed by Valentine in a fog shrouded nightmarish atmosphere

Claude Rains as Sir John and Warren William surrounded by Otterson's fog shrouded sets as shot by Valentine

In 1936, Valentine was one of the less favored cinematographers at Universal, which was on the brink of bankruptcy. He finally got a large scale production in 1935 in James Whale's lavish production, *Remember Last Night?* The photographic virtuosity displayed in this sophisticated murder yarn, especially some unprecedented camera moves through fantastic settings, was the best showcase Valentine's talents had received. Thereafter he was in the big time with such stylish romantic films as *The Moon's Our Home*, *Two in a Crowd* and *The Man I Marry*, all in 1936. He received an Academy Award nomination in 1937 for *Wings Over Honolulu*.

Then he was assigned to *Three Smart Girls* (1937), the first starring vehicle for a teen-aged singer, Deanna Durbin. The girl was pretty, personable and had a fine voice -- but she wasn't quite gorgeous enough by movie star standards. With the help of Valentine's glamour lighting, she sparkled. The inexpensive picture proved an enormous success, and Universal put the youngster on the top star throne formerly occupied by Boris Karloff. The studio paired Valentine with Durbin in all of her increasingly elaborate productions for several years, including *One Hundred Men and a Girl*, *That Certain Age* and *Three Smart Girls Grow Up*. Two of them -- *Mad About Music* (1938) and *Spring Parade* (1941) earned him Academy Award nominations. He joined the Lakeside Country Club (across the river from Universal) and bought a beautiful home in Cheviot Hills (near Twentieth Century Fox).

Between Durbin pictures, Valentine filmed the W.C. Fields - Edgar Bergen classic, *You Can't Cheat an Honest Man* (1939),

the Shakespearean musical-comedy, *The Boys from Syracuse* (1940), several of the early Abbott and Costello pictures and several other high budget productions. And, in the winter of 1941, he shot *The Wolf Man*, one of the finest photographic jewels of the immediate post - *Citizen Kane* era.

Valentine's technique for *The Wolf Man* differed considerably from that of any of his previous films. Influenced, possibly, by the deep focus images achieved in *The Long Voyage Home* and *Citizen Kane* by Gregg Toland, ASC, Valentine used wide angle lenses throughout the picture. This was uncommon during the 1940s because lenses of 50mm or longer were more flattering to the performers than shorter lenses. To have used wide angles on previous films with glamour stars such as Deanna Durbin or Joan Bennett would have been unthinkable. With the cast of character actors that populated *The Wolf Man*, it was a different matter -- and Valentine still managed to bring out Evelyn Ankers' blonde beauty admirably. Agfa, Eastman and Dupont had recently introduced faster films and electro-coated lenses also came into use early in 1941. These innovations made it possible to use smaller lens apertures, a necessity for deep focus photography.

There is also a ceilinged set à la Toland in *The Wolf Man*: The Conliffe antique store and living quarters. This is used to excellent effect in the emotional scenes wherein Larry confesses to Gwen that he is a werewolf and tells her she must never see him again. The play of nocturnal shadows over the low ceiling greatly enhances the feeling of entrapment that is an important aspect of this excellently performed sequence.

The images in *The Wolf Man* that made the greatest impression were those of the fog-shrouded woods where most of the outdoor action took place. The planes of distance maintained in these shots created an impression of aerial perspective that was almost three dimensional.

Phil Lathrop, ASC, the distinguished cinematographer who received the 1992 Lifetime Achievement Award from the American Society of Cinematographers, was Valentine's operative cameraman on numerous pictures, including *The Wolf Man*.

"Joe was a great cinematographer and I learned a lot from him," Lathrop recalled recently. "I don't remember too much about *The Wolf Man* except working on those fog scenes. All those supposed exteriors were actually done on a stage, so the fog could be controlled. The kind of fog they used in those days was nothing like the kind we have today. It was greasy stuff made with mineral oil. We worked in it for weeks and the entire cast and crew had sore eyes and intestinal trouble the whole time. Besides that, we were all shivering with cold because it was necessary to keep the temperature below 50 degrees when using the fog.

"One other thing I remember was that Lon Chaney was usually drunk. In the evenings he and his pals, Broderick Crawford and Andy Devine, would get loaded and trash out their dressing rooms."

The United States declared war on the Axis powers on December 7, just days before the premiere of *The Wolf Man*. In a short time Valentine was in the Army, serving as a captain in the Signal Corps. After the war he resumed his career in Hollywood as one of the most sought after cinematographers in the business. He was also the first director of photography of that time to receive billing on ads and posters.

Robert Boyle

Production designer Robert Boyle, who created the settings for The Wolf Man, has had a distinguished career that includes five Alfred Hitchcock classics: *Saboteur, Shadow of A Doubt, North by Northwest, The Birds* and *Marnie*. Among many other credits are *Flesh and Fantasy, Two Tickets to London, Nocturne, Ride the Pink Horse, It Came from Outer Space, Cape Fear, In Cold Blood, Gaily, Gaily* and *Fiddler on the Roof*. A combat cameraman in Europe during World War II, he was the first American to enter Berlin. Semi-retired, the ruggedly handsome, white-haired artist lives in the Hollywood Hills with his wife, screenwriter Bess Taffel. He teaches at the American Film Institute and has long been active on the Board of Governors of the Academy of Motion Picture Arts and Sciences.

He was born in 1910 and graduated from the U.S.C. School of Architecture just as the Great Depression hit. In 1933, after three successive architectural firms that hired him had gone broke, he began playing bit parts at RKO Radio. Van Nest Polglase, head art director, looked at his drawings and sent him next door to Paramount, where Hans Dreier hired him as an assistant art director, draftsman and sketch artist. There he contributed to the look of numerous films including *You and Me, The Plainsman, Trail of the Lonesome Pine* and *The Ghost Breakers*.

Boyle came to Universal in 1941 to work as assistant to John B. Goodman, art director of a Frank Lloyd production, *This Woman Is Mine*. He remained at Universal as associate to the studio's official art director, Jack Otterson. At that time it was customary to give art director screen credit to the head of the department and list the actual art director of each film as associate. Boyle's first assignment was to a serial, *Don Winslow of the Navy*. Because serials didn't follow the custom of crediting department heads, his first on-screen credit was as art director on the serial. Next Otterson assigned Boyle to *The Wolf Man*, for which the credits read, "Art Director... Jack Otterson; Associate... Robert Boyle". Today the department heads no longer hold sway and the former associates are now called production designers. The former assistant art directors are now listed as art directors.

I did all the work on that since Jack was the head of the art department and did very little work on the films,

Boyle recalled early in 1993:

But these were interesting times. We had almost no money to make these films; but we had access to a lot of tricks: mattes, miniatures, scenic painting and lots of fog. Fog was the saving grace of a lot of films in those days. I remember the story about John Ford, when he was unable to do the big pictures at RKO because he was in bad favor at one time. It's hard to think that John Ford would ever be in bad favor, but he was; he'd been spending too much money. So he said, "Well, I've got this little picture, it's an Irish picture, and I'll do it for such-and-such a sum," which was very little. And he went on the backlot, and he said, "We won't even paint it." They took the backlot streets and made Dublin out of it, and they wet down all the buildings so they'd pick up the highlights, and put a lot of fog on the set. It made it possible for him to recoup because The Informer *became such an instant success and cost almost nothing.*

Very often when we were called upon to make a very inexpensive horror picture, we did it with bits and pieces and a lot of fog,

Boyle chuckled. As for The Wolf Man,

It did have castles, and there were a few stock sets around that we could use, but we needed a forest. And in order to get a forest of this kind and stay in the studio, we had to do it on stage. So, I traveled on the backlot, found a lot of old stumps and pieces of trees and even whole trees that we could move in on the stage. And so we painted the trees. Almost all of them were painted black. And we put a shiny glycerine coat on them so they'd pick up the lights and look damp and forbidding.

Many of the dead trees had done duty on the battlefields of *All Quiet on the Western Front*, on the supposed Austrian-Hungarian border in *The Black Cat*, in the forest kingdom in *Flash Gordon's Trip to Mars* and in the eerie landscapes around Village Frankenstein in *Son of Frankenstein*.

And then we used the fog, which was a low-lying chemical that just hugged the ground,

Boyle said.

Holding the fog was easy on the stage because there was no wind. We had a backing which went all the way around the stage. By moving some of these trees -- turning them around, really, is what it amounted to -- we could get a different set or a different part of the forest with a little bit of a change.

As I recall, after we did this the trees stayed there and they did several other pictures using the same forest, with various different effects. In those days they didn't let anything go to waste. The standing sets were left and then we would revamp them and revamp them. Nowadays there are very few standing sets except for series television. They're inclined to just go in and bulldoze the whole thing out and the next company comes in with a different situation, because so many of the studios are rentals now. They sell a space and that's more valuable than keeping an old set around.

The Wolf Man, you tell me, has become one of the cult movies,

Boyle mused.

One of my assistants one time said that I was becoming the king of the cults! Most of the movies that we thought were dogs turned out to be looked on by the new film students with some reverence. Some of those films were done with a kind of direct simplicity, both in the writing and the playing, a no nonsense approach. I think in many ways that's the success of the recent Clint Eastwood film [The Unforgiven], *that it reminds us of the days of a simple straight line going from point A to point B and beyond.*

The designer remarked that the professionalism of the makers of The Wolf Man was the reason for its lasting qualities.

A very good filmmaker, a man who directed too, was Curt Siodmak, the writer on this. And the director was George Waggner. These were very professional people and they approached it with knowledge of what they could get away with and a sense of simple storytelling. Joe Valentine was a marvelous cinematographer. So it's not surprising that it has been remembered. And then, of course, they made a sequel. You could go on and never end. It still looks good.

Here we see the importance of design in a film, particularly if you have a modest budget. Today a modest budget seems to mean going on a location and just not spending any money on sets. But you spend it elsewhere. You spend it on time-loss and producer shares and transportation and site rentals and lunches and all of the things that don't get on the screen. None of this is reflected in The Wolf Man.

With some of the best technicians that Universal had to offer on his team, Waggner continued with the casting.

Fay Helm as Jenny Williams

There were some fine players in smaller roles. Playing Jenny Williams, wolfbane-picking victim of Bela the Gypsy, was Fay Helm, who later acted in such Universal shockers as *Night Monster* and *Captive Wild Woman* (and who is considered today a "lost" player). J.M. Kerrigan (1885 - 1964), formerly of Ireland's Abbey Players, and who had played in such John Ford films as *The Lost Patrol*, *The Informer* and *The Long Voyage Home*, was cast as Charles Conliffe, Gwen's father. Forrester Harvey (1890 - 1945), Irish character player who had acted as the innkeeper of 1933's *The Invisible Man*, signed to play Victor Twiddle, Col. Montford's comically timid assistant.

Bela the Gypsy is found dead - Forrester Harvey in center takes notes.

Doris Lloyd, (1896 - 1968), the red-haired, blue-eyed British character actress who had starred with Chaney Sr. in MGM's *The Blackbird* (1926), would play in such Universal fare as *The Ghost of Frankenstein, Frankenstein Meets the Wolf Man* and *The Invisible Man's Revenge*, and whose top horror moment came as Jack the Ripper's terrified, twitching victim of 20th Century-Fox's *The Lodger* (1944), signed on as Mrs. Williams, Jenny's mournful (and vindictive) mother. Harry Stubbs (1874 - 1950), the police chief from *The Invisible Man* and policeman of *The Invisible Man Returns* (and who would turn up as yet another police chief in *Frankenstein Meets the Wolf Man*), took the part of Rev. Norman, while Harry Cording (1891 - 1954), memorable as the giant "Thamal" of 1934's *The Black Cat*, acted the role of the suspicious villager, Wykes. Gibson Gowland (1872 - 1951), who had starred in von Stroheim's *Greed* and had played "Simon Buquet," who climactically leads the mob against Chaney Sr. in *The Phantom of the Opera*, found work in *The Wolf Man* as a villager. Playing Mrs. Bally was Ottola Nesmith (1888 - 1972), who would find a footnote in Universal Horror in 1957 - when she hosted an L.A. showing of *Frankenstein*, posing as a delirious old lady who believed she was *Frankenstein*'s leading lady, Mae Clarke. The real Miss Clarke learned about the charade - and successfully sued!

Finally, Universal hired a trained bear for the carnival episode, and signed the bald, Polish character player Kurt Katch (1896 - 1958) to play the bear's Gypsy schpieler.

At long last, the $180,000 budget was blueprinted, the Curt Siodmak script fine-tuned, the sets constructed. *The Wolf Man* would utilize the famous back lot European village - and, for the church sequence, would visit the old Notre Dame Cathedral exterior from Chaney Sr.'s *The Hunchback of Notre Dame*.

On October 27, 1941, Universal began shooting *The Wolf Man*.

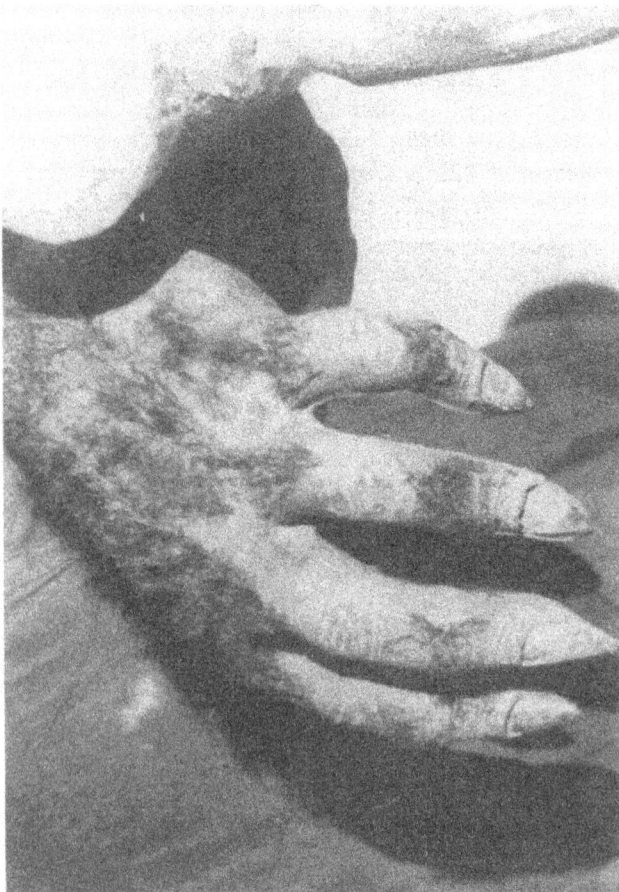

Detail of the wolf claws by Jack Pierce

Is he man or Unholy Beast?
- Universal advertising slogan
for *The Wolf Man*

Come Halloween of 1941, *The Wolf Man* was shooting at Universal City. The lion's share of publicity fell upon Chaney, much of it accenting how Jack P. Pierce, via a T-shaped moulded-rubber nosepiece, shredded kelp, claw-like gloves, padded paws and (naturally) gleaming fangs, turned Chaney into the Wolf Man. It was a tough assignment for young Lon, and Curt Siodmak recalled:

Of course, I had access to the set, and I went over, but I didn't like to go there. Lon wanted to kill me! He was angry because it took 5 to 6 hours to put Chaney into the Wolf Man makeup, and an hour to take it off; he couldn't talk in the makeup, and he had to eat through a straw. Chaney said, "If I find the s-o-b who made up this monster, I'm gonna hit him over the head!" Still, he became a friend of mine...

Pierce later referred to the Wolf Man makeup as "one of the easier ones," eventually refining the application to a two-and-a-half hour job.

Chaney's true baptism of fire was not the makeup; it was the transformation from beast to man, revealed in the film's denouement. Chaney himself later explained how John P. Fulton accomplished this wonderful special effect:

The day we did the transformations I came in at 2:00 a.m. When I hit that position they would take little nails and drive them through the skin at the edge of my fingers, on both hands, so that I wouldn't move them anymore. While I was in this position, they would build a plaster cast of the back of my head. Then they would take the drapes from behind me and starch them, and while they were drying them, they would take the camera and weigh it down with one ton, so that it wouldn't quiver when people walked. They had targets for my eyes up there. Then, while I'm still in this position, they would shoot 5 or 10 frames of film in the camera. They'd take that film out and send it to the lab. While it was there the makeup man would come and take the whole thing off my face, and put on a new one, only less. I'm still immobile. When the film came back from the lab they'd check me. They'd say, "Your eyes have moved a little bit, move them to the right...now your shoulder is up..." Then they'd roll it again and shoot another 10 frames.

Well, we did 21 changes of makeup and it took 22 hours. I won't discuss about the bathroom!

There were some casualties on *The Wolf Man* - one suffered by Chaney. Claude Rains loved acting, so much so that he would beg directors to prevent him from overacting. Come the fog-shrouded climax, George Waggner let Rains go, and when the little actor attacked his huge "son", he got a bit carried away. A Universal press release stated:

A black eye has been accidentally added to Lon Chaney's horror makeup as The Wolf Man... Chaney came off second best in a fight with Claude Rains, although he out-measured his opponent by 60 pounds and five inches... Rains accidentally clubbed Chaney in the right eye with the silver head of the cane, which weighs ten pounds. Ice-pack treatment failed to reduce the swelling, and Chaney was excused for the day. Scenes planned for the afternoon, in which he was to wear "straight" makeup instead of his "Wolf Man" guise, were postponed.

As the beast personality begins to affect him, Chaney attacks the aged bear despite protests from Gwen. The scene destroyed any sympathy for Chaney's character and was cut.

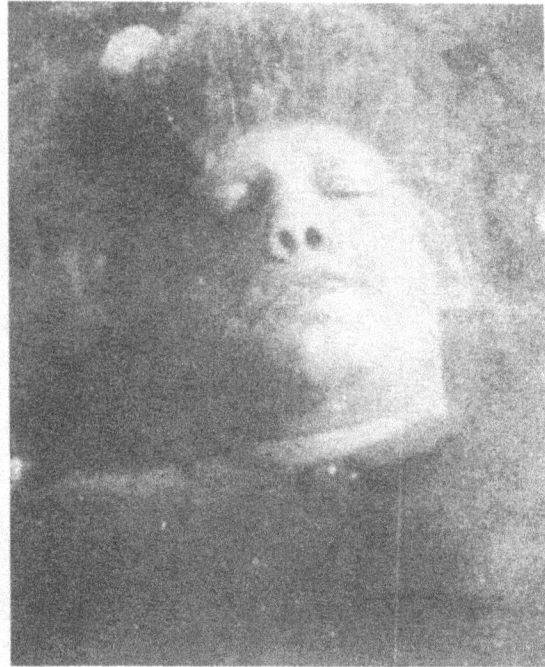

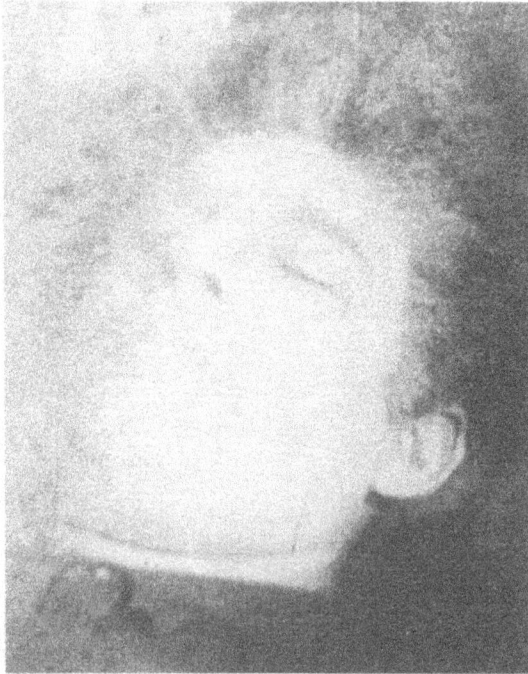

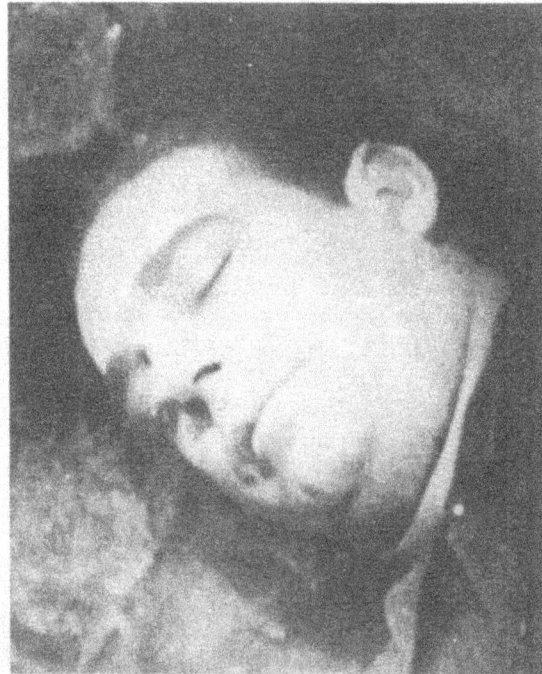

Frame blowups of Chaney transforming from Wolf to Man - He would not be seen turning INTO the werewolf until the sequel 2 years later - Frankenstein Meets the Wolf Man.

Finally, Chaney suffered another injury on *The Wolf Man* - but came to love its perpetrator. Representing Bela the Gypsy in werewolf form was actually a German Shepherd dog named ''Moose'' (See *Frankenstein Meets the Wolf Man* - Volume 5, MagicImage Filmscript Series). Come the scene where Chaney killed the wolf, the actor was wearing three pairs of leather gloves for protection, along with a layer of half-inch thick sponge rubber. Still, Moose bit Chaney so hard on the hand that the dog broke the bones between Lon's thumb and forefinger. Chaney appreciated the dog's spirit, adopting Moose as his special pet, and the two were inseparable at Universal City. Moose later appeared with his master in a Gypsy camp scene in *Frankenstein Meets the Wolf Man*. (When Moose was road-killed on the Universal back lot, while Chaney was co-starring with Maria Montez in *Cobra Woman*, Lon was heartbroken.)

On Tuesday, November 25, 1941, after less than one month of shooting, George Waggner completed *The Wolf Man*. With the release date less than one month away, post-production proceeded rapidly and efficiently.

First of all, there was a major cut. Universal had its revenge on the 600-lb. Gypsy bear: the studio cut his vignette (along with Gypsy Kurt Katch) entirely from the film. While the ebullient bear might have been a real-life nightmare for Universal's Evelyn Ankers, the studio probably cut the scene because the shots of Chaney beating and bellowing at the bear would have upset animal lovers and lost sympathy for Larry Talbot. (A close-up of Chaney from this episode, looking wild-eyed and in his shirt-sleeves, survives in the trailer; Universal has yet to find the cut bear footage in the studio archives.)

Also, in the 2 weeks between final shooting and scheduled preview, Universal added the exquisite musical score - created by Universal's musical director Charles Previn, with associates Frank Skinner and Hans J. Salter. The beautiful score of *The Wolf Man*, dominated by Gypsy motifs, has helped make the Vienna-born Mr. Salter (who had begun his Universal career orchestrating Frank Skinner's epic score for *Son of Frankenstein*) a cult figure, revered for his wonderfully dramatic scoring of Universal chillers of the 1940s and 1950s. As Mr. Salter told Preston Jones in an interview in CINEFANTASTIQUE magazine:

When they presented those pictures to me in the projection room, there was nothing there, just a bunch of disjointed scenes that had no cohesion and didn't scare anybody. You had to create with the music all the tension that was "in between the lines," and didn't come off on the screen. And that was such a tremendous challenge that these pictures interested me, and I developed a very refined technique for this type of picture....

"Who will dare to wrestle with the bear? A florin reward for anyone who can throw him." Cut from the final release print - Chaney (Behind the bear with Evelyn Ankers) begins to feel the effects of the werewolf curse as the animal urges surface. Claude Rains & Ralph Bellamy in foreground.

Publicity shot designed for use on proposed alternate one sheet - for a second variation of the one-sheet - not used - see pressbook

Universal Signature

Jimmy McHugh © 1939

The famous Universal 1940s Theme logo as it appears in musical notation - arranged by Joseph Marcello.

The original Main Title cue from the Wolf Man [Music published in this chapter ©1941 Universal Pictures Co. Motif's and themes to illustrate text were arranged by Joseph Marcello for MagicImage 1993.]

The Music of The Wolf Man
By
Joseph Marcello

"Listen to them! - Children of the night... What music they make!"
                                                  - Count Dracula

"Keep that god-damned music down!"
                          - Unnamed Universal Producer of the 40s

Perhaps no other horror score possesses quite the inspired pathos of *The Wolf Man*. An uncannily seamless -- almost incestuous -- blending of the truine talent of Frank Skinner, Charles Previn, and Hans J. Salter, penned in the prime of their creative spans, it is remarkable as much for its subtleties as for its sheer expressive depths.

To understand the depth of the music for *The Wolf Man* we must first look into the background of the composers who created the scores and their beginnings at Universal.

Steeped in the ethos of the Austro-German school, Messrs. Salter, Previn and Skinner (as most of their Hollywood contempo-raries) spoke the language of the late Romantic with ready fluency - not to mention facility. A composer at Universal at that time was expected to produce a full score-some thirty to forty minutes of orchestral music - in anywhere from one to four weeks. Lest this seem like a reasonable amount of time to court the Muse and deliver the goods, it might be instructive to consider that one hundred fifty three pages of orchestral score for Beethoven's "Pastorale Symphony" requires only some thirty minutes to perform; the contrasted merits of this and a film score quite aside, the feat of conjuring this much even less-than-immortal music in so brief a span is surely somewhat awesome to contemplate. And this, not for one brief shining hour-but consistently, film after film, year after year. In response to a question by writer Preston Jones, who had no technical musical training, Hans Salter took care to emphasize the magnitude of producing three minutes of orchestral music in a day of work. After a beat or two, he affirmed, "Two minutes of orchestral music is a lot of music for one day!"

He continued: *In my early days in Vienna, Richard Strauss and Gustav Mahler had enormous influence on all budding composers and theirs were the styles everyone tried to emulate. Later we became aware of the French School, of men like Debussy and Ravel, followed by the great impact of Stravinsky. And of course Beethoven, Mozart and Brahms were all basic to us. We sort of inhaled them as we grew up.*

Salter had studied privately for at time with one of the most famous scions of the Mahler lineage -Alban Berg, whose teaching style he admits to having found rather weak.

Hans J. Salter

It wasn't that I had any interest in the macabre. These films gave me no thrill. It was just that they were so much in need of music, and for reasons I have never been able to fully explain, I was able to devise a technique of dealing with them. I became known as "The Master of Terror and Suspense" and people could never understand how a nice, mild-mannered fellow from Vienna could become a specialist in such material. Neither could I, except to say that perhaps I had a certain affinity with fantasy

stories. Other than that, it was simply a matter of applied technique. The musical devices at my command were evidently right, and I must admit it was a satisfaction to know that whenever other studios set out to make horror pictures, they usually showed the composers some of ours to give them an idea of what it was all about.

In those days, particularly in the early forties, we had no idea that these pictures would be studied and appreciated years later. There were no thoughts about writing for posterity. We were just trying to keep up with the frantic pace of one picture after the other. For example, a producer would show you his picture on a Monday. You then had one week to write a score, orchestrate it, and be ready to rehearse and record the following Monday. It was like a factory where you had to turn out, say, so many dozens of red socks and so many dozens of green socks. And, of course, we must not forget that, in the order of importance, music was at the very bottom of the heap. It probably still is. Sound effects were always favored over the music. It took a gradual education of the producers until they began to realize that in certain scenes the emotional impact of the music did more for their picture than the tatic sound effects. It was a constant hassle, and once I was even 'asked'' to stay away from the dubbing room so they could finish their picture without any interference. "Keep the Goddamned music down'' was a popular battle cry. I had to speak up for myself because nobody else did. And no matter how well you did the job, the producers rarely made any comment. Perhaps they were afraid that if they paid us a compliment, we would ask for a raise. They were hectic days, and none of us thought that years after people would be studying our work.

Salter's first assignment at Universal came in 1939 when he orchestrated Frank Skinner's *Son of Frankenstein*. This enabled him to absorb, first hand, from Skinner, musical mould - archetypes which he would soon come to replenish with his own invention. It also baptized him to the film world where he had to come to grips with its tight schedules while still creating a musical atmosphere through the ''tricks'' - such as a harmonic devices, timbral and coloristic idioms - which ultimately became a musical trade mark unique to the Kingdom of Universal Mythology.

Much has been written about the scriptwriting technique with regard to the Thalberg method. Thalberg would always have several writers working on the same script and then would incorporate the best of each into the final screenplay. Some of the more famous novelists such as F. Scott Fitzgerald and William Faulkner could not survive in that atmosphere. The same went for the hybrid score demanded by Universal. Aside from immense talent it also involved a sublimation of the ego. Ironically one of the best musical sound-tracks to come out of Universal's 40s Monster films was the remake of *Phantom of the Opera* in which *The Wolf Man*'s star, Claude Rains, portrayed the Lon Chaney role with a twist. Instead of being born hideous, the Phantom's disfigurement was caused by his possessiveness to his music.

Their next joint venture into the genre was *The Invisible Man Returns* which contained some of their most exquisite writing, which, if heard in a concert hall environment would well be considered "inspired."

So successful is the collaboration of *The Wolf Man* score that it almost exists as one oversoul working through three distinct personalities, two European emigres fleeing the approaching storm of the Third Reich in Germany and a shy gifted Midwestern farm boy seeking his expression through music.

While film-scoring technique in general has often relied heavily upon character motifs, it is noteworthy that few protagonists have been blessed with such distinctive musical signatures as the stable of mythological denizens dwelling at Universal spanning the years from 1933-1955.

The tradition of the three-, four-, and sometimes five-note musical motto is virtually a sacred tenet and founding principle in those films.

The motif of the Wolf Man has its musical roots in history, along with the actual folklore. At one time the "Tritone" was a forbidden musical practice. In the *Diabola in Musica* (Devil in Music) of the medievals, this was considered the musical equivalent of a land mine, so volatile was its chemistry. The sound itself was considered to be a muse of the Dark Powers and the unfortunate monk

Frank Skinner

who composed an obvious tritone piece was quick to be put to torture as a black magician.

As man's personal freedom won out over the structure of the old order, so did his musical freedom.

In the realm of film music especially the fantasy genre, the coming of sound provided a perfect home for the once "forbidden tritone." What could not be done with special effects or visually, could be accomplished with music. At first the producers stuck to the well known classical pieces. With the exception of the opening credits, it was thought that no one would accept music coming from the screen unless they could see the source.

With the release of *King Kong* in 1933 the Hollywood producers finally took notice to the strength of music. They no longer insisted on familiar pieces to serve as only background for dialogue and unsure acting abilities of the early talkie casts. Universal responded with a score for *The Invisible Man (1933)*, *The Werewolf of London (1935)*, *Dracula's Daughter (1936)* and *Son of Frankenstein (1939)* just to name a few in the fantasy film category. This leads us now to the music of *The Wolf Man*.

Charles Previn

As the trade mark fades we first hear the tri-toned song of the Wolf Man, unique in its evocation of two simultaneous atmospheres: Menace and Destiny.

Just *how* this is done is the secret of the musical alchemist, but the more deeply one explores the art of film-scoring, the clearer it becomes that the visual narrative track *itself* is a seminal voice in the composer's orchestra-much like a new section of instruments, or a Greek chorus. The 'chorus' generates its own themes, tempi, momentums and counterpoints-about which the composer - much as he would in a concerto setting - conjures a dynamic vortex which pivots on, and illuminates the soloists.

One almost misses the Wolf Man theme in the main title, screaming as it does, wildly above the cascade of rushing parallel chording. Four times it peals, each higher than the previous, when, at its *fortissimo* extremity it suddenly all comes crashing to earth.

What follows takes the form of a mini-suite, journeying rapidly through the themes for the Wolf Man. Bela's death, Maleva's motif, the love theme, the pentagram theme, and finally, the lament, with an unsettling echo of the Wolf Man motif - like an ill-omen.

The first and perhaps most light-hearted cue in the entire Wolf Man canon ''The Telescope'' unfolds a tender but all too brief glimpse of the innocent, boyish, Larry Talbot, a tune drawn from Salter's prior score for *Man Made Monster* (in which Chaney is again featured as a naive, tragic victim of fate). Hans Salter said of this passage:

The Wolf Man motif

I was often able to write musical sequences that were quite complete in form, with a beginning, a middle and an end. In MAN MADE MONSTER, for example, there is a sequence in which Lon Chaney plays with a dog. For this I wrote a scherzo. It stands up itself when heard away from the picture, but it also works well with the visual. It is always pleasing when you can do this because most of the time in scoring you cannot, and neither can you expect to. It's the wedding between the music and the picture that matters.

In three tones its call is full, fateful, and final - elemental like the cry of a beast. In these brief three sounds we can hear not only menace, but the anguished cry of a presence who is compelled by his destiny to do the very things he would not do.

Reverberating through the mists of a widely-voiced E minor sixth cord (with added ninth) it is at once a warning voiced through the horn section, just as the ancient hunter's horns signalled the sighting of the quarry. The hunter's horns evoke the whole beshrouded landscape of the Welsh moors with its lurking mythologies.

Wolfbane-Love Theme

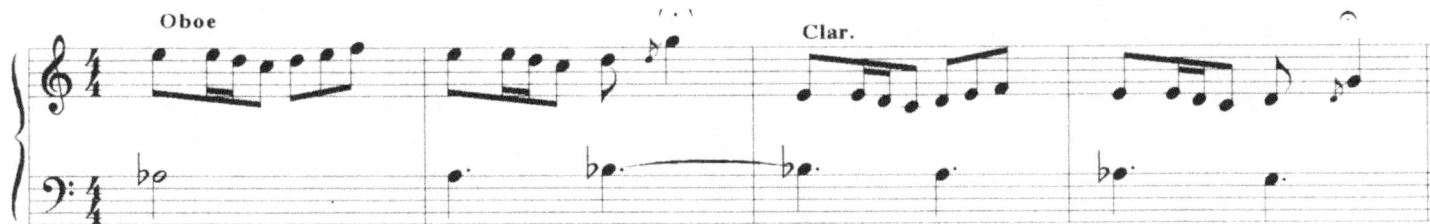

The Telescope (Pt A.)

to her gently undulating theme - a sylph-like tune dressed in parallel string gowns, that dreams its way softly to earth. (A closely voiced line tinged with the lavender scent of sixth chords, a warning dominant seventh, and a final, garrulous diminished seventh).

The most felicitous touch in this twenty bars of tenderness is the seamlessness with which it ushers us from the near end of Sir John's peeping Tom of a telescope, through space and time, to the far end, as a nattily dressed Larry, fulfilling his wishful fancy in person enters the antique shop to find his towered princess.

Once the carefree strains dissolve, it is the end of innocence. We have heard the last we shall ever hear, in the five-film Wolf Man saga of guileless happiness, -or at least, the illusion of it.

Despite the sustained, and in some ways, superior refinements of its sequels, this brief, poignant preamble accounts for the enduring fondness of many, who often gaze back on the film, as if on childhood itself.

The Telescope (B)

Here, however, the tune fades after a mere piquant four bars, and segues to the brief beguilement of a somewhat exotic - if not quite erotic - siren song that beckons beneath the roving eye of the telescope. This, under a tranquil string octave pedal point (a sustained tone or tones) produces one of the most curiously pleasing moments in any of the Universal melodramas: We become, with Larry, willing voyeurs upon the quaint daily life of the rural Welsh village of Llanwelly - which can be found on a good map of Wales, under the spelling ''Llanelly''.

Through Joseph Valentine's cinematography we witness children playing, cyclists passing, wagons gliding by, in silent life, until, discovering Evelyn Ankers in our lens, we are treated

Larry & Gwen at the Gypsy wagon

Wolfbane Pt. A

"Wolfbane" by Charles Previn, Universal's Music department Head, shows this unheralded composer to be a man of exceptional musical sensitivity. It encompasses some of the subtlest and most complex emotional shifts in the film.

The cue occupies a strategic place in the narrative, drawing us for the first time, with the protagonists, from the sunlit lanes of simple Welsh village life into the realms of the mysterious and ultimately, the supernatural. Harmonically daring, it opens with a plaintive series of falling fourth chords (six notes deep) set against a seesawing series of applied dominant bass sequences, drifting in with the evening fog like a huge web. Though not overtly threatening, these impressionistic colors obscure the lines of the commonplace and invoke the presence of the unknown. On a purely harmonic level, one may view the notes of the fourth chords as 'children without a home', yet, though perhaps lost, children who are strangely content in their exile. Traditional triadic chord construction (thirds) tends to generate a sense of musical 'belonging' and the sensation of arrival and homecoming. Previn chooses here just such nebulous fourth-sonorities, hanging like vast parentheses in the path of the narrative, a strangely beguiling shift of mood which clears the mind of all things ordinary.

And then, in pregnant contrast, as the ill-fated trio approaches the campsite, there emerges out of the emptiness, resonant and impassioned, the soulful throb of a gypsy violin, scored in its lowest, darkest, and richest register, between the still audible web of string mists. With it, the emotional waters are suddenly roiled and revealed to be unsettlingly deep. Implicit within this new, but ancient, idiomatic Gypsy dialect drawn from the twin Muses of Passion and Pain - is the world of the fantastic, the mythological. Like seeds borne from the wells of the Eastern European folklore, the gypsies and their musical ethos implant themselves into the New World, the good earth of British reason, and American guilelessness.

During the fortune-telling sequence Jenny's pitiable naivete is beautifully counterposed musically against Bela the gypsy's tragic depth of vision. The wolfsbane leaves have been cast from the table: their destiny is inescapable. An evocative confrontation between the two poles of being, the conscious and the unconscious, the known and the unknown has been laid bare before us.

With a deftness of touch Previn's passages metamorphose instantly; from one to the other; from drifting mists to Hungarian soul-cry, to the two-bar "Beware" motif for Maleva the gypsy woman, the one character who fathoms the tragedy and all its players.

Gwen, Larry & Jenny approach Bela the Gypsy

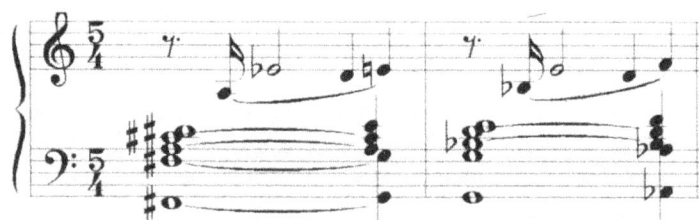

Maleva's Motif

The music now shifts to an exhilarated, almost zephyr-like mysterioso for Gwen and Larry's near - love scene - a wash of sound suffused with a subliminal eroticism yields to Bela's

Wolfbane   The Gypsy Camp

CONDUCTOR

"THE WOLF MAN"

"THE FORTUNE"

by CHARLES PREVIN

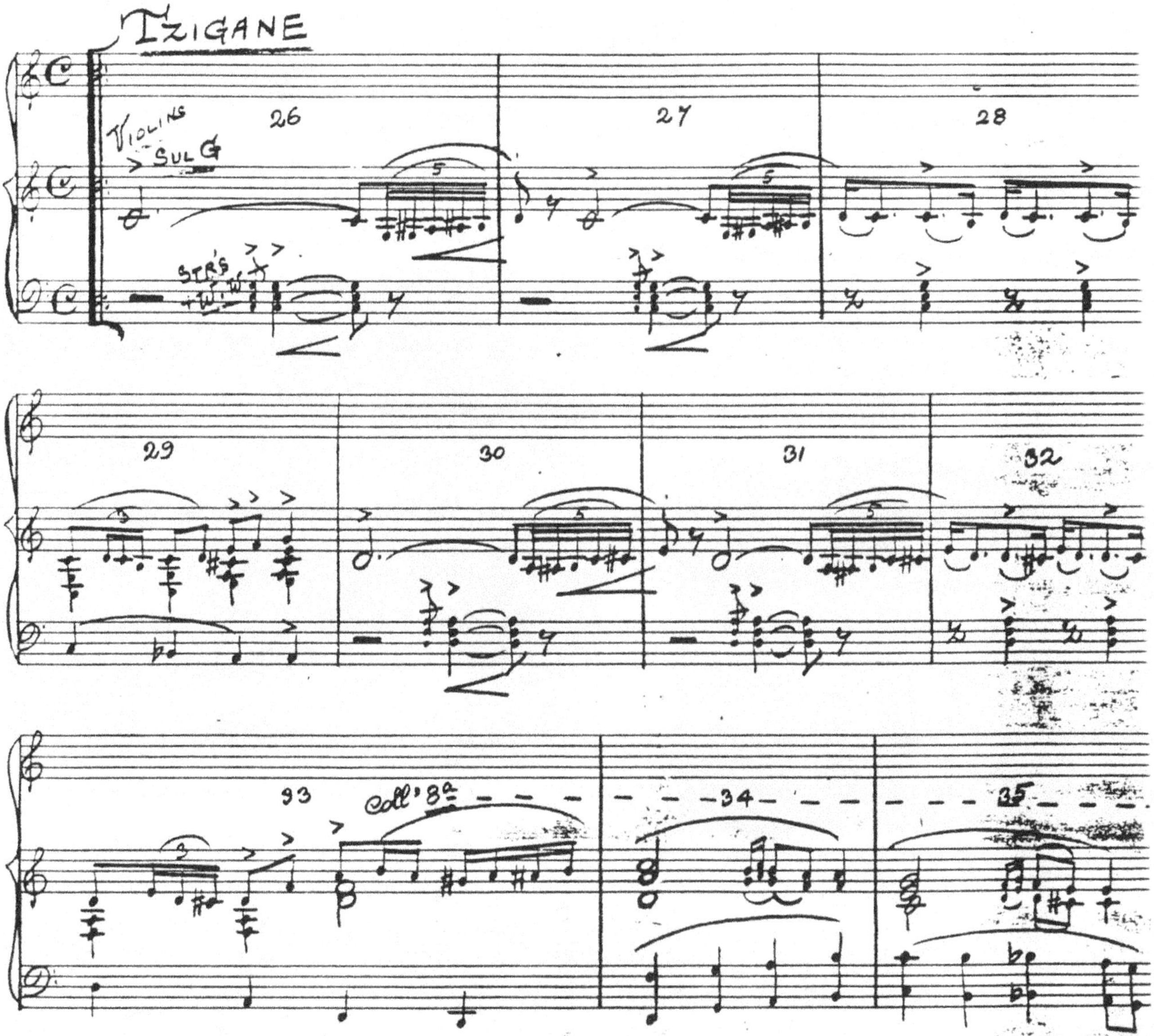

Wolfbane- Love Scene

The rhapsodic strings bestir themselves, through gypsy violin elaborations, into panic as Bela warns Jenny to ''Go Quickly!!'' At this point the music breaks into a terrified run before fleeing wilding into the night. The instinctive impression is of motion into distance as if fading into the perspective of musical space - we can sense the calm before the storm. The Fate-like Wolf Man theme confirms our deepest apprehensions: the hunt is on. Whomever fails to register a chilling rush up the spine at this moment is probably well on his way to a better world than this, for the forces of sight and sound are so electrifyingly choreographed that deep involvement and excitement is virtually inevitable. Without a moment's hesitation or dynamic faltering, Previn has drawn us across the bridge of the Impossible, and from here on, the score (and the film) lives in the dimension of the Tragic, which we now sense to be inevitable.

vibrant, wrathful melody, above a bed of brooding strings, lifting, to poise in shock at Jenny's query: ''Can you tell me when I'm going to be married?'' Bela then brushes aside his hair and revealing, upon his forehead, the sign of the pentagram. Visually as well as musically we now know that he is a werewolf.

Now comes a memorable moment: like the very essence of Jenny's soul-and Bela's- an uneasy ascending line unravels and, betraying its fears, accelerates, until it climaxes in the theme of the

'Wolfbane', Pt. C

Pentagram as it appears within Jenny's doomed palm. (The effect here, to merely glimpse a bit of the alchemist's art, rests upon a dynamic contrast between the initial *legato* (smoothly voice) quality of the ascending arioso, with its febrile but flowing sting tremolando (softly agitated cross-bowing of the strings) as opposed to the sudden, emphatic revelation of the massed horns, stabbing into the emotional fabric with almost military authority.

Bela watches, helpless, as the transformation begins

Maleva watches as her son turns into a werewolf

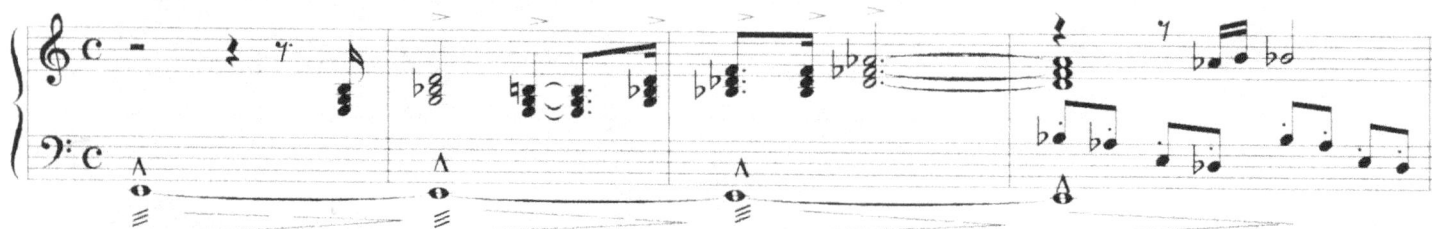

The Pentagram

'The Kill' (Pt. A)

What follows surely qualifies as among Salter's inspired inventions: ''The Kill.'' This theme has forever been intimately associated with the stalk and attack music for the Wolf Man, perhaps even more so that the three note leitmotif itself.

Syncopated, nocturnal, bounding, the wonderfully unnerving momentum of Salter's ''The Kill'' is found, upon analysis, to be the product of a triune activity: 1. The uppermost level: a leaping, tripleted tattoo pealing at length into the cry of the Wolf Man theme, then gyrating restlessly into a dizzying sixteenth note spin; 2. the central level: a tremolando of roaming string chords drawn from the whole-tone scale, pulsating against the higher rhythms, in mirrored parallel motion (6 voices deep), and finally; 3. Below, a classic bogey-man bass figure (largely of mixed whole tone scales), which can only be one thing: - clambering feet in pursuit of prey.

Their darkly dancing rhythms combine and revolve against each other to become a marvelous musical gyroscope which succeeds in galvanizing the nervous system. Salter has, in effect, got his listeners in a three way musical Half-Nelson. The mind neither has the time nor the balance to sort out these queasy, quivering counterpoints before they become parts of our aesthetic domain. Our nerves have beaten our reason to the punch, and we may find ourselves, against our better wisdom casting questioning glances at the nocturnal landscape that looms beyond our own windowsill, for, like it or not, neurologically, we have been programmed for flight.

This leads inevitably to the attack sequence, which climaxes in almost nausea-producing series of jarring syncopations and furious chord-cascades, thudding with brutal finality as the victim on the screen falls to earth. The Wolf Man theme, now in majestic dress, announces the dark work has been done. Wagnerian operatic technique helps here, as the scene plays itself out through the rapid fluctuation of leitmotifs, brief snatches of love theme, Maleva's theme and the Pentagram theme. Even the trundling of Maleva's wagon approaching from the distance blends, with the soundscape.

Larry and Gwen hear the cry of the werewolf.

After Larry kills the werewolf Gwen and Maleva take him back to Talbot Castle.

The Kill (Pt. B)

Troubled Dreams

Larry wakens to find he has killed Bela, not a wolf.

Next there is an exceptionally poignant passage continued midway through the cue, "Bela's funeral" by Frank Skinner. Heard once earlier in the main title suite, we now have an opportunity to cherish the 'meaning' of this grievous brass chorale in full, as we watch the gypsy's coffin being silently borne to its bier as Larry eavesdrops upon the scene in the crypt.

One of Skinner's favorite techniques was the pedal point, sometimes below, and just as often above, the melodic/harmonic center. Here, the brass seems to plow its mighty way up from the depths of the earth, with a power shocking in its grief. Yet, above, a motionless, attenuated pedal point of octave G's gazes into the infinite distance, undisturbed by the earth-shaking tremors of the brass. The lower pedal point, a pair of tolling F sharps, set at the hard dissonance of a major seventh to the upper pair and at an extreme distance of three octaves, creates a seeming harmonic head-on-collision. Through this musical chaos Skinner's background in big-band music prevails.

"Troubled Dreams", which is pure Salter, conveys Larry's disturbed awakening through the expedient of a rising chromatic line layered over itself in canonic imitation - stepping up a ladder of woodwinds; bassoon to bass clarinet to clarinet to oboe, and so on finally peaking on a high, tremulously sweet minor third - a sound immediately polluted by the foul innuendo of three muted horns far below. As Larry's alarm escalates, the canonic layering resumes more rapidly, and scored this time for the strings which add an urgency of tone to the same melodic material. Once Larry is fully awake and able to reason, the need for these "irrational" emotional elements wanes and the cue fades. We are again in the light of day, and of 'common sense'...

"The way you walked was thorny..." in Bela's crypt

CONDUCTOR

BELA'S FUNERAL

"THE WOLF-MAN"
by FRANK SKINNER

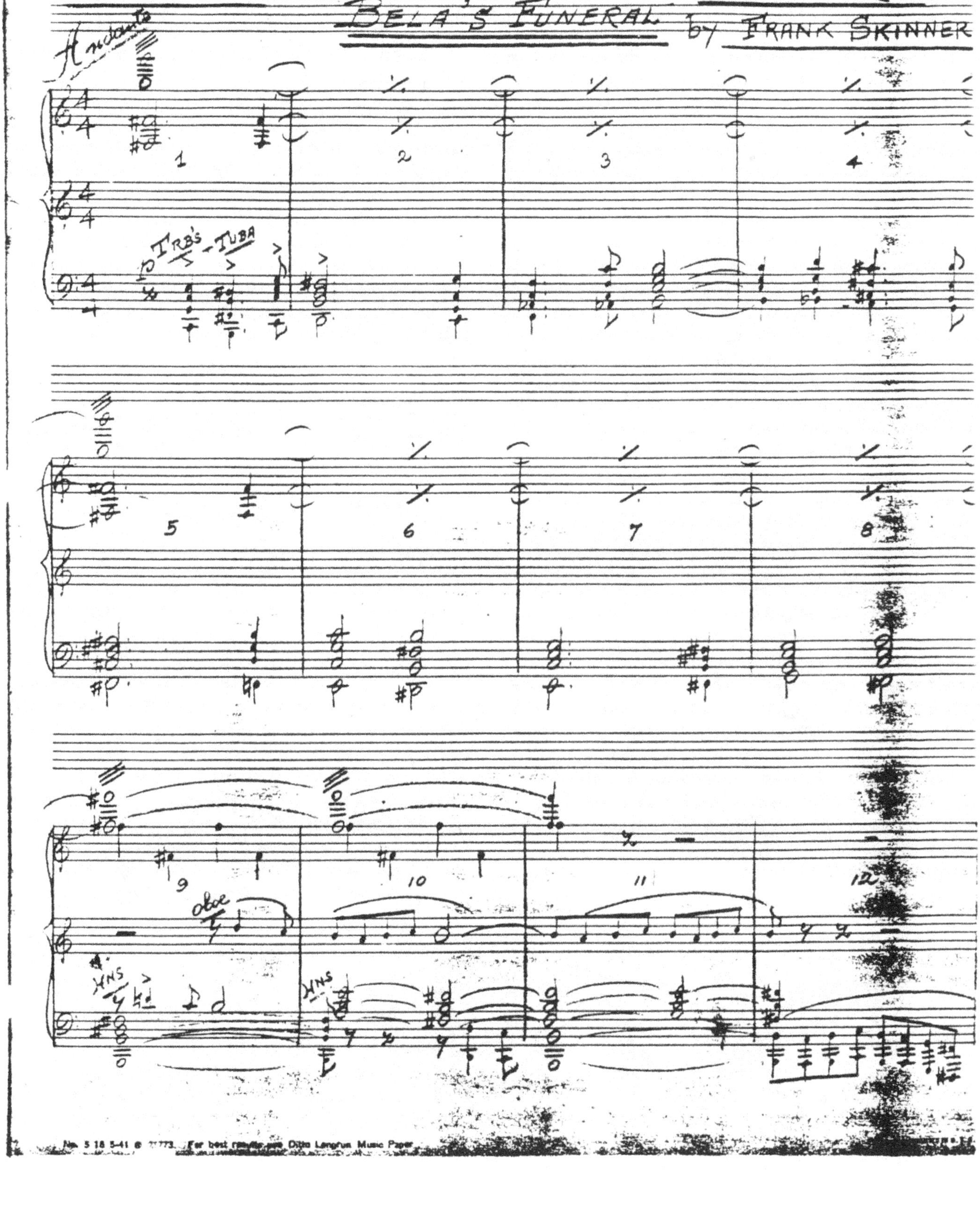

Bela's Funeral -Chorale

He has chosen two different notes for the simultaneous pedal points *each* of which - according to the underlying shifting brass colors, is either benign or alien to the passing harmony. Skinner knew that the brass instruments, even when outpouring a succession of the most dark and brilliant euphonies, will bear and absorb any dissonance from any vying group of instruments in the orchestra - thus allowing for chaos. So at any given moment we find one of them glowing, and the other glowering. On beat one we hear the upper G's are consonant with the brass, but then on beat two they are in disfavor, and harshly dissonant with the brass B Major chord, which in so shifting has made the previously alien F sharp pedal point its dearest of friends. The unconscious mind hears these rapid ''optical'' illusions in the fascinating kaleidoscope of - harsh - beautiful - harsh - beautiful, simultaneously.

Skinner is sounding for us both the fundamental tone, and its *appoggiatura*, at the same time. The fundamental tone is the final tone of the resolution, and its appoggiatura is a neighboring note that ardently seeks to reach that fundamental. But it is just a half step away. To become the fundamental tone, it must give up its life as an *appoggiatura*, and die. It must make the leap to the fundamental. If it refuses to do this, then it creates a sizzling dissonance with the fundamental, like a fallen angel unwilling to return humbly to God's throne.

Spanning the chorale to the following dirge is a short twelve bar apotheosis of submerged pain. The horns offer a benign variant of the Wolf Man theme, now rendered free of menace, and almost prayerful, which an oboe then echoes and possesses as its own, in turn to be echoed and repossessed by the sonorous bass strings. Like much of Frank Skinner's art, it is structurally simple and yet profoundly effective. The theme, echoed in relays by horns, oboe and bassi at a distance of first one, then two octaves, and a time delay of two and a half beats, twines and heaves on both ends of a rocking series of triads: A Minor and B major, C major, B major. The net effect is as if the fact and its reflection were nearly a simultaneous event, or perhaps, as if the past, present and future were one inevitable stream.

A short octave bridge brings us to the lament itself. Below Maleva's confrontation with the vicar, we hear a doleful *cantus firmus* in exquisite passing chromatic colors, against which the Wolf Man theme grieves in counterpoint, first in the vibrant sorrow of the trombone as it peals down, then echoed - like the wolf howl in the distance - by the English horn's answering cry. When it is reprised at the scene's end, the more puissant French horn answers the trombone before fading, as Larry weeps.

This lament along with its following elegy, like a thrice-tragic refrain, tolls the chimes of Destiny through the film, beautifully binding the three phases of the narrative together - implied tragedy, the contamination of Larry's soul and the freeing of Bela's - and finally in Larry's release in death.

Dirge (Bela's Funeral))

In the conductor score for this cue there is about a page and a half of music which has been cut from the final print. Siodmak's original script gives us a fascinating revelation: In the film we only behold Larry gazing upon Bela as third persons: what Larry sees remains a mystery. However, in the original script, we have Larry's angle on Bela, and we see that below Bela's bandaged skull, his eyes are open, his mouth grinning, seemingly at Larry. As the grave diggers bear the coffin away, we suddenly view the world from Bela's recumbent point of view, as sky and treetops pass our lens. Only later does Maleva's incantation administered with the sacrament of flowers, candles and wolfbane - draw the diabolic features into repose. The omitted music is in the nature of a mediation in the style of a grave gypsy improvisation, setting up the little epiphany of a moment that is to follow:

Bela's Funeral   Wolf Man Variant

Bela's Funeral: Elegy

"The way you walk", Maleva's benediction, and arguably the score's most luminous moment. A plangent elegy, this, nothing more than a softly praying violin weaving its way above a footpath of longing progressions, and both these as before embraced above and below by two pedalpoints, the lower constant, the higher intermittent. Their net effect bears the inescapable imprint of time's irrevocable flow. As the 'prayer' culminates, the harmonies becloud, and the bass begins its irretrievable descent, but the violins carry the upper line out of sight -- in an evocative metaphor of transcendence.

Gwen and Frank arrive at the Gypsy camp.

The source music for the gypsy fair "In a Gypsy Camp" is listed only as "Arranged by Bela Schaeffer." It is at least certain, given this and other scores, that these ethnic pieces were not the product of Skinner, Salter or Previn; however, one might easily mistake Previn's ethnically derivative tzigane (Rumanian Dance Song), "The Fortune", which underscores Larry's rendezvous with Maleva in her tent, as yet another genuine Gypsy reel. A case of scoring against the mood, designed, it seems, as source music, with its strangely gay tenor in the midst of this fateful confrontation, in which Larry's darkest apprehensions are confirmed.

When Larry purposely misses a metal wolf in a carnival rifle shoot that the Gypsy camp provides, he runs into Maleva.

Larry's mind gives in to the reality - "Go and Heaven help you!"

From the moment Maleva utters the words, "And Heaven help you!" when Larry flees her tent, the atmosphere is charged with the winds of Destiny: no longer is it a matter of 'will it happen' but rather of 'when' and 'how'.

A strangely poignant, delicately scored love scene between Larry and Gwen follows. At the penultimate moment of intimacy a mounting anxiety fractures their fragile tryst as the gypsies hurriedly break camp. Echoing Maleva's fateful revelation with a final blow, a terrified gypsy informs Larry that they are fleeing because there is a werewolf in camp. At this point an unraveling orchestral crescendo gives way to contagious panic, actually a passage from a much longer, final, cue, "Sir John's Discovery". In both occurrences it performs the almost identical function of evoking an awakening terror in Larry, who, until this moment, has kept the temptation of fear locked safely within his own bosom. When we hear it again, it hastens the unraveling of Sir John's brittle courage into stark terror.

Vns., Vle, Cl.

Hns.

Bass. Cl.
Bass'n. Cello/Bass

Sir John's Discovery (Pt

Skinner achieves this in a very effective and time-honored fashion - by generating the melodic dynamic contour of a fanning web of sound, the treble and bass like two great spreading wings, the upper ''wing'' a chromatically soaring arc consisting of high strings and graduated winds, and the lower ''wing'' consisting of bassoon, bass clarinet and deep strings. Between these mirrored flights, the horns peal, augmenting the Wolf Man theme far beyond its three note cell. From a unison middle C, the two fugitive currents of sound yaw to a dizzying three octave span before spiralling in upon a return arc, merging into the same tone octaves apart.

As Larry's reason flees, the acceleration of tempo and accumulation of textural density keep apace, segueing into what is without doubt the most orchestrally sumptuous moment in the film. A breathless, polyphonically hyperactive agitato, with instrumental forces fleeing in a furious maelstrom of late Romantic passion, it allows no time for reflection, sweeping us irrevocably onward, like a flash-flood, into the eye of the hurricane.

A montage-like sequence follows where Larry's hallucinatory visions haunt the screen as he peers, frozen, into the nightmare. A blur of sound washes by, depicting a stream of consciousness pastiche that is invaded by the next cue by Skinner and Salter, called ''Desperation''.

Here, pulsating feverishly, the strings describe a tightening series of diminished seventh chords in sequential suspensions, gyrating over a throbbing octave pedal bass. Harkening back to the 'Creation' scene of *Bride of Frankenstein*, the throbbing tympani (kettle drums) pulsate and accelerate the tempo, like a troubled heart, throughout the cue. The sense of angst becomes well-nigh unbearable as these urgent strains quicken, intensifying into a pleading 'stringendo' before poising.

In five distinctive phases, the cue carries us through unrest, anxiety, agony , desperation and surrender. And for all its tortures, it possesses a strangely compelling lyricism.

As Larry's spiritual resistance subsides, a deadly serious tone invades the sound climate as we witness the surreal moment when reality becomes possessed by myth: Man becomes Beast. A deep falling chromatic bass suggests the immersion into darkness, while a trio of muted - almost strangled - horns lifts in parallel six four-chord inversions. However the muted horn sonority, bespeaking distortion and contamination - would achieve its sinister effect, with or without melodic contour. The scene is an eerily

COPYRIGHT 1941
· BY ·
UNIVERSAL MUSIC CORPORATION
NEW YORK, N. Y.

"The Wolf Man"

CONDUCTOR

"Desperation"

by Hans J. Salter and Frank Skinner

-15746-

No. 5 15 5-41 ℗ 11773 For best results use Ditto Longrun Music Paper
PRINTED IN U.S.A.

Desperation (Pt A)

frozen moment, the horror withheld, suspended as it were, by the utter fascination of its coming. It is virtually devoid of feeling, perhaps due to the way in which the camera's eye steers itself out of the human realm, allowing only the vision of the lower half of the body in a strangely clinical, creaturely view of events. A little inspired moment is the cold thonking of the Wolf Man theme on the xylophone as we witness the anomaly of animal feet. Perhaps this is the mind of the creature that we are hearing - an alien mentality under brute compulsion.

The "Destiny" cue fulfills itself in the transformation as the stalking music of "The Kill" leads us to the creature's first hunt, and victim.

Desperation (Pt. B)

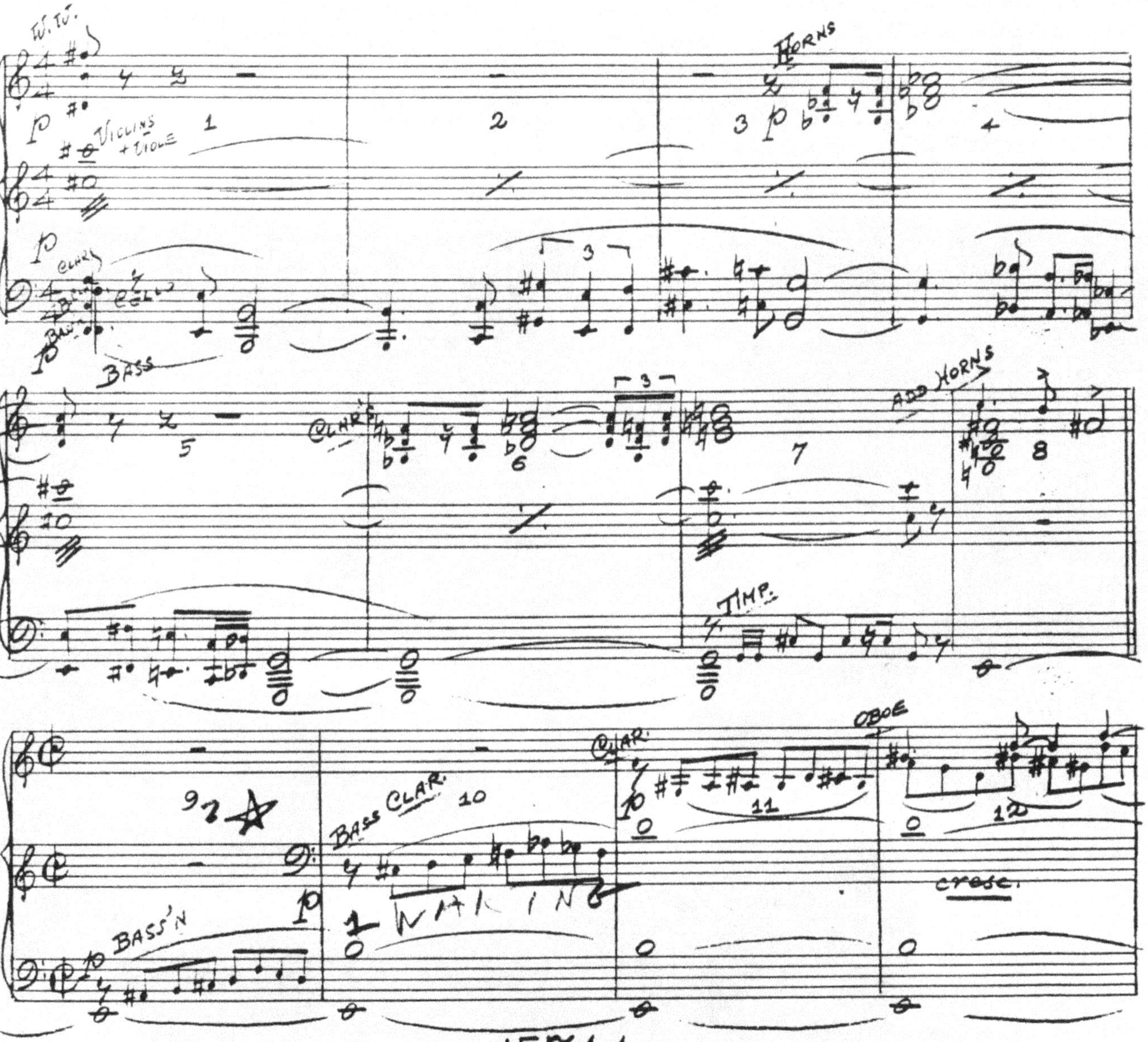

Wolf Tracks

"Wolf Tracks" by Hans Salter traces Larry's nightmare, as waking the following morning he confronts the reality of his fears. A muddy trail of lupine footprints leading from the window sill to his own bed. This passage is remarkable for its novel coloristic contrasts - a subtle protrayal of waring psychic elements - dread and hope. It is composed of an ominous two-part polyphony of octave bass elaborations on the Wolf Man theme. Plying against a variant of the Hunting theme - again in the trio of horns - these mutually resistant strains speak of the two simultaneous realities before us: the unconscious Larry, dreaming dark dreams (bass Wolf Man theme variants) and the approaching party of inquisitors (Hunting theme) outside the window.

"Troubled Dreams" picks up here, with its wakening shafts of light and as Larry sobers to the appearance of dried wolf tracks in his room, the stalking theme subconsciously reminds us of the previous night, adding its note of hasty malaise.

One of the most arresting scenes in *The Wolf Man* is Larry Talbot's confrontation of the sacred, and his paralysis and alienation in the face of his fellows and, one is tempted to imagine, his God. The built-in scoring of the organ hymn whose source remains unknown, is deeply effective in exposing Talbot's doubt and guilt or self banishment.

The werewolf is caught in the trap.

Attributed to all three composers "The Wolf Trap" is to a great extent a reprise of the stalking and attack music of "The Kill". We now arrive at the centerpiece, the second in the thrice-refrained incantation of Maleva the gypsy, who intercedes for Larry, caught in the wolf trap as the huntsmen approach. At Maleva's benediction "The way you walk is thorny" we hear the same exquisite elegy that tolled Bela's entrance into eternity. In one and the same moment it resonates the shared destiny of Larry and Bela, and ultimately, their shared fate. We shall hear it but once more. Like a dark Pieta, the icon of the wise gypsy woman, her wounded 'son' upon her lap, leaves an image which, harbored now within us, causes the tale's climax to be felt as truly predestined.

Deep in the nightmare now, Larry seeks a rendezvous with Gwen in a pathetic farewell attempt to spare her his agony. And it is the appropriately titled "Desperation" which reappears here to recreate its fevered pulse, swelling beneath the couple's troubled tryst, until the Pentagram reveals itself in the palm of Gwen's upraised hand.

Larry finds himself more the outcast. He is deluged with the supernatural suggestions that Director George Waggner presents on the screen. On one side is his father who insists on the down-to-earth explanations and on the other is Maleva, who presents him with the truth as unbelievable as it is.

From here on the touch of Frank Skinner is everywhere - his passion for chromatic lines, for mirrored melodic contours, his restrained, yet ominously Mythical orchestrations.

The last two cues, both fairly extended, form a compelling mini-tone poem, and are overwhelmingly the work of Frank Skinner - with some moments of the last cue recognizable as Salter's. Skinner fertilizes the film's climax with a wizardly array of compelling musical inventions, not a few of which, incompletely realized here due to the dictates of the dramatic timetable, were to be handsomely utilized by Hans Salter in his next two landmark scores *Ghost of Frankenstein* and *Frankenstein Meets the Wolf Man*.

Several lovely, pungent new themes are heard. A cantilena of three clarinets (one a bass) wanders homelessly beneath the scene of Sir John in his final appeal to Common Sense, binding Larry to the arm chair. This is immediately followed by the arcing English horn/viola aria which was destined to become the main title for *House of Frankenstein*. Toward the end there is a stabbingly poignant string outburst - echoed by the oboe: a remarkable evocation of Larry's terminal anguish on his father's behalf.

Desperation (Pt. C)

Sir John's Discovery

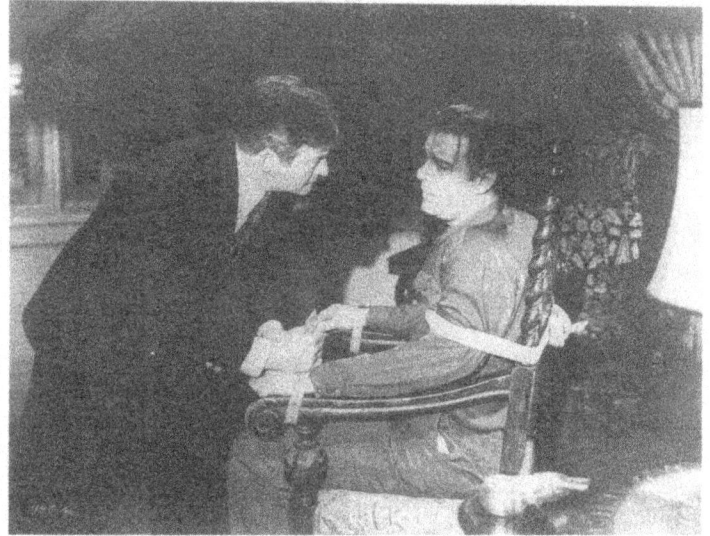

Sir John's Discovery -Pt   1

It sounds like nothing less than what it is - a desperate farewell cry, brought up short by the Wolf Man motif. Much like the climax of Bernstein's *West Side Story*, we have a massing and gathering of forces, primal and subtle, drawing together a tapestry of fate: Sir John, Montford, Dr. Lloyd, Gwen, Maleva, and the Wolf Man. During the striking confrontation between Sir John and Maleva, Reason and Wisdom, the composer baits us on the hook of softly anxious tremolando strings - a rising apprehensive oboe lifting above as their conversation escalates to a breaking point, when gunshots shatter their dark tryst. Skinner is unafraid to make abundant use of a good thing, now, as once again, the two great spreading wings of sound engulf the emotional canvas, laying bare the suppressed terror, climaxing in their fullest most furious, flight of Sir John's Discovery.

Gwen is told to run before Larry finds HER!

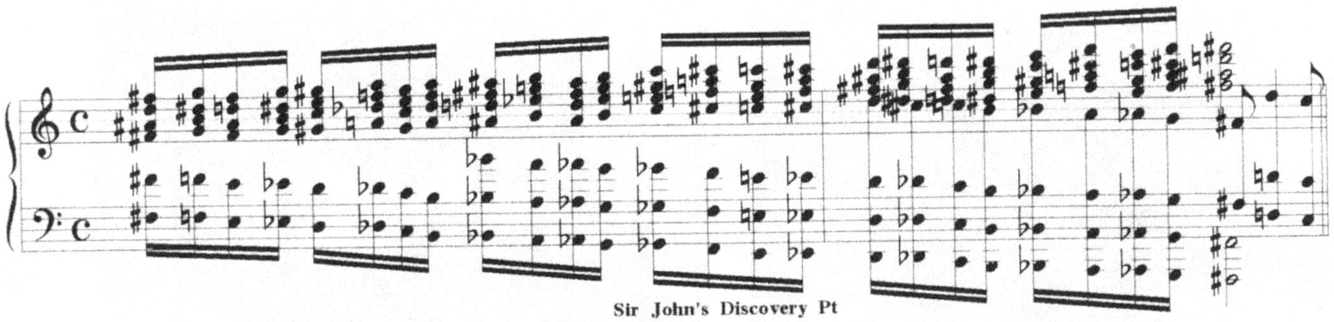

Sir John's Discovery Pt

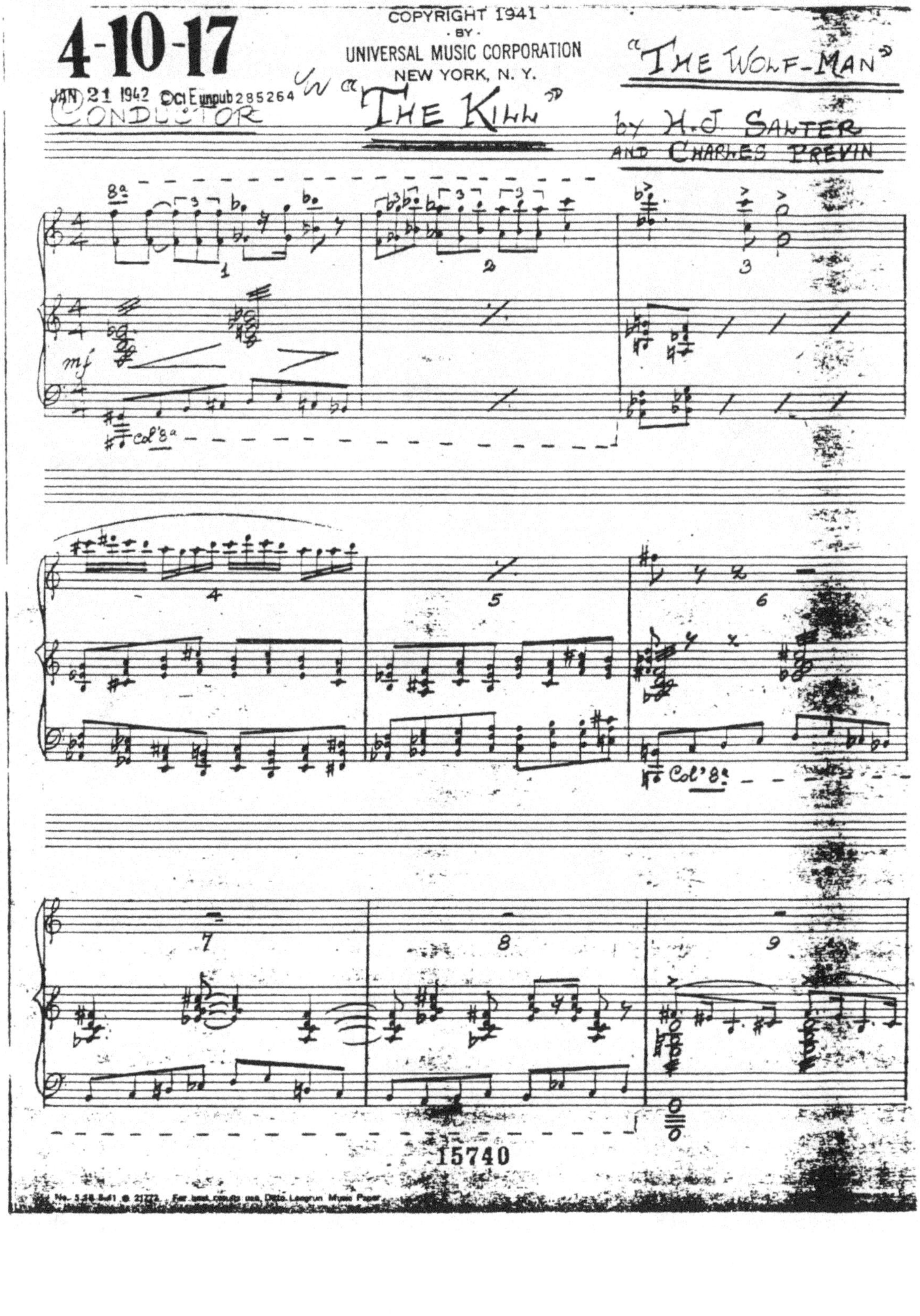

4-10-17
COPYRIGHT 1941
· BY ·
UNIVERSAL MUSIC CORPORATION
NEW YORK, N. Y.
JAN 21 1942 ©Cl Eunpub285264
CONDUCTOR
"THE KILL"
"THE WOLF-MAN"
by H.J. SALTER
AND CHARLES PREVIN
mf
Col'8a
15740

Sir John begins to doubt.

The Wolf stalks Gwen.

Gwen at the Wolf's mercy.

After sighting Gwen, the werewolf slowly turns to pursue his predestined prey. At this point parallel, octaved diminished chords, four lines of sound --race breathlessly upward against the accumulating weight of a triple octave chromatic bass plunge, again pealing forth in a Wolf Man variant. For the final encounter, "The Kill", Sir John slays the beast in the identical manner as Bela was slain, watching incredulously as it is revealed to be his own son. Now the secret cross is Sir John's to bear.

Here at last the fulfillment of destiny is played out, as Maleva emerges from the mist to cast her final benediction upon the becalmed Larry.

"...So do tears run to a predestined end ..."

For the last time we hear the inconsolable violin praying over the tranquil tolling harmonies, as dying into a diminuendo, their two paths depart, one to earth, the other heavenwards, to their respective homes - that of the flesh and that of the spirit.

Above and below, left and right - Sir John attacks the Werewolf

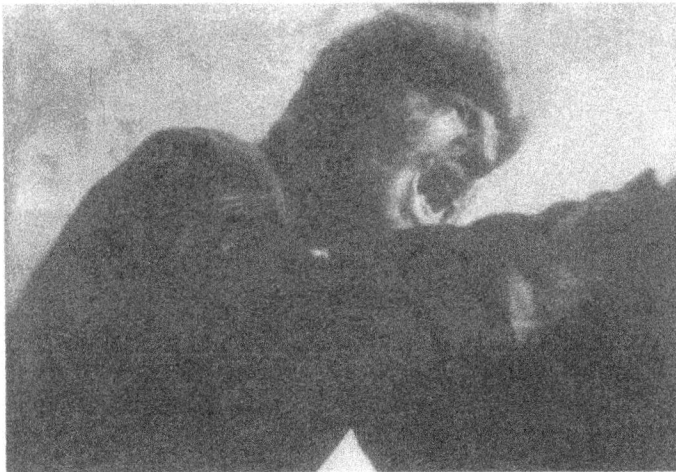

These gone, the mystic elements vanish, and we are returned to the level of simple human grief as the earthly chorale laments the death of a son. In a curious bit of almost abrupt editing, the moment is interrupted by a fade-out and the end title music makes its impassioned summation with an almost regrettable suddenness.

As Salter admits:

I think film music is an art form and so is the horror film, and the wedding between the two is necessary. And the scoring of these films gives composers more opportunity than people may *imagine... to bring these two things into unison is not easy. Sometimes it almost made me cry to see how well the music fit the scene, how much it did for it, how it lifted the scene to a dimension not even the writer or director imagined. I sometimes could hardly believe the effect the music had... Even in some of the horror scores, some of the sequences affected me deeply.*

This is why these wonderful gentlemen, each of whom went on to do excellent work in subsequent years, rose to unimaginable heights. Heights that, a half-century later, appear unmistakably as the finest moments of a life's work.

There would be resurrections and returns and other Wolf Man scores, some four of them by the end of the era, an archive remarkably rich in invention and skill. But never again would there be - even amidst the coming of darkness - quite the purity of innocence, the promise of youth, nor the beckonings toward a benign eternity that rend the heart so openly and so humanly as in the tragic fairy-tale, *The Wolf Man*.

Joseph Marcello is an active concert composer and the founder of Music for Life Studio in Northfield, Massachusetts. He is currently finishing an operatic version of Mary Shelley's Frankenstein, *and has transcribed concert suites of classic film scores such as* The Werewolf of London *and* Dracula's Daughter. *He is also the music director for Sunapee Arts Camp.*

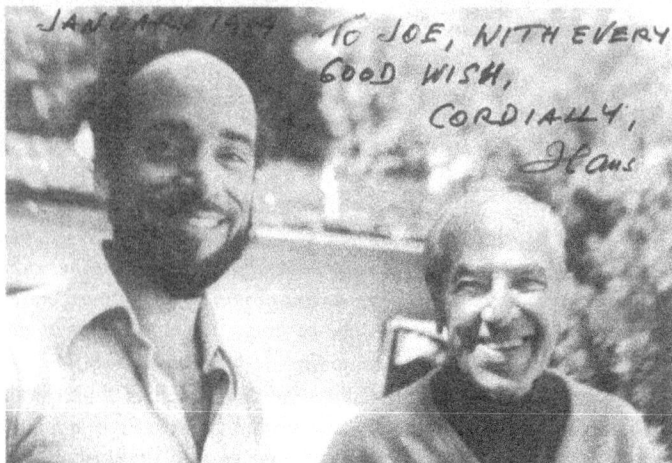

Joe Marcello with Hans Salter

Author Preston Jones with Hans Salter and MagicImage's Ghost of Frankenstein - *Horror Volume 5* for which Mr. Salter wrote the introduction.

LISTEN TO THAT BOX OFFICE HOWL!

He's ready to outscream "Frankenstein" and "Dracula" in that Pre-Christmas date!

Here it is all set for you to sell hard . . . that horror magic that brings you hot profits out of cold shivers!

The WOLF MAN

with

**CLAUDE RAINS
WARREN WILLIAM
RALPH BELLAMY
PATRIC KNOWLES
BELA LUGOSI
MARIA OUSPENSKAYA
EVELYN ANKERS**

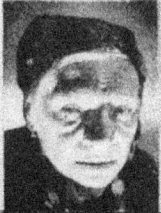

and the new master character creator

LON CHANEY

as "The Wolf Man"

Directed by GEORGE WAGGNER
Associate Producer, GEORGE WAGGNER

LON CHANEY · WARREN WILLIAM · RALPH BELLAMY · CLAUDE RAINS · PATRIC KNOWLES · BELA LUGOSI · EVELYN ANKERS · MARIA OUSPENSKAYA

YOUR UNIVERSAL DATE! READY NOW!

Universal also showered Chaney with publicity, treating him to special billing on the film credits, and hailing him on the posters as ''the new master character creator.'' But the inevitable was bound to happen. On December 4th, the New York Morning Telegraph ran the following:

Chaney Jr. Role Similar To Man of Thousand Faces

HOLLYWOOD, Dec. 3. - Lon Chaney Jr., who for a long time was cast in conventional roles, finally is creating a character to equal any played by his late father, the ''man of a thousand faces.''

Chaney has the title role in Universal's ''The Wolf Man,'' and is transformed by makeup artistry into one of the strangest characters ever seen on screen.

In a picture its makers hope will give audiences the shudders, Chaney will appear as a werewolf- half man, half wolf.

Task of turning Chaney from a respectable citizen into a werewolf fell to Jack Pierce, creator of the Frankenstein monster, ''The Mummy'' and others.

Pierce had considerable difficulty finding out just what a werewolf looked like.

''I combed numerous histories of England without finding a practical description of a werewolf,'' he said.

''About all I learned was that the legend began, and still persists among the people of Wales who live around the ancient castles.

''Sometimes the wind produces sounds like the howling of wolves. Apparently the werewolf legend started with these noises.''

Unable to find a workable description of a werewolf, Pierce designed one of his own. He started with a plaster bust of Chaney, practicing in the application of yak and kelp hair before starting on the actor.

It takes four hours to get the makeup on, and 45 minutes to get it off again. Getting it off doesn't take so long, but sometimes is painful, if the hair sticks too tightly.

A strange nose piece aids the ''wolf'' illusion, and even ears, hands, and feet have to be hairy. The werewolf wears shirt and trousers, so Chaney is spared having the rest of his body made up.

On December 9, 1941 - 10 years and 3 days after the release of Universal's *Frankenstein*, and 2 days after Pearl Harbor - *The Wolf Man* previewed in Hollywood. THE HOLLYWOOD REPORTER noted:

THE WOLF MAN serves its horror straight. A very substantial cast undertakes to sell believably a tale of superstitious folklore...producer-director George Waggner dresses it up with all the craft at the command of a studio practiced in spinning horror yarns... Lon Chaney assumes the really terrifying makeup created by Jack P. Pierce and bears favorable comparison to his esteemed father. And he is pleasantly personable as the untransformed Larry...Evelyn Ankers is a lovely intelligent heroine...Smart is the touch of Gypsy mysticism introduced in the character played by Maria Ouspenskaya... low key photography by Joseph Valentine and the stunning art direction by Jack Otterson and Robert Boyle.

THE HOLLYWOOD REPORTER, however, wouldn't dare guess the box office appeal of a horror film previewed the week America went to War.

In fact, the box office power of *The Wolf Man* would surprise everybody.

NIGHT MONSTER!
Prowling...Killing...Terrifying a countryside!
- Poster copy for *The Wolf Man*

Universal sold *The Wolf Man* with an all-out chiller campaign. ''HIS HIDEOUS HOWL A DIRGE OF DEATH!'' proclaimed one poster, elucidating:

Not a ''Thing'' - but a mortal man - a LIVING horror - with its unearthly body a twitching tomb of strange desires!

Saturday, December 20, 1941. *The Wolf Man* premiered at New York City's Rialto Theater. The New York TIMES panned the movie mercilessly:

Universal which must have a veritable menagerie of mythological monsters, all with an eye on stardom and five -year contracts, is now sponsoring the debut of its latest pride and joy, The Wolf Man, at the Rialto... nobody is going to go on believing in werewolves or Santa Clauses if the custodians of these legends don't tell them with a more convincing imaginative touch... the wolf man is left without a paw to stand on... he looks a lot less terrifying and not nearly as funny as Mr. Disney's Big, Bad Wolf.

Hollywood's tradepaper *Variety* however was more favorable.

Previewed in Studio Projection Room, Dec. 9, '41

The English legendary werewolf provides basis for another cinematic adventure in the horrific chiller-diller realm. ''The Wolf Man'' is a compactly-knit tale of its kind, with good direction and performances by an above par assemblage of players, but dubious entertainment at this particular time. It's a B dual supporter, which must depend on bookings for audience receptivity in each particular booking.

Young Lon Chaney (who drops the Jr. in films for the first time here) returns to the family's English castle after long absence in America to stand in as heir to the estate. According to legend, a person bitten by a werewolf assumes the dual personality of the latter -- and Chaney is the victim of a bite. The psychological effect of Chaney's mental and physical transitions provides the dramatic elements until he is killed by his father.

Young Chaney gives a competent performance both straight and under makeup for the dual role. Strength is added by good cast consisting of Warren William, Ralph Bellamy, Bela Lugosi, Maria Ouspenskaya and Evelyn Ankers. The script stresses the tenseness of the fabled tale in both action and dialog with George Waggner piloting in Okay manner.

"The Harrison's Report," which accepted no advertising and therefore could be as independent and detached as it wanted reported on December 20th:

(Universal, December 12; time, 70 min.)

This horror melodrama, which deals with werewolves and witchcraft, is suitable mostly for theatres catering to audiences that enjoy entertainment of this kind. It is a little too harrowing and somewhat depressing for the general run of picture-goer, for the hero, who becomes infected with the werewolf disease, is a pitiful character for whom one feels sympathy. There are a few scenes that are properly frightening. And the production values are good, particularly the photography, which gives the picture an eerie atmosphere. The romantic interest is unimportant... Not for children.

Yet business was a smash. *The Wolf Man*, with its Gypsy curse and foggy forest and powerhouse Chaney performance, proved just the type of escapism craved by the war-conscious public, and the film became Universal's biggest money-maker of the season. "...the studio received more mail for me during that period than any other star," Lon Chaney proudly remembered. Indeed, before *The Wolf Man* even opened in New York, George Waggner had rushed Chaney into the role of Frankenstein's Monster in his new production *The Ghost of Frankenstein*, directed by Erle C. Kenton and featuring *The Wolf Man* veterans Evelyn Ankers, Ralph Bellamy, Doris Lloyd, Harry Cording and - back as "Old Ygor" - Bela Lugosi.

The Wolf Man became a $1,000,000 hit.

✸

It established George Waggner as one of Universal's major powers; the phenomenal success of this venture into rampant lycanthropy made Waggner the studio's fair-haired boy. In 1942 he produced, but didn't direct, *The Ghost of Frankenstein*, a smoothly made episode in the *Frankenstein à la Universal* saga. A good show in itself, but it and Chaney's monster suffer in comparison to Karloff's towering creation and the three predecessors. He was associate producer to executive producer Frank Lloyd on the handsomely staged but rather absurdly written *Invisible Agent* (1942). Then he produced, but again didn't direct, the immensely popular *Frankenstein Meets the Wolf Man* (1943), a fine vehicle for Chaney's werewolf but a letdown as far as the Frankenstein legend was concerned, and was producer and librettist of his *magnum opus*, *Phantom of the Opera* (1943).

He produced, directed and wrote the operatic libretti for a *Phantom* follow-up (but not a sequel), *The Climax* (1944), which was visually elegant but lacked the hoped-for charm despite the presences of Boris Karloff, Susanna Foster and Gale Sondergaard. He produced and directed a pair of rather good musicals, *Frisco Sal* and *Shady Lady* (1945) and a fairly good spy thriller, *Tangier* (1946) before leaving Universal.

As a free-lance, Waggner directed *Gunfighters* (1947), a good Randolph Scott Western, for Columbia; wrote and directed Republic's *The Fighting Kentuckian* (1949) and Warner Bros.' *Operation Pacific* (1951), both starring John Wayne; co-wrote and directed Republic's *Pawnee* (1957), wrote and directed Allied Artists' *Destination 60,000* (1957), and co-directed with Jacques Tourneur three obscure MGM pictures in 1959: *Frontier Ranger*, *Mission of Danger* and *Fury River*.

In his later years Waggner was active in TV. His most conspicuous success was at Warner Bros., where he wrote and directed more than 50 one-hour episodes of the detective series, *77 Sunset Strip*, and contributed as writer and/or director to some 20 other shows. Incidentally, his billing in the titles of his TV shows was in the unusual style of his signature; george waGGner.

He was 90 when he died on December 11, 1984.

✸

Curt Siodmak became the top fantasy writer of Hollywood's war years. The obvious success of *The Wolf Man* brought about a long term writer's contract. Not to be taken in by success, the next title he turned in was called "The Invisible Man Reclaims His Head", released as *Invisible Agent* (1942). His wonderful imagination sparked *Frankenstein Meets the Wolf Man* (1943), *Son of Dracula* (1943), *The Climax* (1944) and *House of Frankenstein* (1944). He also found time to pen the classic science fiction novel, *Donovan's Brain* (1943). Siodmak co-scripted (with Ardel Wray) Val Lewton's *I Walked with a Zombie* (RKO, 1943); scripted such late 1940s escapism as Warner's *The Beast with Five Fingers* (1946) and RKO's *Tarzan's Magic Fountain* (1949). Eventually he became a director, working on the scripts of all his films, including Realart's *Bride of the Gorilla* (1951), which featured Lon Chaney and ingredients reminiscent of *The Wolf Man* and Universal's *Curucu, Beast of the Amazon* (1956). As of this writing (Spring 1993), the 91 year-old Siodmak appeared as a guest at the FAMOUS MONSTERS 35th Anniversary Convention in Crystal City, Virginia over Memorial Day Weekend, 1993. He is currently enjoying the success of his new novel *Gabriel's Body* - the final part of his *Donovan's Brain* trilogy - published by Dorchester, 1992.

✸

Jack P. Pierce continued as Universal's Director of Makeup until 1947, later free-lancing on films such as Monogram's *Master Minds* (1949) working on the television series *Fireside Theatre*, *You Are There* and *Mr. Ed*. Pierce died July 19, 1968.

✸

John P. Fulton collected four Special Effects Academy nominations for his work at Universal: *The Boys from Syracuse* and *The Invisible Man Returns* (both 1940), *The Invisible Woman* (1941) and *Invisible Agent* (1942). He would take home Oscars for Goldwyn's *Wonder Man* (1945), and for parting the Red Sea in Paramount's Cecil B. DeMille epic *The Ten Commandments* (1956). John P. Fulton died in 1965.

✸

During the next several years Joseph Valentine photographed two memorable Alfred Hitchcock productions, *Saboteur* (1942) and *Shadow of a Doubt* (1943). There were more slick romantic star vehicles as well as two classics of mood and atmosphere, the artistic psychological dramas *Possessed* (1947), with Joan Crawford, and *Sleep My Love* (1948), with Claudette Colbert. The most unusual was *Rope* (1948), Alfred Hitchcock's first Technicolor film. *Rope* was an *almost* successful experiment at telling a story in real time in what was made to seem a single take, the only picture of its kind in history. Valentine became ill before the stressful picture was completed. No less trying was Victor Fleming's spectacular *Joan of Arc*, with Ingrid Bergman. The picture earned Valentine an Academy Award, but his health was deteriorating rapidly.

He was only 45 years old in 1949, when his heart gave out. He had just completed his last picture, RKO Radio's *Bride for Sale* with Claudette Colbert and Robert Young. He was survived by his wife, Katherine, a two-year-old son, Joseph Francis, his parents and a sister.

❀

Claude Rains followed *The Wolf Man* with his wily Police Chief of 1943's *Casablanca*. A shy man, for all his on-screen flamboyance, he escaped Hollywood between films to his Pennsylvania farm, taking the train to the movie capital for films such as Universal's 1943 Technicolor hit *Phantom of the Opera*, with Rains displaying powerful pathos in the title role.

In his lifetime, Rains would collect four Best Supporting Academy nominations (for 1939's *Mr. Smith Goes to Washington*, 1943's *Casablanca*, 1944's *Mr. Skeffington*, and 1946's *Deception*), many theatre prizes (including Broadway's Tony Award for the 1951 play *Darkness at Noon*), and six wives. He is best-remembered for his movie villains, once remarking:

Good men, while slated to inherit the Earth and the Kingdom of Heaven, too, are rarely as captivating to the eye as a polished blackguard. Or to mind, for that matter. People can't help saying, ''My, my. If only the rascal had turned his talents in the proper channels - what a power for good he would have become!'' It's the reforming instinct in mankind, I guess.

Rains' career was non-stop. His last part was as Herod in *The Greatest Story Every Told* - fittingly the ultimate villain for the Christian world as the man who killed all of the children in Bethlehem so that the Messiah's coming could be prevented.

He died on May 30th, 1967 at the age of 77. His tombstone reads:

CLAUDE RAINS
1889-1967
''All things once
are things forever.
Soul, once living,
lives forever.''

❀

The beautiful Evelyn Ankers followed her legendary years of screaming at Universal with such films as 20th Century-Fox's *Black Beauty* (1946), RKO's *Tarzan's Magic Fountain* (1949) and Columbia's *The Texan Meets Calamity Jane* (1950). She did some guests spots on such 1950s TV shows as *Cavalcade of America, Screen Directors Playhouse* and *Cheyenne*, and made her final film appearance in 1960's *No Greater Love*, a Lutheran Church-sponsored featurette. Her favorite role was Mrs. Richard Denning, and she spent her retirement years happily in Hawaii, living (in her words), ''...a life more like we think God intended us to live: quiet, clean, healthy, but most of all peaceful - away from the man-made rat race!'' However, Evelyn is best-remembered today for her perils in melodrama - her screams inspired by *The Ghost of Frankenstein* (1942), *Captive Wild Woman* (1943), *The Mad Ghoul* (1943) and *The Invisible Man's Revenge* (1944).

Evelyn Ankers Denning died of cancer in Hawaii in August of 1985. *The Wolf Man* remains her most famous performance - and gave her the honor of being the first player to recite Siodmak's famous folklore.

❀

Warren William, who played Dr. Lloyd in *The Wolf Man* died in Encino, California on September 24, 1948. A victim of multiple myeloma, he had been able to work in just three films after 1943.

❀

Perhaps best-remembered for his Tony Award-winning performance as Franklin Roosevelt in the Broadway play *Sunrise at Campobello* (a role he reprised in the 1960 film), Ralph Bellamy never lost his affection for his Universal horror movies, *The Wolf Man* and *The Ghost of Frankenstein* (providing the introduction for the MagicImage Filmbook on the latter title).

Bellamy was a founder of the Screen Actors Guild and President of Actors Equity in New York for 12 years. He starred in four tele-series: *Man Against Crime* (1949 - 1953, the first live weekly half-hour dramatic show in network television), *The 11th Hour* (1963-1964), *The Most Deadly Game* (1970-1971) and *The Hunter* (1976), and later added to his horror repertoire by playing the satanic obstetrician of *Rosemary's Baby* (1968). He received an honorary Oscar in 1987 for his screen career, and at the age of 86, enjoyed new success in *Trading Places* as the biggoted commodities broker with Don Ameche; in 1990 he was prominently featured in the box office smash *Pretty Woman*.

Ralph Bellamy was unfailingly kind to movie buffs. Less than a month before his death, Bellamy left his sick bed to give a telephone interview to writer Doug McClelland; when Bellamy became short of breath, he asked McClelland to call him back in a week. Bellamy completed the interview, and died two weeks later - November 29, 1991, at Saint John's Hospital and Health Center in Los Angeles. He was 87 years old.

❀

Patric Knowles would star as the obsessed ''Dr. Mannering'' in *The Wolf Man*'s 1943 sequel, *Frankenstein Meets the Wolf Man*. He remained one of motion picture's most popular character actors and leads in comedies, musicals and drama for the next 4 decades. His impressive appearances, as listed in Katz's Film Encyclopedia, include *Of Human Bondage* (1946), *From Earth to the Moon* and *Auntie Mame* (1958), as Lord Mountbatten in *The Devil's Brigade* (1967), and his last horror film was listed as *Terror in the Wax Museum* in 1970.

Today, one of the Movies' ''Great Survivors,'' Knowles laughs: ''People come up and ask me, 'Didn't you USED to be Patric Knowles?' When I confirm this, they say, 'Never got the girl, did you?''

Indeed, *The Wolf Man* would be one of the films in which Knowles, as gamekeeper of the Talbot estate, DID get the girl. As of this writing, he remains busy in Los Angeles, still wed to his wife of nearly 60 years, and doing volunteer work at the Motion Picture Country House.

❀

Bela Lugosi would play Ygor again in *The Ghost of Frankenstein* (1942), portray the Frankenstein Monster (a role he had scorned in 1931) in *Frankenstein Meets the Wolf Man* (1943); his final visit to Universal was as a magnificent Count Dracula in *Abbott & Costello Meet Frankenstein* (1948). Although financially poor and neglected by Hollywood, Lugosi had the great personal triumph of overcoming a narcotic addiction at the age of

72 and making a brief appearance in a film, *Plan 9 From Outer Space,* which now has a cult following and is affectionately known as one of the *worst* pictures ever made.

He died on August 16, 1956 of a heart attack. Yet the glory of his screen persona waxes today more brilliantly than ever, and many are the horror buffs who pay homage at Holy Cross Cemetery near Hollywood where, in tribute to the character that made him famous, Bela Lugosi was buried in his Dracula cape at the request of his wife and son.

✪

Although Marie Ouspenskaya looked very venerable, she was in truth, only 54 when she made *The Wolf Man* - 5 years younger than her "son" Bela! She would wonderfully reprise Maleva, in Universal's *Frankenstein Meets the Wolf Man* (1943).

Madame Ouspenskaya was devoted to acting; and in 1944, she insisted on going on in the last 5 performances of the Broadway play *Outrageous Fortune* despite lobar pneumonia and a 103-degree temperature; "Would a soldier refuse to go into battle if he sneezed?" she demanded. She would make only a few more films, *Tarzan and the Amazons (1945), I've Always Loved You (1946), Wyoming (1947)* and *A Kiss in the Dark (1949)*. On December 3, 1949, the seemingly indestructible actress at the Motion Picture Country House Hospital.

✪

As for *The Wolf Man* himself: Lon Chaney became Universal's Horror Dynamo of the War Years: playing the Mummy in *The Mummy's Tomb* (1942), *The Mummy's Ghost* (1944) and *The Mummy's Curse* (1945); proving a subtle, all-powerful vampire in *Son of Dracula* (1943); headlining a series of *Inner Sanctum* mysteries. However, his most memorable work always was as the Wolf Man. In *Frankenstein Meets the Wolf Man* (1943), Lon's Larry Talbot returned, freed from the Talbot crypt by grave-robbers who happen to plunder the mausoleum on the night of a full moon. He meets Patric Knowles' Dr. Mannering; once again seeks the help of Maria Ouspenskaya's Maleva; beseeches Ilona Massey's Baroness Frankenstein for aid; meets Lionel Atwill's Mayor of Vasaria and - of course - battles the Frankenstein Monster, played by Bela Lugosi. *House of Frankenstein* (1944) saw Karloff's Mad Doctor and his assistant, J. Carrol Naish's homicidal hunchback, pirating George Zucco's traveling Chamber of Horrors. They resurrect John Carradine's Count Dracula (who is chased into a fatal dawn by Inspector Lionel Atwill and his mounted gendarmes), then head for the Frankenstein ruins - where they thaw Chaney's Talbot and the Monster (now played by Glenn Strange) from the icy caves. In this "Monster Rally", Chaney's Wolf Man perished by a silver bullet fired by Elena Verdugo's Gypsy girl - who "loves him enough to understand." A happier fate awaited him in *House of*

Dracula (1945) - Chaney's Wolf Man, Carradine's Dracula and Strange's Monster all arrived at the seaside castle of Dr. Franz Edelmann (Onslow Stevens), seeking a cure. Dracula and the Monster perished, as did Stevens' Jekyll & Hyde mad doctor, his hunchbacked nurse (Jane Adams), and even Lionel Atwill's police inspector; but Chaney survived a brain operation to escape his Lycanthropy and exit the fiery climax clasping leading lady Martha O'Driscoll.

Chaney's Larry Talbot came back (just for fun) in Universal International's 1948 *Abbott and Costello Meet Frankenstein*, joining Lugosi's Dracula and Strange's Monster in this wonderful horror/comedy. Chaney also played a Wolf Man in the 1959 Mexican film *La Casa del Terror*, and - on October 26, 1962 - played on the famous *Route 66* episode "Lizard's Leg and Owlet's Wing", along with Karloff as the Monster and Peter Lorre in cape and top hat. On this show, Chaney masqueraded not only as the Wolf Man, but also as the Mummy and Quasimodo. Pierce assistant Abe Haberman recreated the famous group of monsters.

The Wolf Man became part of Universal's wondrous Monster Mythology. He was the only monster to find a cure; the only monster character consistently played by the same actor.

"He was my Baby!" proudly remembered Lon Chaney.

Lon Chaney Jr.'s own path was "thorny". In 1948, just after completing *Abbott and Costello Meet Frankenstein*, there was a suicide attempt; alcohol remained a lifelong problem. Yet he was always a professional, accumulating scores of film and TV credits and forever taking pride in his milestone portrayal of The Wolf Man. Indeed, Chaney's "baby" even ultimately provided him a mask for his illness. In October of 1969, Chaney appeared on *Tonight*, with Johnny Carson. The actor's voice was disturbingly hoarse - for he had the same disease that killed his father, throat cancer. Yet Chaney would invite no pity. He claimed that, during Halloween of 1968, so many Trick-or-Treaters came to his house, begging to hear "The Wolf Man" growl, that he had been hoarse ever since.

Lon Chaney Jr. died of a heart attack in San Clemente, California July 12, 1973, at the age of 67.

THE WOLF MAN

STUDIO: Universal
ASSOCIATE PRODUCER/DIRECTOR: George Waggner
SCREENPLAY: Curt Siodmak
CINEMATOGRAPHER: Joseph Valentine
ART DIRECTOR: Jack Otterson (Associate, Robert Boyle)
FILM EDITOR: Ted Kent
MUSICAL DIRECTOR: Charles Previn
MUSICAL SCORE: Charles Previn, Frank Skinner
                & Hans J. Salter
ASSISTANT DIRECTOR: Vernon Keays
MAKEUP ARTIST: Jack P. Pierce
SOUND DIRECTOR: Bernard B. Brown
                (Technician, Joe Lapis)
GOWNS: Vera West
SET DECORATIONS: R.A. Gausman
SPECIAL EFFECTS: John P. Fulton
RUNNING TIME: 71 Minutes

Filmed at Universal City, California, 27 October - 25 November, 1941. Opened at the Rialto Theatre, New York City, December 20, 1941.

THE PLAYERS

Sir John Talbot	Claude Rains
Dr. Lloyd	Warren William
Col. Paul Montford	Ralph Bellamy
Frank Andrews	Patric Knowles
Bela the Gypsy	Bela Lugosi
Maleva	Maria Ouspenskaya
Gwen Conliffe	Evelyn Ankers
Larry Talbot, the Wolf Man	Lon Chaney
Jenny Williams	Fay Helm
Kendall	Leyland Hodgson
Charles Conliffe	J. M. Kerrigan
Gypsy with Bear	Kurt Katch*
Mrs. Williams	Doris Lloyd
Villager	Olaf Hytten
Rev. Norman	Harry Stubbs
Richardson, the Grave Digger	Tom Stevenson
Chauffeur	Eric Wilton
Wykes	Harry Cording
Phillips	Erie Stanton
Mrs. Bally	Ottola Nesmith
Mrs. Wykes	Connie Leon
Gypsy Dancer	La Riana
First Woman	Caroline Cook
Second Woman	Margaret Fealy
Gypsy Woman	Jessie Arnold
Churchgoer	Eddie Polo
Villager	Gibson Gowland

* Footage Deleted.

Behind the Scenes

Claude Rains

Evelyn Ankers

Bela Lugosi

Ralph Bellamy

Patric Knowles

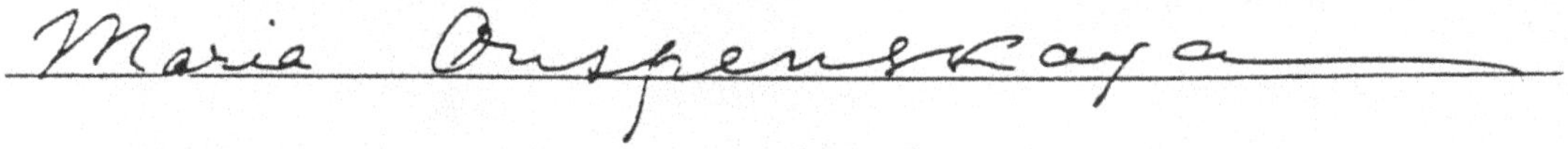

Maria Ouspenskaya

Lon Chaney

Curt Siodmak

Hans Salter

Jack Pierce

Frank Skinner

Robert Boyle

Clifford Work - Head of Production - 1941

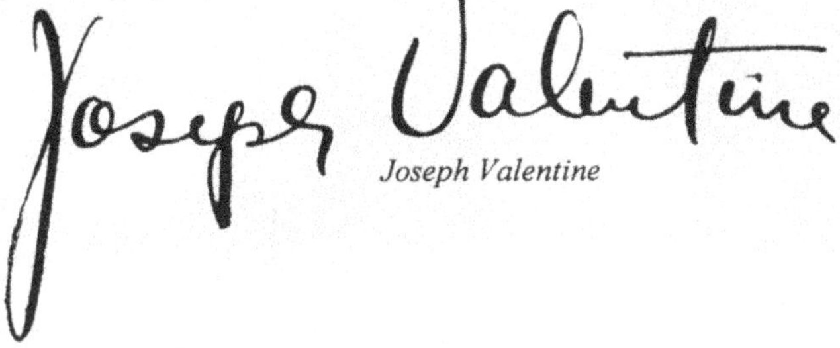

Nat Blumberg - President Universal

Joseph Valentine

Lon Chaney and Bela Lugosi pose for publicity shots -
The Wolf Man *cane was still in the Prop Department as of 1991.*

Evelyn Ankers has her palm read by Maria Ouspenskaya.

Kadja, a well known Hollywood psychic palmist in real life tells Evelyn Ankers her future.
(Kadja was often seen at parties given by Basil Rathbone, Mary Pickford and Goldwyn Executive Abraham Lehr.)

Two real gypsies, who also appeared in the film with Miss Ankers.

Surviving cast and crew members who were on the set, admit that there was some tension between Chaney and Ankers - however everyone was a professional during the publicity shots.

Madame Ouspenskaya - Maleva adds wolfbane to the pot.

Patric Knowles finally got the girl - in real life both were happily married to their respective spouses - Mr. Knowles is to this day.

Portrait of Larry's older brother - obviously Chaney - This painting is stored in the prop department at Universal.

Larry arrives at Talbot Castle.

Miniature of Talbot Castle - seen only for a few seconds in the opening

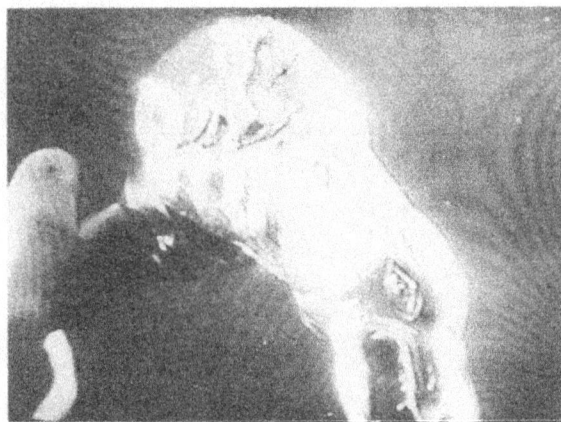

The Wolf Man's cane - Of 4 made for the film only one remains at the Universal Prop Department.

Publicity poses of the Wolf Man's attack

1195-89AB

The Original Screenplay by Curt Siodmak

T H E   W O L F   M A N

ORIGINAL SCREENPLAY

By

KURT SIODMAK

*
***
*****
***
*

October 9, 1941

1195-8AB

"WOLF MAN"

1   The screen is dark. The low frightful HOWL OF A WOLF IS HEARD, increasing in strength, then suddenly stopping.

Now the dark screen is slit by white moonlight, which falls through a window, visible as a hand opens a curtain. The pale light of the moon shines upon a row of big volumes - THE ENCYCLOPEDIA BRITTANICA - and the hand chooses a volume.

While the CAMERA MOVES INTO A CLOSE-UP, the hand opens the book, and the heading "WOLF MAN" fills the screen.

The CAMERA PULLS BACK a few inches so that a part of the page becomes legible, and we read:

      WOLF MAN or WEREWOLF, a man transformed
      temporarily or permanently into a wolf.

A Welsh song, "MEN OF HARLECH" IS HEARD, faintly at first, then increasing, a score of male voices coming closer, while the hand whirls the pages of the book, and under the heading

CAST

we read the names:

      LARRY GILL...............LON CHANEY

      GWEN CONLIFFE............

etc., etc.

The hand moves the pages again, giving the other credits under the different headings, as if they were to be found in the ENCYCLOPEDIA.

The song, which accompanies the credit titles, mingles with the far-away SOUND OF A CAR, and the WHINE OF THE WIND. The whine becomes louder now, the motor of the car more distant.

CONTINUED

1   CONTINUED

The hand indicates the column of print under the heading

WOLF MAN
Werewolves were often found
in Wales...
                    (in italics)

THE CAMERA APPROACHES the word WALES, until it fills
the page completely. THE LENS BURSTS THROUGH the
page. The SONG FADES OUT.

2   EXT. - COUNTRY-SIDE - LONG SHOT - DAY

We are in Wales. Through the landscape which unfolds
before our eyes, a Rolls Royce is driving fast. It
is a modern chauffeur-driven car. The car races along
a narrow winding highway, through a dense forest which
covers the mountain side.

                              DISSOLVE TO:

3   EXT. - COUNTRY - LONG

The car passes towering hills, shrouded in low-lying
clouds. THE WIND WHISTLES AND WHINES.

                              DISSOLVE TO:

4   EXT. - COUNTRY - LONG

The car drives through a moor - a wide dark plain,
bare of foliage.

5   EXT. - CAMERA ON CAR HOOD - MED. CLOSE - (PROCESS)

The uniformed chauffeur, a middle-aged man, turns and
points to the right. Behind him, his 6' 3" frame
leisurely stretched out, his eyes watching the landscape with interest, sits LARRY GILL, a man of about
thirty. To make himself heard above the WHINE OF THE
WIND, the chauffeur shouts:

                              CONTINUED

3   CONTINUED

CHAUFFEUR
Talbot Castle!

Larry at once bends forward and looks in the direction
indicated.

6   EXT. - MOOR - THROUGH WINDOW OF MOVING CAR -(PROCESS)

Out of the moor, which has an unreal quality, through
waves of rolling mist, a massive edifice of grey stone
looms up, with turrets and terraces and sinister
bastions, - a castle whose outer walls were built
during the 14th century.

DISSOLVE TO:

7   EXT. - TALBOT CASTLE - LONG SHOT - DAY

The car sweeps up the driveway and stops in front of
the stone balustrade. A footman is waiting there.

8   EXT. - TALBOT CASTLE - MED. CLOSE

The car comes to a stop. The footman approaches the
Rolls and opens the door. Larry steps out.

CUT TO:

9   EXT. - THE WIDE OPEN DOOR OF TALBOT CASTLE - MED. CLOSE

It is an oaken door, dark with age, and opens into a
big hall. In the doorway waits a distinguished-looking
man of about 55 - SIR JOHN TALBOT. As Larry enters
the picture, Sir John smiles and greets him with outstretched hand. He speaks with the pronounced clipped
accent of the English gentry:

SIR JOHN TALBOT
Welcome to Wales, Mr. Gill!
I'm John Talbot.

Larry takes Sir John's hand and shakes it vigorously.

CONTINUED

                         LARRY
              Glad to meet you, Sir John.

They step inside.

10   INT. - CASTLE - PAN SHOT FROM LARRY'S ANGLE - <u>DAY</u>

A big fire is burning in the fireplace, throwing
lambent shadows on the stone walls, covered by large
Gobelins. A broad carved staircase leads to the upper
floors. The room is furnished with massive antiques
in 17th century style.

                         LARRY'S VOICE
                         (with awed
                          admiration)
              It's out of this world!

11   INT. - CASTLE - MED. CLOSE - LARRY AND SIR JOHN

Sir John looks at Larry with some amusement, intrigued
by the American's enthusiasm.

                         SIR JOHN
                         (amused)
              On the edge of it, perhaps -
              but within telescopic distance!

                         LARRY
              Oh - has the telescope arrived
              already?

They walk on, THE CAMERA TRAVELING in front of them.

                         SIR JOHN
                         (nodding)
              I was afraid to unpack it
              without you.

He rubs his hands in eager expectation.

                         SIR JOHN
                         (continuing)
              D'you think it's weathered
              the crossing?

11   CONTINUED

                         LARRY
              Better than I have...
              A telescope is made of steel -
                         (grins
                          sheepishly)
              -- my stomach's only cast-iron...

                                        DISSOLVE TO:

12   INT. - A MODERN OBSERVATORY - FULL SHOT - <u>DAY</u>

     Larry and Sir John enter the latter's observatory,
     which is equipped with the latest instruments, but
     without a telescope. A cupola which can be opened
     mechanically, forms the ceiling. Charts of the sky
     cover the walls.

     Broad daylight streams through the wide windows, which
     look down over the countryside.

     A huge wooden crate, clasped with iron bands, stands
     in the middle of the room.

13   INT. - OBSERVATORY - MED. CLOSE - LARRY AND SIR JOHN

     Larry looks around approvingly.

                         LARRY
              They told me you were an
              amateur astronomer!

                         SIR JOHN
                         (lightly)
              Where the heavens are concerned,
              God alone is a professional!

     Larry smiles appreciatively. He looks at:

14   INT. - OBSERVATORY - THE CRATE - CLOSE

     On the crate is the caption:

                    STAR OPTICAL COMPANY

                      NEW YORK, N.Y.

                         U. S. A.

         GLASS!   FRAGILE!   HANDLE WITH CARE!

15   INT. - OBSERVATORY - LARRY AND SIR JOHN - MED. CLOSE

                          SIR JOHN
                          (eagerly)
                  I feel like a child before
                  Christmas -- let's open it!

        As Larry and Sir John begin to open the crate,

                                                DISSOLVE TO:

16   INT. - OBSERVATORY - DAY - MED. LONG SHOT - LARRY

        The telescope has been unpacked, the crate removed
        from the observatory. The cupola is closed. Larry
        stands on the platform where the telescope has been
        placed. He adjusts a lens. He then presses a switch.
        The cupola opens.

17   INT. - OBSERVATORY - MED. LONG SHOT FROM LARRY'S ANGLE

        The cupola opens, showing the sky.

18   INT. - OBSERVATORY - MED. CLOSE - ANOTHER ANGLE

        Larry presses another switch, the clock-work of the
        refractor moves and the huge instrument lowers its eye.
        Larry steps to the telescope sight and looks through
        the glass.

19   INT. - OBSERVATORY - TELESCOPE - CLOSE SHOT

        Larry looks through the glass, adjusting the focus.

20   EXT. - LANDSCAPE - AS SEEN THROUGH THE TELESCOPE BY
        LARRY

        The picture is misty at first, but quickly clears up
        as Larry adjusts the focus. The landscape becomes
        visible, the marshes, hills, forests.
        (The motor, WHICH HUMS DEEPLY, moves the platform on
        which the telescope is standing.)

                                                CONTINUED

A few rabbits are seen to run through the marsh; in
the forest a deer can be observed, looking toward the
castle, unaware of being watched...

The lens glides over the plain - and a small town comes
within our vision, enclosed behind 14th century walls,
following the line of its ancient Roman foundation.
We see the small streets and dark arcades, behind which
diminutive shops are hidden. Narrow-chested houses
with pointed gables bend their gargoyles (tin dragons)
toward the little streets. The house entrances are low,
the windows tiny, as if dwarfs had built the shadowy town.

The telescope lowers its eye a fraction... and we see
women with baskets walking along the streets, and men in
caps and loose coats. A dog is barking playfully at a
child - but NO SOUND can be heard, as the town is two
miles away.

The refractor's eye moves up, glides along the house
walls... It passes an open window, and for the fraction
of a second, the picture of a girl can be seen. At once
the HUM of the motor stops, the refractor stops, and then
the motor STARTS again, moving the eye of the telescope
back to the window, where we saw the girl (GWEN CONLIFFE).
The HUM OF THE MOTOR CEASES and the telescope comes to a
rest.

A bedroom is clearly visible. The pretty girl, in a
dressing gown, is speaking, with little gestures, to an
elderly man (CHARLES CONLIFFE). The man smiles, pats
her cheeks, and leaves the room. The girl steps over to
the mirror which hangs above a chest of drawers. She
opens a drawer, takes out a small leather case, and opens
it. Picking out a pair of ear rings - golden half-moons
- she clips one on her ear lobe and appraises herself
critically in the glass. Seeming to be dissatisfied with
her appearance, she picks up another pair - pearl buttons
this time - and now she is content. She starts to move
away - but bumps her knee against a small stool standing
near the dresser. Annoyed, she pushes the stool out of
the way, then begins to unbutton her gown...

(Into the silence comes the SOUND OF A DOOR OPENING in
the observatory, and STEPS COMING CLOSER.)

21   INT. - OBSERVATORY - MED. CLOSE - LARRY AND SIR JOHN

Larry is looking through the glass. Sir John approaches him and puts his hand on Larry's shoulder. Startled,
Larry wheels around. Seeing Sir John, he forces a smile.

                    SIR JOHN
          Beautiful thing, isn't she?

He pats the telescope admiringly.

                    LARRY
               (smiling -
                thinking of the
                girl he's just seen)
          Swell!

Sir John steps closer.

                    SIR JOHN
               (very eagerly)
          May I? May I see - ?

But Larry at once presses the button and the telescope
moves.

                    LARRY
          Not yet... I have to stabilize
          the worm-gear wheel first. It's
          still out of balance.

                    SIR JOHN
          Oh - right you are... But you'll
          have it in working order by tonight?

                    LARRY
          I'll try, sir...

Sir John nods happily and leaves. Larry follows him
with his eyes, until he has closed the door. Then
Larry immediately returns to the telescope and looks
through the glass again, moving the telescope back into
its former position.

22   EXT. - GWEN'S HOUSE - AS SEEN BY LARRY THROUGH THE
      TELESCOPE

The telescope (O.S.) moves along the houses again and
stops at the window, as before. But the window is
closed now - the pretty girl can no longer be seen...
The HUM OF THE TELESCOPE IS HEARD as the telescope's
eye slides down the house wall, and stops.

                                        CONTINUED

22   CONTINUED

A small antique shop can be seen, with a sign on the
window:

CHARLES CONLIFFE

ANTIQUES BOUGHT AND SOLD

DISSOLVE TO:

23   EXT. - STREET IN TOWN - DAY - MED. CLOSE - LARRY

Larry, dressed in a blue suit, stands in the street,
looks at the shop and reads the sign. CAMERA MOVES with
him as he steps closer and stops in front of the shop.

24   EXT. - STREET - OUTSIDE SHOP - MED. CLOSE - LARRY'S ANGLE

We see Larry's reflection in the glass window of the
shop, as he looks in at old English furniture, silver
salvers, and miscellaneous trinkets. The display is
neat and well arranged. Larry peers through the window
to catch a glimpse of the girl inside.

25   EXT. - SHOP - THROUGH WINDOW TO INTERIOR

The girl, Gwen Conliffe, whom Larry saw through the
telescope, is alone in the shop, busily polishing a
silver vase. She is wearing the pearl button ear rings,
as we saw her before, but now has on a day dress.

26   EXT. - STREET OUTSIDE SHOP - MED. CLOSE - LARRY

He turns and enters the store. THE BELL ABOVE THE DOOR
CHIMES.

27   INT.-CONLIFFE'S ANTIQUE SHOP - MED. CLOSE - LARRY AND GWEN

The girl looks up, a polite smile on her face, as Larry
comes into the picture.

                    GWEN
          Good afternoon, sir.

CONTINUED

                    LARRY
               (smiling shyly -
                but he has his
                campaign all mapped out!)
          Hello!

He looks around as if he were a serious connoisseur
of antiques.

                    GWEN
          May I help you? Perhaps
          there's something special
          you're looking for?

                    LARRY
          H'mm... well, yes. I'd like
          to buy a present... some ear rings -

The girl at once opens a glass case and, taking out a
velvet tray of ear rings, puts it on top of the showcase.

28   INT. SHOP - CLOSER - TWO SHOT

Larry bends over the various ear rings, then shakes his
head.

                    LARRY
          Mmm... no... the kind I want
          are sort of half-moons...golden -

                    GWEN
          I'm sorry... We haven't any
          like that - just now.

                    LARRY
               (poker-faced)
          You'll find them in your room
          upstairs. In the left-hand
          drawer of your dressing-table.
          In the little leather case,
          you know...

                    GWEN
               (astonished)
          In... my room?!!

                                        CONTINUED

                              LARRY
                          (airily)
               Yes...

                          (suddenly
                            solicitous)
               But be careful not to bump your
               shin on the stool again... I'd
               hate to have you hurt yourself.

The girl stares at him, amazed, wondering how he knows
all this, trying to remember if she's ever seen him
before. But she can't make out how he got all this
intimate information about her:

                              LARRY
                          (maddeningly
                            nonchalant)
               Would you mind getting 'em
               for me?

                              GWEN
                          (at a loss)
               Why... they... they're not
               for sale...

She continues to look at him wonderingly. Larry shakes
his head and sighs.

                              LARRY
               I don't blame you. They
               look so pretty on you...
                          (looking
                            around)
               Well, if I can't get the
               ear rings...

CAMERA PANS: the store, filled with furniture, wooden
medieval statues, silver plates, etc. In a corner
stands a huge vase filled with an assortment of walking-
sticks.

29   INT. SHOP - CAMERA BEHIND THE VASE FULL OF STICKS

       Larry walks toward it and, picking out a stick, says:

                                                  CONTINUED

                              LARRY
                    ... then I'll buy a cane...

He chooses one, a heavy ebony walking-stick with a
pointed silver handle and a round knob.

                              LARRY (cont'd.)
                    The guys back home'd get a
                    kick out of me wearing a cane. -
                    How much?

He takes a swaggering step or two, flourishing the
cane, smiling with amusement, pretending he has forgotten all about the girl. But she is burning up with
curiosity!

                              GWEN
                    Tell me, please! How did
                    you know about the ear rings
                    ... and my room?

                              LARRY
                           (playing with
                            the stick)
                    Oh... I'm psychic. When I
                    see a pretty girl, I know
                    everything about her -
                           (snaps his
                            fingers)
                    - just like that!

30   INT. SHOP - CLOSE - TWO SHOT

          Their eyes meet and hold for a moment - Larry unable
          to take his gaze off her - she is so pretty - and Gwen,
          in spite of herself, strongly attracted to this surpris-
          ing stranger. Then, embarrassed, they both look away
          and Larry quickly turns his scrutiny on the cane in his
          hands.

31   INT. SHOP - THE STICK IN LARRY'S HANDS - CLOSE

                              LARRY'S VOICE
                    That's a funny-looking handle
                    - a wolf - and a star...
                    What's it mean?

          The knob on the stick shows a five-pointed star - a
          pentagram - enclosing a jumping wolf.

INT. SHOP - MED. CLOSE - LARRY AND GWEN

The girl has regained her composure and smiles pertly:

                    GWEN
          I thought you said you
          were psychic....

Larry smiles back, then shakes his head, weighing the
stick in his hand:

                    LARRY
          But this is only wood...
                    (He inspects the
                    head closely)
          - and it doesn't have blue eyes!

Gwen is flustered, but, putting on a very business-
like air, she says:

                    GWEN
          The stick is priced at three
          pounds.

Larry whistles, surprised.

                    LARRY
          Fifteen bucks for an old cane?

                    GWEN
          It's a rare piece... early 18th
          century... and it shows the wolf
          and the pentagram... the sign of
          the werewolf...

She points to the knob, bending her head over it, the
fragrance of her hair very close to him. Larry looks
at her, fascinated, then jerks his thoughts back to
the conversation.

                    LARRY
          The werewolf? What's that?
          Some kind of coyote?

                    GWEN
                    (smiling)
          A werewolf is a human being
          who changes at a certain time
          of the year into a wolf!

                              CONTINUED

                    LARRY
                 (admiringly)
          'What big eyes you have,
           grandma!'

Gwen disregards the jesting compliment and goes on,
serious.

                    GWEN
          'Little Red-Riding-Hood' was
          a werewolf story... There have
          been many others - in many lands
          - but especially in Wales.

                    LARRY
                 (smiling
                  indulgently)
          You people are pretty
          superstitious, aren't you?

                    GWEN
                 (in earnest)
          I'm not so sure it's superstition.
          ... There's an old poem...
                 (reciting)
          'Even a man who is pure in heart
          And says his prayers by night,
          May become a wolf when the wolfbane blooms,
          And the autumn moon is bright'....

                    LARRY
                 (laughing
                  it off)
          Brr - take it easy - you'll scare
          your customer out of the store!

He starts to take some money out of his pocket. Gwen
realizes he will be going soon... she may never see
him again. She must know the answer to the mystery of
the ear rings!

                    GWEN
          Please tell me... have you
          ever seen me before?

                    LARRY
          Of course! How else could
          I know about the ear rings?
                 (then -
                  business-like)
          I'll take the cane.

                                        CONTINUED

32   CONTINUED - 2

Larry puts down three one-pound notes.

                    GWEN
                 (nonplussed)
        But I can't remember...

                    LARRY
                 (pressing his
                  advantage)
        Look - I'm a stranger here.
        Let's take a walk tonight -
        show me a little of the town
        - and maybe I'll tell you!

                    GWEN
                 (suddenly
                  distant)
            No!

Larry feels the sudden barrier between them and doesn't
understand it - but decides to ignore it. He picks up
his stick and starts to leave.

33   INT. SHOP - NEAR STREET DOOR - MED. CLOSE

Larry approaches the door, the girl following him closely.

                    LARRY
                 (serenely)
        I'll see you at eight...

                    GWEN
                 (opening the
                  door for him)
            No!

(THE BELL CHIMES over the door as she opens it.)

OVER COMES THE SOUND OF OTHER BELLS ringing in the street
- and the NOISE OF AN APPROACHING CART CAN BE HEARD.
Larry and Gwen look out toward the street.

34   EXT. - THE STREET - DAY - FROM LARRY AND GWEN'S ANGLE -
      LONG SHOT

Down the street walks a gypsy, pushing a wheel-cart,
decorated with bells, and laden with colorful rugs.
He is followed by a few curious children.

                                        CONTINUED

34   CONTINUED

As he comes close, the gypsy (BELA) shows his big white teeth in a smile at Gwen and Larry, then THE CAMERA PANS, following him as he walks out of scene.

35   INT. SHOP - DOORWAY - MED. CLOSE - LARRY AND GWEN

                    LARRY
         I didn't know you had gypsies
         over here...

                    GWEN
         They pass through our town
         every autumn... They're fortune-
         tellers -

                    LARRY
               (wistfully)
         I haven't had my fortune told
         in years. Let's go tonight!

                    GWEN
               (wanting to, but
               knowing she mustn't)
               firmly)
     No!

                    LARRY
               (smiling into
               her eyes)
     Okay... at eight!

He walks out, swinging his cane. CAMERA PANS, following him for a moment.

36   EXT. STREET - NEAR SHOP DOOR - MED. CLOSE ON GWEN

She looks after him, bewildered, then shakes her pretty head, and closes the door. (THE DOOR BELL CHIMES.)

37   EXT. STREET - CAMERA TRUCKING IN FRONT OF LARRY

Larry walks along, whistling and flourishing his cane. He looks down at it, amused, as we

                           DISSOLVE TO:

38   INT. OBSERVATORY - ~~DAY~~ NIGHT - CLOSE - ON THE KNOB OF THE
      WALKING-STICK

      showing the wolf jumping through the pentagram.

                              SIR JOHN'S VOICE
                    Yes... That's the sign of the
                    werewolf...

      CAMERA PULLS BACK INTO:

39   INT. - OBSERVATORY - MED. FULL SHOT - LARRY AND SIR JOHN

      Larry is working at the counterweight of the telescope,
      adjusting it carefully. Sir John is sitting in a chair
      nearby, holding the cane Larry bought.

                              LARRY
                         (as he works)
                    You know, my people were Welsh.
                    They left here in 1822... My
                    grandmother used to tell me a
                    lot of wild stories about Wales
                    ... but I don't remember any
                    werewolves...

      He presses the switch which opens the cupola. It is
      DARK outside and a full moon hangs in the sky.

40   INT. - OBSERVATORY - CLOSER - TELESCOPE

      showing the cupola, the evening sky, and the full moon.

41   INT. - OBSERVATORY - MED. CLOSE - LARRY AND SIR JOHN

                              SIR JOHN
                         (reciting)
                    'Even a man who is pure in heart
                    And says his prayers by night,
                    May become a wolf when the wolfbane blooms,
                    And the autumn moon is bright...'

      Larry stops working and looks at Sir John.

                              LARRY
                    That's funny... The girl in the
                    antique shop said the same thing!

                                              CONTINUED

                              SIR JOHN
                            (rising)
                    Fast workers, you Americans!
                    Only here a few days and met
                    the nicest girl in town -
                    hot off the wicket - as you
                    Americans would say!

Larry bends over the telescope, to hide his embarrass-
ment. He says, very matter-of-fact:

                              LARRY
                    You can use the telescope
                    tonight, if you want to,
                    Sir John...

                              SIR JOHN
                            (moving toward
                             the door)
                    Very well, my boy. I recognize
                    the language of diplomacy.
                    You're excused for the evening!

He smiles and leaves.

Larry, pleased, at once lowers the telescope. THE
MOTOR HUMS.

42   INT. - OBSERVATORY - CLOSE - ON TELESCOPE

The telescope lowers its eye until it looks straight
into CAMERA.

43   EXT. - TOWN - NIGHT - MOVING SHOT - AS SEEN THROUGH
         THE TELESCOPE

THE CAMERA WANDERS along dark house walls, and stops
at a lighted window (Gwen's). (THE MOTOR HUM OF THE
TELESCOPE CEASES).

There, in her room, Gwen is talking to another girl
(JENNY WILLIAMS), who sits in the corner near the door
on the little stool. Jenny, a bony spinster of about
35, is hanging on Gwen's every word, as the girl
obviously talks about Larry. Standing on her toes,
Gwen indicates his height, pantomines his manner, re-
lates what happened between them in the shop today.
(Of course, we can only see, not hear, this conversation.)

                                        CONTINUED

43   CONTINUED

Gwen, still talking about Larry, picks up a pair of
ear rings from her drawer, points to them, then fixes
them over her ear lobes. Suddenly she looks at her
watch. Jenny, wagging her head in astonishment, watches
Gwen, then asks her a question. Gwen shakes her head
emphatically (she certainly will not keep a tryst with
this stranger!) and walks to the window...

The picture enlarges as GWEN IS SEEN IN CLOSE-UP. On
her ears are the ear rings Larry admired: the golden
half-moons. Gwen closes the curtains - and the picture
becomes dark.

44   INT. - OBSERVATORY - NIGHT - CLOSE ON LARRY

He takes his eye from the telescope sight, smiling in
happy triumph.

                                       DISSOLVE TO:

45   EXT. STREET - IN FRONT OF CONLIFFE'S SHOP - NIGHT +
       MED. CLOSE

A roll curtain is let down inside the shop window. The
wrought iron gas-lamp in front of the shop sheds its
yellow light in a circle on the pavement. THE CHURCH
BELL not far away TOLLS - EIGHT TIMES.

At the fourth stroke of the bell, the door of the shop
opens carefully (SLIGHT CHIME OF THE DOOR BELL) - and
Gwen looks out.

CAMERA SWINGS a yard to the left, still keeping Gwen in
the picture. There, at the left side of the door, waits
Larry.

                         GWEN
                    (surprised, but
                     not displeased)
              Oh... you!

                         LARRY
              Sure - who did you expect?

                         GWEN
                    (embarrassed)
              Why - nobody...

                                       CONTINUED

                              LARRY
                    Well, everything's under control!
                    Let's go...

He offers her his arm, but Gwen steps back.

                              GWEN
                    I told you I couldn't go out
                    with you!

CAMERA PULLS CLOSER INTO:

46   EXT. - CONLIFFE'S SHOP - <u>NIGHT</u> - CLOSE TWO SHOT

                              LARRY
                    Now don't give me that!
                    After putting on the ear
                    rings I like - and telling
                    your girl-friend all about me!

Gwen is speechless with surprise. She opens her mouth
to ask "How....?!" - but he goes on quickly:

                              LARRY (cont'ing)
                    You even made fun of my size...

                              GWEN
                         (giving her-
                          self away)
                    I did not. I spoke very nicely
                    about you... better than you
                    deserve -

Then she realizes she's admitted her interest in him.
Flustered, she hesitates. He quickly takes advantage:

                              LARRY
                         (persuasively)
                    Come on, Gwen... I don't
                    want to go alone. I'm
                    afraid of the dark!

Gwen can't help laughing, utterly defeated, and
intrigued by this strong big American, with his funny
way of talking and his strange knowledge of herself!

                                        CONTINUED

                              GWEN
            So am I!
                          (she turns
                           and calls)
            Jenny!

Jenny appears behind her, smiling. Larry gulps and
swallows his disappointment. So there's to be a girl-
friend taken along as chaperone! Gwen has a twinkle
in her eye as she sees his discomfiture.

                              GWEN
                          (mockingly)
            This is Jenny Williams...
            She's been dying to have
            her fortune told, too!

                              JENNY
            Very pleased to meet you.

                              LARRY
                          (with an effort)
            Me too - Lawrence Gill's the
            name - just call me Larry.

                              JENNY
                          (coquettishly)
            If you don't mind... Larry...

They begin to move off, and we

                                              DISSOLVE TO:

47   EXT. - A PATH IN THE WOODS - NIGHT - LONG SHOT

        A small light shines through the trees.

                                              DISSOLVE TO:

48   EXT. - THE GYPSY'S TENT IN THE WOODS - NIGHT - MED. CLOSE

        The gypsy's cart, unloaded, stands close by.

                                              DISSOLVE TO:

49   INT. - INSIDE THE TENT - NIGHT - MED. CLOSE

BELA, the gypsy, has fixed up his tent. In a corner,
a sack stuffed with hay indicates his sleeping place.
Some small horrid wax effigies are scattered about,
and heaped on the floor, all around, are the soft
colorful hand-made rugs the gypsy sells. On the walls
of the tent hang silver chains, amulets, and charms.
A lamp hangs in the middle of the tent.

Bela places a crystal globe on a small table. The
glass globe deflects the light, throwing prismatic
effects on the canvas walls.

Bela is a dark, sad-faced man with melancholy eyes.
He suddenly stops and listens, then smiling, moves to
the entrance of the tent.

50   EXT. - PATH BEFORE THE TENT - NIGHT - MED. LONG SHOT

Larry and the two girls, one on each side of him, walk
toward the tent, talking and laughing.

51   EXT. - THE TENT - NIGHT - MED. CLOSE

The gypsy appears at the opening of the tent, looking
toward them. Larry and the girls stop a few feet from
Bela.

                    JENNY
                 (excited)
           There he is --
                 (calling
                  toward Bela)
           We've come to have our fortunes
           told... Can you really read the
           future?

The gypsy bows solemnly.

                    BELA
           I will not disappoint you, my
           lady... Step inside, please...

He opens the canvas, so that a broad stream of light
falls on his visitors. Jenny turns to Larry and Gwen.

                                        CONTINUED

                              JENNY
                          (breathlessly)
                    Wait for me - but not too
                    close to the tent - no eaves-
                    dropping, please... You don't
                    mind if I go in first?

                              GWEN
                          (laughs)
                    Go ahead, you silly...

Jenny quickly disappears into the tent, and the
entrance closes, after Bela goes in too.

52   EXT. - OUTSIDE TENT - <u>NIGHT</u> - MED. CLOSE

                              LARRY
                    Let's take a little walk - so
                    we won't be tempted to listen
                    in on Jenny's big romance.

Gwen smiles up at him, and the CAMERA PANS with them
as they walk away along the path. Larry has his cane
on one arm; he is too shy to offer the other arm to
the girl... For a moment there is silence... The young
people are self-conscious about being alone together
in the woods.

53   EXT. - WOODS - MOVING SHOT - CAMERA IN FRONT OF COUPLE
        <u>NIGHT</u>

                              GWEN
                          (hesitatingly)
                    Now... tell me. How did you
                    know about - my room - and -

                              LARRY
                    I - I can't tell you...
                    You'll be sore at me -

                              GWEN
                          (convincingly)
                    Oh - I never would!

                              LARRY
                    Promise? Cross your heart?

                                        CONTINUED

                         GWEN
               I promise...

They stop. Larry looks at her uncomfortably. But
she is so expectant that he has to speak up.

                         LARRY
               Well... I was sent to Wales
               to instal a telescope - at
               Sir John Talbot's place, you see...

                         GWEN
               Yes...

                         LARRY
               And a telescope's got a mighty
               sharp eye... It brings the stars
               so close you feel you can almost
               touch 'em...

                         GWEN
                    (beginning to
                     understand)
               Yes...?

                         LARRY
               And people in their rooms, too -
               even miles away - if you point
               it in their direction...

The girl sees it all now.

                         GWEN
                    (taken aback)
               Oh - you wouldn't!

                         LARRY
                    (embarrassed)
               Oh, yes, I would... In fact,
               I did.
                    (quickly)
               I really only started to test
               the refractor. I didn't know
               about you - and all of a sudden
               - there you were!

Gwen is silent.

                                        CONTINUED

                         LARRY
                     (in despair)
              Now you're angry. But honest -
              I only looked twice! The first
              time when you put on your ear-
              rings - and the second time
              when you were with Jenny -

                         GWEN
                     (relieved)
              Oh... Well - but you mustn't
              ever... From now on, I shall
              draw the curtains even in
              daytime!

Larry breathes more easily.

                         LARRY
              Forgive me?

                         GWEN
              There's nothing to forgive,
              really...

She lifts her head and smiles. Larry sighs deeply in
relief.

                         LARRY
              I was afraid you wouldn't
              speak to me again...

He takes her arm and they walk on together.

54   EXT. - WOODS - MOVING SHOT - IN FRONT OF GWEN AND LARRY
       Night

                         GWEN
                     (quietly)
              I don't believe in quarreling
              with the people I like...

                         LARRY
                     (awkwardly)
              Gee... thanks! You're the
              swellest girl I ever met...
                     (catches
                      her eye)
              I mean it!

                                        DISSOLVE TO:

55   INT. GYPSY TENT - <u>NIGHT</u> - MED. CLOSE - BELA AND JENNY

        Jenny sits expectantly on a folding stool in front of
        the small table on which Bela has spread his magic
        paraphenalia: the crystal globe, some cabalistic
        charts, etc. Jenny looks at him trustingly.

                        JENNY
               Tell me... when am I going
               to be married?

        Bela looks up. His dark eyes are narrow slits. He
        mumbles in a strange language, then pulls the globe
        close and looks into it.

                        JENNY
                 (spell-bound)
               What do you see?

        CAMERA MOVES CLOSER INTO:

56   INT. GYPSY TENT - CLOSE-UP - BELA

        Bela's head is bent over the crystal. He pushes back
        his dark hair which has fallen over his forehead. A
        scar becomes visible on his forehead, a five-pointed
        star, a pentagram, deeply cut into the bone.

        CAMERA PULLS BACK INTO:

57   MED. CLOSE - SAME AS 55

        Bela looks up and demands:

                        BELA
               Your hands...

        Jenny puts her hands on the table, palms up.

                        BELA
               The left hand shows your past...
               the right hand shows your future...

        The pentagram on his forehead becomes more distinct,
        as if penetrating more deeply into his skin. Bela
        takes Jenny's left hand and studies it. But he suddenly
        seems disturbed,- he puts his left hand over the
        pentagram as if in pain. Abruptly he gets up, dropping
        Jenny's hand. His face is distorted.

                                              CONTINUED

                          JENNY
                        (alarmed)
                  What's the matter?

She gazes at her hand - then at Bela. The man standing before her seems to be in the throes of some
dreadful suffering. His left hand presses his hair
hard against his forehead, as if to hide the pentagram
and ease the pain of it. He trembles - his eyes are
glassy.

                          BELA
                     (speaking with
                       difficulty)
                  I... can't tell you anything
                  tonight... come back tomorrow -

Jenny grows more alarmed.

                          JENNY
                  What did you see?
                  Something evil?

Bela answers in a tortured voice:

                          BELA
                  No, no... Now go away...
                  go quickly...
                        (shouting)
                  GO!

Jenny jumps up and retreats backwards to the entrance
of the tent.

                          JENNY
                        (terrified)
                  Yes... yes... I'm going...

She runs out of the tent. Bela puts both hands before
his face, his shoulders convulsed, as if in pain.

58   EXT. - OUTSIDE THE TENT - NIGHT - MED. CLOSE - JENNY

Jenny rushes out of the tent, and calls:

                          JENNY
                  Gwen!... Gwen! Where are you?

She runs away quickly.

                                        CONTINUED

58   CONTINUED

                                    JENNY'S VOICE (O.S.)
                    Gwen...!

                                            WIPE TO:

59   EXT. - A SMALL CLEARING IN THE WOODS - <u>NIGHT</u> - LONG SHOT

        Brightly lit by the moon. Larry and Gwen are walking
        along, talking.

60   EXT. - SAME AS ABOVE - MED. CLOSE - LARRY AND GWEN

        Larry stops and looks at Gwen.

                            LARRY
                    You know - I don't understand
                    it. I never lost my head before...
                    But with you...

        He puts his hands on her shoulders and bends down to
        kiss her - but Gwen steps back.

                            GWEN
                    No, Larry...

        He drops his hands at once.

                            GWEN
                    I - I'm engaged, Larry...
                    I'm going to be married soon.

                            LARRY
                    Oh.... Well, that's that.

                            GWEN
                    I like you, Larry... but...

                            LARRY
                    Sure... I might've known it -
                    nobody'd pass up a girl like you...

        Gwen tries to change the subject.... She looks around...
        Suddenly Jenny comes into her mind.

                                            CONTINUED

60   CONTINUED

All at once the silence is broken by a strange SOUND -
a low, fitful WAIL, like a signal from afar.

                    LARRY
                  (stopping)
          What was that... a coyote?

Gwen clutches his arm in fright. THE HOWL IS REPEATED,
rising swiftly, until it reaches its crescendo in a
scream.

                    GWEN
          I don't know! I've never heard
          anything like it before!

Jenny's VOICE COMES OVER, faintly but in terror:

                    JENNY'S VOICE (O.S.)
          Help!.... Help!.....

Larry stares at Gwen, who trembles.

                    GWEN
          Jenny!

                    LARRY
                  (hurriedly)
          Now don't get scared -
          I'll be back -

He runs off. Gwen starts after him - but he is much
faster than she. CAMERA PANS, as both run in the direction
they came from, Larry considerably ahead.

                    GWEN
                  (calling)
          Larry... Wait... Larry!

                                        CUT TO:

61   EXT. - THE PATH LEADING TO BELA'S TENT - NIGHT - LONG SHOT

In the moonlight, below a great tree, lies Jenny. Above
her stands a huge animal, a wolf. Larry runs into the
scene.

62   EXT. - WOODS - <u>NIGHT</u> - MED. CLOSE - LARRY AND THE WOLF

Larry stops as he sees the wolf and Jenny. The beast
turns, and looks at him with eyes like burning coals.
Larry sees the animal crouch - he lifts his cane,
ready to smash it over the animal's head. The wolf
springs forward to attack him.

63   EXT. - WOODS - ANOTHER ANGLE

The animal jumps at Larry. Larry crashes the silver
handle of his stick down on the wolf's head, but the
beast hangs on.

64   EXT. - WOODS - CLOSE SHOT

The wolf's head, his teeth tearing Larry's coat right
over his heart, to shreds. Larry hits the animal with
his left fist, and stumbles back.

CAMERA PULLS BACK TO:

65   EXT. - WOODS - MED. CLOSE

The beast attacks him again, but Larry crashes his
stick over the animal's skull... once... twice...
The wolf collapses.

                                        CUT TO:

66   EXT. - WOODS - <u>NIGHT</u> - LONG SHOT - GWEN

Gwen is running through the woods, shouting in deadly
fear:

                              GWEN
                Larry! Where are you...?
                Larry!...

She passes the camera, suddenly stops:

67   EXT. WOODS - LONG - FROM GWEN'S ANGLE

Larry comes stumbling toward her, his hands pressed
over his heart, his clothes torn, his breathing labored.

                                    CONTINUED

Gwen runs up to Larry (CAMERA FOLLOWING). When he reaches her, he collapses, sinking to his knees.

                    GWEN
          Larry! What happened!

She kneels beside him, looking at his hand, covered with blood. Larry stares at her - he tries to talk - but suddenly crumples over in a faint, falling on his face.

Gwen, terrified, tries to move him, but she is not strong enough. She gets up, looks around, controlling herself with an effort.

Suddenly she hears the CREAKING OF CART WHEELS AND THE CLOP-CLOP OF A HORSE'S HOOFS. THE CAMERA PANS TO:

68   EXT. - ROAD NEAR WOODS - <u>NIGHT</u> - MED. LONG SHOT

Along the moonlit country road which leads to Bela's tent, a horse-drawn cart is moving. An oil lamp dangles from the driver's seat, where an old woman sits, wrapped in heavy blankets against the night's chill.

                    GWEN'S VOICE (O.S.)
          Help!.... Help!...

The old woman stops the horse and listens.

69   EXT. - ROAD - CLOSE - MALEVA

She is dark-eyed and dark-haired; her face is heavily lined. Big rings hang from her ear lobes, and silver necklaces tinkle when she moves. She is MALEVA, the gypsy woman.

                    GWEN'S VOICE (O.S.)
          Help!.... Help!....

The gypsy woman pulls the reins and the tired horse moves on, toward the spot where the voice comes from.

70   EXT. - ROAD - MED. CLOSE - MALEVA

The cart moves off.

                                        DISSOLVE TO:

71   EXT. - WOODS - NIGHT - MED. LONG

Gwen stands in the f.g. beside Larry's body. She
looks toward the cart, which approaches quickly,
the oil lamp throwing a yellow beam on the ground.

                    GWEN
          Here.... Come quick!

                    MALEVA
          Coming...

The cart stops.

72   EXT. - WOODS - CAMERA ON THE CART - MED. CLOSE

Maleva stops the cart close to Gwen, and steps down
from the seat, taking a voluminous bag with her.

                    GWEN
          Help me... he's wounded...

The woman kneels down at Larry's side, and with Gwen's
help, she turns Larry over. Larry opens his eyes and
looks at Maleva and Gwen, dazed. Fearfully he touches
the torn shirt over his heart.

                    MALEVA
          What happened?

                    LARRY
          A wolf attacked me...
          he bit me... he killed Jenny.

                    GWEN
                (paralyzed
                 with shock)
          Jenny...!

She gets up, to look for Jenny, but Maleva orders her
in a stern voice:

                    MALEVA
          Don't go away... Stay here
          and help me...

The girl stops at once and looks at her. Larry gets
to his feet, slowly, staggeringly, supported by Maleva
and Gwen.

                                        CONTINUED

72   CONTINUED

                        LARRY
             The wolf... I killed him...

73   EXT. - WOODS - <u>NIGHT</u> - CLOSE TWO SHOT - LARRY AND MALEVA

    Maleva looks at him, her eyes narrow. Then she says,
    kindly:

                        MALEVA
          Come on... I'll take you home...

74   EXT. - WOODS - MED. CLOSE

    Helped by Gwen and Maleva, Larry climbs into the cart.

                                 FADE OUT.

    FADE IN.

    EXT. - THE WOODS - WHERE LARRY KILLED THE WOLF - <u>DAY</u>
75   LONG SHOT

    It is early morning, and a low mist is hanging between
    the trees and bushes. A few men are moving about.
    FRANK ANDREWS, the game-keeper, a young, good-looking
    man of twenty-five, in high boots, riding breeches and
    leather jacket, leading a dog on a leash. With him is
    MR. TWIDDLE, the policeman, in uniform. About 20 yards
    to the right, KENDALL, the police inspector, COTTON,
    his assistant, and DR. LLOYD, the physician, are examin-
    ing Jenny's body.

76   SAME AS ABOVE - MED. CLOSE

    Frank Andrew's dog sniffs the ground, pulling at his
    leash. Frank holds it short and bends down.

77   SAME AS ABOVE - CLOSE - ON GROUND

    Clearly marked in the humid ground are the traces of a
    big dog's or wolf's claws.

    CAMERA PULLS BACK INTO:

78   EXT. - WOODS - SAME AS 75 - <u>DAY</u> - MED. CLOSE

Frank, holding the dog, says to Twiddle, pointing to
the wolf tracks:

                    FRANK
            Look, Mr. Twiddle...
            Wolf tracks!

                    TWIDDLE
              (doubtfully)
            But, Mr. Andrews! You know
            we have no wolves around here.
            The last one was killed in the
            Middle Ages!

                    FRANK
            Just the same - there's no
            question about these marks.

The dog tears at the leash, eager to follow the scent.
He pulls Frank along. Twiddle stops and looks after him
wonderingly.

79   EXT. - WOODS - NEAR JENNY'S BODY - MED. CLOSE

The body cannot be seen, as the men stand in front of it.
Inspector Kendall, in bowler hat and the typical outfit
of an English plain-clothes policeman, turns to his aide,
Cotton, a young hungry-looking man who holds a pad and
pencil. But under the pad he hides a flat whiskey bottle
and takes a quick drink, secretly, when he is unobserved.

                    KENDALL
            Take a note, Mr. Cotton...
            Jenny Williams - attacked
            by some large animal. From
            the evidence I'd say -
                    (hesitates)
            - a wolf.
                    (turning to
                    Dr. Lloyd)
            Is that right, Dr. Lloyd?

                    DR. LLOYD
              (getting up)
            Her jugular was severed by the
            bite of powerful teeth. The
            cause of death was internal
            hemmorhage.

                                        CONTINUED

                    KENDALL
              (to Cotton, who
               seems faint)
         What's the matter with you,
         Mr. Cotton?

                    COTTON
              (with difficulty)
         I feel a little queer, sir.

                    KENDALL
              (angrily)
         Don't feel queer! Write down
         what I told you!

                    COTTON
              (frightened look
               toward Jenny's body)
         Very well, sir!

He takes a secret swig, lifting the flask to his mouth
as the others turn away from him.

80   EXT. WOODS - DAY - NEAR JENNY'S BODY - ANOTHER ANGLE

      Twiddle, the policeman, bends down to look at the ground
      more closely. He calls out excitedly:

                    TWIDDLE
         Inspector! Have a look
         at this!

81   EXT. WOODS - FROM TWIDDLE'S ANGLE - LONG

      Inspector Kendall, Dr. Lloyd, and Mr. Cotton hurry over
      toward Twiddle, and look at where he points:

82   EXT. WOODS - CLOSE SHOT - LARRY'S CANE LYING ON THE
      GROUND

      CAMERA PULLS BACK INTO:

83   EXT. WOODS - THE GROUP - MED. CLOSE

      Twiddle points to the cane, as the men come into scene.

                                        CONTINUED

83 CONTINUED

TWIDDLE
A cane - with a silver handle!

Twiddle bends down, picks up the walking-stick and passes it to Kendall, who scrutinizes it, then dictates:

KENDALL
Take a note, Mr. Cotton...
Found - on scene of tragedy:
a silver-handled stick -
engraved.

COTTON
(with an
effort)
Very well, sir.

OVER THE DIALOGUE, A DOG'S BARK IS HEARD. THEN FRANK ANDREW'S VOICE COMES OVER.

FRANK'S VOICE (O.S.)
Inspector! Inspector!

The men turn in the direction of his voice - while Cotton takes another surreptitious nip from his flask.

84 EXT. - ANOTHER SPOT IN WOODS - DAY - MED. CLOSE

Frank Andrews holds the barking dog, which tries to approach the body that is lying deeply embedded in the humid moss. The body (Bela) lies with its naked feet toward the camera. As the four men enter the scene, Andrews calls out in horror:

FRANK
It's the gypsy!

Kendall stops, looking at the body, while Dr. Lloyd bends over it.

KENDALL
Yes - that's Bela. Was he
killed by the animal, too,
Dr. Lloyd?

Dr. Lloyd gets up.

CONTINUED

                        DR. LLOYD
               No. His skull was crushed
               by heavy blows - with a
               pointed instrument.

Kendall turns the walking-stick in his hands, and
dictates:

                        KENDALL
                   (to Cotton)
               Bela, the gypsy, found dead
               about 30 yards north of Jenny
               William's body. Cause of death:
               heavy blows inflicted with some
               pointed instrument... Put that
               down, Mr. Cotton.

                        COTTON
                   (half-drunk,
                   writing with
                   difficulty)
           Very well, sir.

Dr. Lloyd, surprised, points to the dead man's feet.

                        DR. LLOYD
           Look - his feet are bare!

Kendall bends down to look more closely.

                        KENDALL
           So they are... and he's fully
          dressed otherwise. Make a
          note of that, Mr. Cotton.

Cotton drops his hands, unable to write any more. His
eyes are glassy and he whispers:

                        COTTON
          Very well, sir....

Then, before the eyes of the others, Cotton swoons and
passes out completely.

                                  DISSOLVE TO:

85   INT. - LARRY'S ROOM IN TALBOT CASTLE - DAY - MED. CLOSE

Larry lies asleep in an old Tudor bed. Opposite the
bed stands a Tudor cupboard, with a large mirror in
the center of it. The sun streams broadly through the
curtains.
Larry wakes up, and for a moment, he lies there, open-
eyed and without moving.

86   INT. - LARRY'S ROOM - CAMERA BEHIND LARRY - MED. CLOSE

He sees himself in the mirror, lying in bed. Slowly he
gets up and sits on his bed, covering his face with his
hands, to organize his thoughts. Then he gingerly
touches his pajamas over his heart. He feels no pain.
He hits the spot harder where the wolf bit him -- still
no pain! Larry steps over to the mirror and bares his
chest.

CAMERA MOVES INTO:

87   INT. - LARRY'S ROOM - CLOSEUP AT MIRROR

Larry looks at his chest - but where he expected to find
a wound, only a scar can be seen, faintly irregular.
He looks at it wonderingly and touches it.

STEPS COME CLOSER - AND THE CAMERA PULLS BACK TO:

88   INT. - LARRY'S ROOM - MED. SHOT

He grabs a morning-gown and puts it on. Somebody
KNOCKS ON THE DOOR.

                         LARRY
                       (turning
                        toward door)
             Come in...

89   INT. - LARRY'S ROOM - MED. CLOSE FROM LARRY'S ANGLE

The door opens and Sir John, followed by Kendall and
Dr. Lloyd, stand in the doorway.

                         LARRY
             Good morning, Sir John.

                                        CONTINUED

                              SIR JOHN
                        (alarmed at seeing
                        Larry up already)
                  Good morning, Mr. Gill.
                  But why aren't you staying in bed?

90   INT. - LARRY'S ROOM - MED. CLOSE - THE GROUP

                              LARRY
                          (nervously)
                  Oh, I'm all right...
                  Please come in.

The men enter the room.

                              SIR JOHN
                  This is Inspector Kendall,
                  and this is Dr. Lloyd, whom
                  you won't recall, I'm sure...

                              LARRY
                  How do you do...
                          (to Sir John)
                  No...I don't. Have I met him
                  before?

                              DR. LLOYD
                          (with forced
                          heartiness)
                  You frightened us last night,
                  my boy. When the two women
                  brought you in - you were
                  apparently quite dead!

                              LARRY
                  Dead? But there's nothing
                  wrong with me!

He looks at the Inspector, inquisitively.

                              LARRY (cont'ing)
                  Or... is there?

Kendall produces the walking-stick.

                              KENDALL
                  Is this your stick?

                                        CONTINUED

Larry takes the stick from Kendall and looks at it.

                    LARRY
          Yeah - that's mine... I
          reckon it saved my life.
          I killed the wolf with it.

Kendall watches him professionally. The other men
exchange glances.

                    KENDALL
          A man was killed with this
          stick!

                    LARRY
                (astonished)

          A man?

                    KENDALL
                (slowly)
          The gypsy, Bela, is dead,
          his skull crushed by that cane!

                    LARRY
                (amazed)
          Bela? He wasn't there!
          I only saw a wolf -- he bit me
          -- here - right over the heart.

                    DR. LLOYD
                (interested)
          Is that so? I couldn't find
          any wound last night! Let
          me see...

Larry opens his shirt over his heart. The Doctor steps
closer.

91   ANOTHER ANGLE - FAVORING LARRY, THE CENTER OF THE GROUP

                    LARRY
                (indicating
                his chest)
          Here's where it was. But
          it healed up over-night...
                (with a
                forced laugh)
          Your climate must be healthier
          than California's.

                                        CONTINUED

Dr. Lloyd looks at the wound and shakes his head.

                    DR. LLOYD
          This scar is one you had
          before, my boy. It's an
          old one.

Larry looks at him irritatedly, buttoning his shirt
again.

                    LARRY
          But, Doc, I ought to know
          my own scars.
                    (tries to
                    joke)
          I always take my shower with-
          out a bathing suit - I'm
          funny that way!

Inspector Kendall cuts in, addressing Larry.

                    KENDALL
          May I ask you a few questions?

                    LARRY
          Sure... go ahead.

He sits down, tired, his face worn. Dr. Lloyd watches
him attentively.

                    DR. LLOYD
                    (with authority)
          We'd better leave Mr. Gill
          alone... He needs a rest.

                    LARRY
                    (flaring up)
          What's the matter with you all?
          If you want to ask me questions,
          go ahead. But don't try to tell
          me I killed a man - when I know
          I killed a wolf!

                    DR. LLOYD
                    (soothingly)
          Yes, yes... Now lie down and
          relax.

                                        CONTINUED

                         LARRY
              Okay, Doc. But don't treat me
              like I was loco. I'm O. K. -
              up here, anyway.
                    (taps his
                    head)

                         DR. LLOYD
                    (laughs pro-
                    fessionally)
              I'm sure you are, Mr. Gill...
              Have a good rest.

92   INT. - LARRY'S ROOM - WIDER VIEW

        The men leave the room. Larry looks after them and
        picks up the walking-stick the Inspector left behind.
        Irritatedly he stares at the crest - the wolf and the
        pentagram...

                                        DISSOLVE TO:

93   INT. - LIBRARY OF TALBOT CASTLE - DAY - FULL SHOT

        The library is a panelled room, the walls partly covered
        with book shelves. Stuffed heads of African animals
        stare from the corners. Sir John stands near the hearth
        where a coal fire is burning. Kendall is sitting in a
        deep chair, smoking a cigar with relish. Dr. Lloyd
        stands near the window, thoughtfully looking at the
        Inspector.

94   INT. - LIBRARY - MED. CLOSE - THE GROUP

                         SIR JOHN
              I can vouch for the man's
              integrity, Mr. Kendall.

                         KENDALL
                    (amicably)
              I don't accuse him of foul
              play, Sir John... I have solved
              the case in my own mind, and I
              don't think I can be wrong...

        He looks through the smoke of his cigar, his eyes half-
        closed, to test the effect of his words on Sir John.

                                        CONTINUED

                         SIR JOHN
                        (curious)
               You mean you have a theory,
               Inspector?

                         KENDALL
                        (with relish)
               It's more than a theory. A
               dog or wolf attacked Jenny
               Williams. That's proven.
               When she cried for help, Gill
               and Bela came to her rescue...
               It was dark. In the excitement
               and confusion, he didn't see the
               gypsy. Without knowing it, he
               hit Bela over the head...

95   INT. - LIBRARY - ANOTHER ANGLE - KENDALL IN F.G. -
        DR. LLOYD IN B.G.

        Dr. Lloyd listens with interest, but doubtfully.

                         DR. LLOYD
               But Bela's bare feet...
               That's strange, isn't it?

        Kendall turns toward him with a smile.

96   INT. - LIBRARY - MED. CLOSE - FROM LLOYD'S ANGLE,
        FEATURING KENDALL AND SIR JOHN

                         KENDALL
                        (patiently)
               Not at all...Most gypsies
               go bare-footed...

97   INT. - LIBRARY - BACK TO THE GROUP

                         DR. LLOYD
               I grant you that... But what
               about Gill's wound...?

                         KENDALL
               Clear as daylight! Gill
               imagined he had been bitten!
               The beast jumped at him and
               tore his coat to shreds...

                                             CONTINUED

Kendall looks around triumphantly, but Lloyd looks
sceptical.

> DR. LLOYD
> (emphatically)
> Yes, but what about that scar?
> It's at least ten years old,
> yet he insists he received it
> last night, - wound and recovery
> all in twelve hours!

> SIR JOHN
> And what do you make of that
> fact, _Doctor_?

> DR. LLOYD
> (slowly)
> The patient is mentally disturbed
> ... Perhaps the shock did it -
> perhaps he's always been un-
> balanced... Don't question him
> any more until I know for certain.
> (turning to
> Kendall)
> You policemen are always in a
> hurry, as if dead men hadn't
> time for all eternity.

Kendall gets up, and throws his cigar into the fireplace.

> KENDALL
> Well! You'll be declaring me
> a mental case, next!

> DR. LLOYD
> (smiling)
> Oh, no... I shouldn't dare...

> KENDALL
> (wryly)
> Thank you. In return, I'll
> not question your patient again
> until you think fit. The case
> is clear to me, however....

WIPE TO:

98   EXT. - STREET NEAR CONLIFFE'S SHOP - <u>DAY</u> - THE WOMEN

CAMERA TRAVELS in front of five middle-aged females,
who, led by a fierce-looking woman, walk down the
street. The woman in front wears a black hat and
carries an umbrella. Her name is Mrs. Williams and
she is Jenny's older sister-in-law.

                    MRS. WILLIAMS
                 (belligerently)
            If the police thinks the case
            is clear - it's not to me!

Miss Bally, an old spinster who walks at her side,
half a step behind the fast-moving leader, asks avidly:

                    MISS BALLY
            What are you going to tell her?

                    MRS. WILLIAMS
                 (with grim
                  determination)
            Just watch me!

                                        CUT TO:

99   INT. - CONLIFFE'S SHOP - <u>DAY</u> - MED. CLOSE # GWEN AND
      FATHER

Gwen is standing near the door which leads to the back
room, leaning unhappily against the door frame. Her
father is dusting a shelf on which old English mugs
are displayed.

                    CONLIFFE
                 (worried)
            But there is nothing they can
            accuse you of... Why don't you
            go to your room and lie down?

But the girl slowly shakes her head.

                    GWEN
            I'm afraid to be alone, father.
            As soon as I close my eyes,
            I see Jenny...
                 (shudders)
            Please let me stay...

                                        CONTINUED

                         CONLIFFE
              Of course, my child...

He looks at her through the corners of his eyes,
worried, then goes on polishing the porcelain, which
clatters in his hands...

Suddenly Gwen stares with fright toward the window.

100   INT. - THROUGH THE SHOP WINDOW - FROM GWEN'S ANGLE

         The five women appear and enter the shop. (TEE DOOR
         BELL CHIMES.)

101   INT. - SHOP - MED. CLOSE - THE GROUP

         Conliffe steps forward as if to protect his daughter
         from the five women.

                         CONLIFFE
              Mrs. Williams...

The woman steps close to the counter and puts her
umbrella on it. She looks threateningly at the frightened girl. The other women watch eagerly.

                         MRS. WILLIAMS
              There she is!...

                         GWEN
                      (trying to
                       be brave)
              What do you want?

                         MRS. WILLIAMS
              Just tell me why you left my
              poor sister-in-law all alone
              with that gypsy!

                         GWEN
              But... She didn't want anyone
              to hear her fortune -

                         MRS. WILLIAMS
                      (scornfully)
              What a lie! YOU wanted to walk
              off in the dark with that American!

                                        CONTINUED

Conliffe steps in front of his daughter, as Mrs. Williams
says above, and addresses her angrily:

                    CONLIFFE
          How dare you talk to Gwen
          like that!

                    MRS. WILLIAMS
                  (turns to her
                   entourage)
          Listen to him! A fine father
          he is!

Miss Bally, hiding behind Mrs. Williams like a small dog
behind its mistress, peers out at Conliffe and squeaks:

                    MISS BALLY
          How dare you permit her to walk
          out with other men when she's
          engaged to my nephew!

                    GWEN
                  (flaring up)
          I didn't do anything wrong!

                    MRS. WILLIAMS
                  (shouting)
          Anything wrong! It was because
          of you that poor Jenny was killed!

The girl stares at her, then bursts into tears.

                    GWEN
                  (sobbing)
          It's cruel of you to say that!

Conliffe steps forward, and says wildly:

                    CONLIFFE
          Now that's enough!

                    MRS. WILLIAMS
          She's to blame, the little chit.
          I always knew her innocent face
          was just a mask -

Gwen backs away, horrified, and rushes into the back
room. Conliffe approaches the women threateningly. He
says hoarsely:

CONTINUED

101   CONTINUED - 2

                                    CONLIFFE
                    Get out of here - all of you.

        (THE DOOR BELL CHIMES)

                                                    CUT TO:

102   INT. - SHOP - NEAR DOOR - CLOSE ON LARRY

        Larry enters. Astonished, he looks toward the group
        and hears Mrs. Williams shouting:

                                    MRS. WILLIAMS' VOICE (O.S.)
                    You won't get rid of me before
                    I knew the truth! What was she
                    doing with that man, while poor
                    Jenny was being murdered?

        Larry moves forward, scowling.

103   INT. - SHOP - BACK TO GROUP (EXCEPT GWEN WHO HAS LEFT)

        Larry enters group while Mrs. Williams continues:

                                    MRS. WILLIAMS
                    I'll tell you what she was
                    doing - !

        Larry cuts in behind her back:

                                    LARRY
                    Tell me too!

        Mrs. Williams at once breaks off and wheels around,
        staring at Larry open-mouthed. He steps toward her
        through the group of women, who draw back in fear.

                                    LARRY (cont'ing)
                    Come on, spill it!

        Larry looks down at the woman with an expression that
        makes Mrs. Williams tremble - as if he were going to
        strangle her any moment. She subsides and cringes.

                                                    CONTINUED

                    MRS. WILLIAMS
          Don't you dare to touch me!

                    LARRY
                (contemptuously)
          I wouldn't touch you with a
          ten-foot pole!

In quiet fury he turns to the other women:

                    LARRY (cont'd.)
          Now scram - all of you!

Mrs. Williams looks at him, seething, but he stares her
down and her courage deserts her. She turns, and snatch-
ing her umbrella, she retreats, trying to put up a brave
front.

                    MRS. WILLIAMS
                (turning on
                Conliffe)
          You and your fine daughter -
          you haven't heard the last
          of this!

The women walk quickly past Larry, staring at him with
antagonism. THE DOOR IS HEARD TO CLOSE behind them.
(DOOR BELL CHIMES as they go out.)

                    LARRY
          Whew! What's got into them?

                    CONLIFFE
                (helplessly)
          I - I really don't know...

                    LARRY
                (sincerely)
          I'm sorry I got Gwen into such
          a mess - but really, there was
          nothing wrong -

                    CONLIFFE
                (resenting
                Larry)
          I trust my daughter.

                                        CONTINUED

103   CONTINUED - 2

                              LARRY
                         (apprehensively)
                    I hope Gwen didn't hear all
                    that row... Is she here?
                    Could I see her?

Conliffe wipes his forehead with a trembling hand. He's
too upset -- there's no more resistance left in him.

                              CONLIFFE
                         (wearily)
                    She's in there...

He points to the back door and Larry walks toward it.

                              LARRY
                    Thank you, sir.

104   INT. - LIVING ROOM BEHIND CONLIFFE'S SHOP - FULL SHOT

The room is stuffed with antiques, but there is a table
and some chairs in front of a small fireplace.

Larry enters and looks at Gwen, sitting near the fire.

105   INT. - CONLIFFE LIVING ROOM - MED. CLOSE - GWEN & LARRY

Gwen's face is sad and wet with tears; her hands lie
limp in her lap. As he approaches, she smiles pathet-
ically:

                              GWEN
                    Hello, Larry.

She motions him to a chair opposite her.

                              LARRY
                    Hello, Gwen...

He sits down.

106   INT. - CONLIFFE LIVING ROOM - CLOSE TWO SHOT

                              LARRY
                         (smiling to hide
                          his distress)
                    I - couldn't find you with my
                    spyglass. So I had to come my-
                    self, to see if you were all right.

                                        CONTINUED

Gwen looks up at him listlessly.

> GWEN
> Oh - I - that's not important.
> But how about your wound?

Larry takes her limp hand in his own, and looks at her tenderly.

> LARRY
> (with forced
> cheerfulness)
> It was just a scratch...

Gwen closes her eyes, overwhelmed by the memory, and says softly, shudderingly:

> GWEN
> What a dreadful night!

> LARRY
> I still don't know what to
> make of it. I saw Jenny -
> and the wolf... But now
> they say I killed Bela!

> GWEN
> (seriously)
> There couldn't have been a
> wolf. The story I told you -
> about the werewolf - and the
> flower - must have confused you.

They look at each other and Larry shakes his head, trying to free himself from the confusing, awful thoughts preying upon him.

> LARRY
> I thought I was old enough
> to laugh off things like that...

He gazes at her with a far-away look, bewildered and wondering. Gwen nods.

> LARRY (cont'ing)
> There are a lot of things I
> used to laugh at, that I'm
> beginning to take seriously...

But with a sudden optimism, he smiles and puts his hand on her arm.

                                    CONTINUED

                    LARRY
          Gwen... In a few days I'll be
          through with my job here and
          going back home. Why not
          clear out with me? We can be
          married on the boat...

She looks at him wide-eyed with surprise.

                    LARRY (cont'ing)
                  (with a derisive
                    laugh)
          I saw those old hags outside.
          Let's run away together and
          really give them something
          to talk about!

                    GWEN
                  (rising,
                    shaking her head)
          No, Larry... I must stay with
          Father.

107   INT. - CONLIFFE LIVING ROOM - ANOTHER ANGLE - CLOSE

Larry rises too. He says eagerly:

                    LARRY
          The old man? He's no problem.
          We'd just sell all this stuff
          here and take him along...
          He'd love it over there!

But Gwen only smiles sadly and shakes her head.

                    LARRY
          What else is it, then?
          Don't you like me?

(Faintly, from outside, we HEAR THE DOOR BELL CHIME.)

                    GWEN
          It's not that, Larry.
          You know it...

Larry steps closer to her.

                              CONTINUED

>   LARRY
>   All my life I've been looking
>   for a girl like you... Now
>   I've found you... Come along
>   with me, Gwen.

He stops, hearing a man's voice (Frank's) out of scene.

>   FRANK'S VOICE (O.S.)
>   Is Gwen in, Mr. Conliffe?

>   CONLIFFE (O.S.)
>   Yes, Frank. But she has a
>   visitor - Mr. Gill -

>   FRANK (O.S.)
>   That's all right. I want
>   to meet him!

STEPS COME CLOSER.

>   LARRY
>   (indicating
>   Frank's voice)
>   Is that --- why?

He looks at the girl, who casts down her eyes, without
replying. Larry turns as Frank enters.

108   INT. - CONLIFFE LIVING ROOM - WIDER ANGLE

Frank has his dog, Peter, on a leash. The dog, seeing
Larry, suddenly begins to snarl and show his teeth,
his hair bristling up as if in fear. Gwen starts to
introduce the two men:

>   GWEN
>   Frank, this is -

She is cut short by the dog, who starts to bark and
tries to rush at Larry, tearing at his leash.

109   INT. - CONLIFFE LIVING ROOM - CLOSE ON THE DOG

Snarling in fear and furiously barking toward Larry.
FRANK'S VOICE COMES OVER.

                                        CONTINUED

> FRANK'S VOICE
>> Quiet, Peter!

110   INT. - CONLIFFE LIVING ROOM - BACK TO THE GROUP

Larry steps back, surprised at the dog's conduct.
Gwen looks surprised, too. Frank tries to quiet it.

> FRANK
>> Quiet, I say!

The dog, works himself up into a frenzy, refusing to
be stilled.

> GWEN
> (frightened)
>> You'd better tie him up
>> outside.

Frank turns, struggling to get the dog out.

> FRANK
>> Come on, you fool!

He gets the dog out of the room. Larry looks after
it, disturbed.

> LARRY
>> Funny... Dogs always used
>> to like me!

(OFF SCENE we hear the faint CHIME of the door as it
opens.)

111   INT. - CONLIFFE LIVING ROOM - TWO SHOT - GWEN & LARRY

Larry, still looking after the dog, troubled. Then
he shakes off this thought. Going close to Gwen, he
points his head toward the door and continues:

> LARRY
>> The real reason you want
>> to stay here is because
>> of Frank, isn't it?

The girl nods, perturbed. She is strongly drawn to
Larry - but... She tries to explain:

CONTINUED

                    GWEN
          We grew up together -
          I've always known him...

                    LARRY
                  (jokingly)
          But that's no reason...
          You'd have to marry the
          whole town...

Gwen shakes her head. She doesn't want to hurt Frank
- she doesn't want her life uprooted - she fights against
the power of this strange man.
(The door CHIMES outside again as Frank comes back.)

                    GWEN
          I've given Frank my promise!

Dejectedly, Larry picks up his cane, ready to leave.
He feels there is nothing more he can do.
Frank re-enters the scene (without the dog). With an
effort at good sportsmanship, Larry stretches out his hand
to Frank.

                    LARRY
          Glad to meet you, Mr. Andrews.
          Gwen has told me about you -

But Frank disregards Larry's hand.

                    FRANK
                  (coldly)
          I'm glad she did!

There is an uncomfortable silence for a moment.

                    LARRY
          I just came for a second to
          see if Gwen was all right.
          Well, I'll be going -

Frank is silent. Gwen, watching the two men with growing
distress, steps forward.

                    GWEN
                  (kindlily)
          Wait, Larry -

Larry pauses, looks at her, then at Frank's antagonistic
expression.

                                        CONTINUED

                          LARRY
                       (awkwardly)
                  I've got to go - back to
                  my telescope... Sir John
                  is waiting -

                          GWEN
                       (unhappily)
                  I'll see you again, I hope?

                          LARRY
                       (makes up
                        his mind)
                  I - don't think so...
                  Goodbye. Good luck -
                  to both of you!

He turns to go.

112   INT. - CONLIFFE LIVING ROOM - WIDER ANGLE - CAMERA
        NEAR GWEN AND FRANK

Larry walks out of the room without looking back.
Gwen and Frank are silent for a moment.
(The door bell, out of scene, faintly CHIMES as Larry
leaves the shop, and the dog outside begins to BARK
again.

                          FRANK
                       (gruffly)
                  Humph. Your American has
                  more sense than I thought.

                          GWEN
                  Why were you so rude?
                  What has he done to you?

                          FRANK
                  What's happened to you since
                  he arrived? I don't know
                  what to think!

Gwen steps closer to him.

113   INT. - CONLIFFE SHO LIVING ROOM - CLOSE - TWO SHOT

                          GWEN
                       (quietly)
                  There's only one thing for you
                  to think. If you love me, you'll
                  protect me - in spite of what
                  everyone thinks!

                                              CONTINUED

                    FRANK
                 (sincerely)
          I'm sorry, Gwen. Forgive me.
          You're right - I should have
          realized -

He takes her hand. Gwen looks him in the eye.

                    GWEN
          Promise me never to be
          jealous again!

                    FRANK
          But what can I do? Whenever
          another man talks to you -
          I can't bear it!

                    GWEN
                 (beginning
                  to smile)
          Well - now that the women
          won't talk to me, and you
          don't want me to talk to men -
          what's left?

                    FRANK
                 (taking her
                  in his arms)
          This - !

As he starts to embrace her,

                                        DISSOLVE TO:

114   EXT. - THE CHURCH - <u>DAY</u> - LONG SHOT

      At the end of the main street where Conliffe's shop is
      situated, stands a very old church, built of square-
      cut rock, and with a compact tower.
      The church yard, at the rear, is surrounded by a low
      wall, overgrown with ivy. A second entrance leads along
      the inner church wall to a small building - a crypt
      where the corpses are laid out before burial. A pergola
      connects the crypt with the back entrance to the church.

                                        DISSOLVE TO:

115   EXT. - CHURCH - <u>DAY</u> - MED. LONG - LARRY

        It is high noon when Larry passes the church entrance
        as described in previous scene. The square is de-
        serted - the church door open.

116   EXT. - CHURCH - MED. CLOSE - LARRY AND GRAVE-DIGGERS

        A carriage with two men on the driver's seat rattles
        past Larry and stops at the door leading to the church
        yard.
        Larry pauses, as he sees a coffin, covered with a sheet,
        lying on the carriage.
        The two men, dressed in shabby black coats, step down
        from the seat, take a wooden support to set it up inside
        the crypt for the coffin to rest on, and disappear in-
        side the church yard.

        CAMERA DOLLIES:

117   EXT. - CHURCH - CLOSER - LARRY

        Larry steps closer and stops in front of the coffin.
        He looks around guiltily, to make sure he is unobserved.
        Driven by a morbid curiosity, he lifts the sheet.
        Larry sees that the lid of the coffin has a square hole
        just above the dead man's face.

118   EXT. - CHURCH - CLOSE ON COFFIN - FROM LARRY'S ANGLE

        It is Bela lying in the coffin, looking just as Larry
        had seen him last, with the exception of a bandage now
        wrapped around his head like a turban. The dead man's
        eyes are open; he seems to be looking at Larry with a
        malevolent grin, as if he were not dead at all. The
        pentagram on his forehead stands out like a dark imprint.

        Larry quickly drops the linen and steps back.

119   EXT. - CHURCH - MED. CLOSE - LARRY AND GRAVEDIGGERS

        The undertakers return. Larry watches them and the
        coffin, hypnotized. One man takes the sheet off the
        coffin and folds it. Then both lift the coffin on their
        shoulders and walk inside the church yard.

120   EXT. - CHURCH - <u>DAY</u> - MED. CLOSE - LARRY'S ANGLE

Larry looks after the grave-diggers, profoundly disturbed at having seen this man he is supposed to
have killed. He follows them slowly.

121   EXT. - CHURCH - TRUCK SHOT - CAMERA IN COFFIN

The impression will be given that Bela is alive - but
unable to move. From his point of view, we are looking through the hole of the coffin, as it is borne
along on the shoulders of the undertakers. Above,
are the swaying tops of the trees in the church yard.
On the right is the stone wall of the church building
- and now, bent in an angle towards Bela, the big tower
passes by. Its BELLS CHIME OUT a simple Elizabethan
melody.
The coffin travels on. It enters the crypt. The box
is lowered and the men, seen for a moment from Bela's
point of view, towering and distorted. disappear.

122   EXT. - CHURCH - THE CRYPT ENTRANCE - FULL SHOT

Larry approaches and watches the men, who deposit the
coffin and come out of the crypt again, passing Larry
and throwing him dark suspicious looks. They then
hurry away, without looking back again. Larry looks
after them a moment, then enters the crypt.
(THE CHIMES are still playing from the church tower.)

123   INT. - INSIDE THE CRYPT - FULL SHOT - LARRY

It is a cool half-dark chamber with stained-glass
windows. Bela's coffin stands in the middle, on the
wooden stand which the men brought in previously.
Slowly Larry enters the shot and moves toward the
coffin. (CHURCH CHIMES)

124   INT. - CRYPT - CLOSE TWO SHOT - LARRY AND BELA

Larry bends over Bela's coffin. (THE CHIMES ARE STILL
PLAYING - THEN CEASE - AND THE BELL BEGINS TO TOLL
THE MID-DAY HOUR.)
Bela seems to stare at Larry with a fiendish smile.

CAMERA PULLS BACK:

125   INT. - CRYPT - MED. CLOSE - LARRY

        Larry looks frightened and he steps backward, his eyes
        on the coffin. Suddenly he listens - VOICES AND STEPS
        COME CLOSER.

126   INT. - CRYPT - WIDER ANGLE - CAMERA NEAR COFFIN -
        LARRY, MALEVA AND REVEREND NORMAN

        Larry steps behind a stone pillar. Through the door
        leading from the pergola, Maleva, the gypsy woman, and
        THE REVEREND NORMAN enter.
        Rev. Norman, white-haired and distinguished-looking, is
        dressed in his surplice. He is talking to Maleva, who
        carries a bag and a bunch of white flowers (wolfbane).
        They walk towards the coffin. Just before they reach
        it, they stop.

                          REV. NORMAN
                But my dear woman, we can't
                bury this man like a heathen
                - without a prayer!

                          MALEVA
                There's nothing to pray for, sir.
                Bela has entered a much better
                world than this...
                          (then, slyly)
                At least, so you ministers always
                say, sir!

                          REV. NORMAN
                          (slightly
                          irritated)
                And so it is... But that's no
                reason to hold a pagan celebration!
                I hear your people are coming to
                town, dancing and singing and
                making merry! It's a shocking
                disrespect to the dead!

                          MALEVA
                          (seriously)
                For a thousand years we have
                buried our dead like that, sir.
                I couldn't break the custom,
                even if I wanted to!

        Norman sees there is nothing to do but give in.

                                              CONTINUED

> NORMAN
> (with a sigh)
> Fighting against superstition
> is as hard as fighting against
> Satan himself!

He shakes his head and walks out. Maleva turns to
the coffin.

127   INT. - CRYPT - FROM LARRY'S ANGLE - MALEVA

at the coffin. Putting the white flowers on the wooden
cover, she takes two candles from her bag, fixes them
above Bela's head, and lights them with a taper.

128   INT. - CRYPT - CLOSE ON MALEVA - CAMERA IN COFFIN

Maleva's face is seen from below, lighted by the
candles. She mumbles in a low voice:

> MALEVA
> The way you walked was thorny
> - through no fault of your own.
> But as the rain enters the soil,
> the river enters the sea, - so
> tears run to a predestined end.
> Your suffering is over, Bela,
> my son. Now you will find peace...

129   INT. - CRYPT - CLOSE TWO SHOT - MALEVA AND BELA (SUPERIMPOSE)

Maleva takes one of the white flowers from the bunch
and touches Bela's mouth... It relaxes, the grin disappears... She touches his eyes... they close... She
touches the pentagram on his forehead... and the design FADES AWAY, leaving the skin smooth and without
a trace of its former mutilation.
Bela lies there, a happy smile on his face, as if he
had found peace at last.

130   INT. - CRYPT - MED. CLOSE - FROM LARRY'S ANGLE

Maleva bows toward the coffin and starts to go.
CAMERA FOLLOWS HER until she has left the crypt.

131   INT. - CRYPT - CAMERA BEHIND BELA'S COFFIN - LARRY

Larry steps from behind his hiding place and approaches
the coffin. He looks with astonishment at the change
in the dead gypsy's face.

132   INT. - CRYPT - CLOSE-UP - BELA

His face at peace.

OVER THE CHIMES BEGIN TO PLAY AGAIN, a majestic hymn
("Come Again, Sweet Love".)

Then - THE CHIMES CHANGE INTO WILD GYPSY MUSIC, as we

                                        DISSOLVE TO

133   EXT. - THE SQUARE IN FRONT OF THE CHURCH - DAY - LONG

The square and the market street - as seen from the
church. The gypsies have put up their tents around
the square and along the market street. A gay crowd
flows through.

GYPSY MUSIC IS HEARD.

134   EXT. - MARKET SQUARE - CAMERA BEHIND THE ORCHESTRA

The orchestra consists of violins and a cymbal. The
"primas" (First Violin) plays a wild gypsy dance.
In front of the orchestra, a girl is dancing on a rug,
accompanying her graceful movements with a tamborine.
A crowd is gathered around, watching her.

135   EXT. - MARKET SQUARE - ANOTHER ANGLE - MED. CLOSE

Frank and Gwen are part of the crowd. Frank is neatly
dressed in a dark suit, and Gwen is pretty in a simple
white frock. They watch the gypsy dancer.

136   EXT. - MARKET SQUARE - EDGE OF CROWD - MED. CLOSE

Behind Gwen and Frank, at the edge of the crowd, stands
Larry, looking toward Gwen. Taller than the townspeople, he can see her plainly. They haven't seen him
and he doesn't want them to. He doesn't intend to come
between Gwen and her fiance any more - but he's glad
he can look at her loveliness once more, unobserved.

137   EXT. - MARKET SQUARE - NEAR THE ORCHESTRA - MED. CLOSE

The gypsy girl finishes her dance - the MUSIC STOPS -
THEN BEGINS AGAIN QUICKLY. The crowd rains coins on
the rug, which the girl picks up. Frank throws a coin,
too.

138   EXT. - MARKET SQUARE - MED. CLOSE - FRANK AND GWEN

He looks at her happily and says:

                    FRANK
          Now aren't you glad I
          brought you?

                    GWEN
          I should have stayed home.
          People will say it's too
          soon after Jenny's...

He takes Gwen's arm, as the crowd moves on. CAMERA PANS
with them.

                    FRANK
          Oh, no, they won't. I saw
          old Mrs. Williams at the
          pub today. Just let her
          open her mouth about you!

The crowd is pushing them; Gwen has to hold on to Frank.

                    GWEN
          What a crowd!

Frank suddenly stops and looks in the direction of a
shooting gallery.

139   EXT. - MARKET SQUARE - SHOOTING GALLERY - FRANK'S ANGLE

Larry's head and shoulders can be seen moving in the crowd.

140   EXT. - MARKET SQUARE - BACK TO GWEN AND FRANK - Med. CLOSE

                    FRANK
          There's your American...

                                        CONTINUED

140   CONTINUED

Gwen looks in the direction Frank indicates but she is
too small to see Larry.

                         GWEN
            Where?

                         FRANK
            Over there...

Frank steps behind the girl and lifts her up. Eagerly
Gwen looks at Larry out of scene.

141   EXT. - MARKET SQUARE - LARRY - CLOSE

H e turns and sees Gwen. He looks embarrassed.

142   EXT. - MARKET SQUARE - BACK TO GWEN AND FRANK

Gwen catches Larry's expression ~~looki~~ (O.S.) She
blushes and says to Frank:

                         GWEN
            Let me down.

Frank drops her gently. Then he says:

                         FRANK
            Let's call him...

Gwen looks at him, surprised.

                         FRANK
            I'd just like to prove to you
            I'm not jealous any more...

Smiling, they push through the crowd, Frank leading.

143   EXT. - MARKET SQUARE - NEAR SHOOTING GALLERY - MED. CLOSE

Larry walks along, when he hears a voice calling:

                         FRANK'S VOICE (O.S.)
            Mr. Gill!

Larry stops and turns, then sees Frank and Gwen coming
toward him.

                                              CONTINUED

                          LARRY
                     (embarrassed)
           Hello...

Frank and Gwen stop in front of him:

                         FRANK
                     (friendly)
          We saw you walking along by
          yourself... Why don't you
          join us?

Larry looks at him and Gwen. She smiles at him, happy
to see him again.

                         LARRY
                     (undecided)
          No, thanks... I - I was
          just going home...

He avoids meeting Gwen's eyes. But Frank, finding himself in the position of showing off to Gwen, pats
Larry's shoulder.

                         FRANK
          Now don't say 'no'...
          Come along... We'll have
          a good time together...

                         GWEN
          Yes, do, Larry.

Larry looks at her, uneasily. But Gwen, to settle the
issue, turns and calls out:

                         GWEN
          Look... A bear!

The men turn and look. Gwen pulls Frank out of scene,
Larry following.

144   EXT. - MARKET SQUARE - A GYPSY WITH A BEAR - MED. CLOSE

The gypsy holds the bear on a chain, fastened to the
animal's nose. The gypsy makes the bear stand up and
bow.

145   EXT. - MARKET SQUARE - THE CROWD - MED. CLOSE

watching the gypsy and the bear, amused, interested.

146   EXT. - MARKET SQUARE - GYPSY AND BEAR - MED. CLOSE

After putting the bear through some little tricks,
the gypsy turns toward the crowd and announces a
contest:

>   GYPSY
>   Who will dare to wrestle
>   with the bear? A florin
>   reward for anyone who can
>   throw him!

147   EXT. - SQUARE - THE CROWD, THE GYPSY AND BEAR - FULL

The crowd is suprised and thrilled at the thought of
wrestling with the bear; but nobody stirs to take up
the challenge.
Larry, Gwen and Frank enter the scene.
The gypsy is making the bear throw kisses to the public,
while the gypsy shouts:

>   GYPSY
>   Such a gentle animal --
>   nothing to be afraid of!
>   A florin to any man, young
>   or old, weak or strong, who
>   can throw the bear!

148   EXT. - SQUARE - ANOTHER ANGLE - SHOWING LARRY, GWEN
         & FRANK IN F.G., GYPSY AND BEAR AT EDGE OF CROWD IN B.G.

While the gypsy displays his bear to the interested
crowd, Larry forces himself to forget his fright over
the wolf and enter into the spirit of the festivities.
He turns to Frank and says:

>   LARRY
>   Show us what you can do
>   without your gun!

>   FRANK
>   Not very much, I'm afraid -
>   but what about you?

They look at each other in friendly rivalry. The
gypsy approaches Gwen and says:

CONTINUED

                        GYPSY
            I bet you a florin, lady,
            neither of your brave
            gentlemen will dare to
            fight the bear!

Gwen does not take him seriously - just smiles polite-
ly and shakes her head. But Larry looks at the bear.

149   EXT. - SQUARE - THE BEAR - CLOSE

The bear bows toward Larry.

150   EXT. - SQUARE - THE GROUP - SAME AS 148 - MED. CLOSE

Larry suddenly drops his stick, and jerks off his coat
- but before it can fall to the ground, Frank catches it.
Larry steps forward, a wild expression in his eyes.

                        LARRY
            I'll take that bet!

Frank and Gwen are surprised.

151   EXT. - SQUARE - FULL SHOT - GYPSY AND BEAR IN F.G.
        WITH LARRY, GWEN AND FRANK -- CROWD IN B.G.

The crowd, surprised, thrilled, makes way for our three
main characters as they push toward the cleared center.
Gwen tries to dissuade Larry from fighting the bear,
but he disregards her. Frank looks amused. The gypsy
is pleased to have found a challenger. He says:

                        GYPSY
            Ha! A brave man steps forth
            to match his strength and
            skill with the wrestling bear!

The crowd murmurs excitedly. Frank, holding Larry's
coat, and Gwen, watch as Larry steps into the cleared
circle with the gypsy and the bear. Gwen suddenly
calls out:

                                        CONTINUED

                              GWEN
                 Larry - don't! You'll
                 get hurt!

Frank looks at her, jealous again, but she does not
notice. Larry has not heard her. The gypsy silences
the crowd and speaks:

                              GYPSY
                 Now - all who love good sport -
                 throw out a bit of silver
                 to buy the bear some honey..!

                                        CUT TO:

152   EXT. - SQUARE - CLOSE ON FRANK AND GWEN

Frank is concerned because Gwen looks so anxious about
Larry's safety.
OVER COMES THE MURMUR OF THE CROWD AND THE GYPSY
wheedling coins out of them.

                         GYPSY'S VOICE (O.S.)
                 Money for honey,
                 money for honey,
                 just a little money
                 will buy the bear some honey!

                                        CUT TO:

153   EXT. - SQUARE - CLOSE ON LARRY

looking at the bear. He looks strange, tense, as if
he were beginning to go into a trance.

OVER COMES THE NOISE OF THE CROWD AND THE GYPSY.

                                        CUT TO:

154   EXT. - SQUARE - GYPSY AND EDGE OF CROWD - MED. CLOSE

Coins being tossed toward the gypsy from the spectators.
He picks up a few with a broad smile. The crowd is
roaring for action.

                                        CONTINUED

> CROWD
> (ad lib)
> Let him earn his honey...!
> Never mind the money -
> let's get on with the fight!
> Ten to one on the bear!
> (Etc., etc.)

The gypsy hurries toward Larry and the bear.

155   EXT. - SQUARE - LARRY, THE GYPSY AND BEAR IN F.G. --
CROWD IN B.G. - GWEN AND FRANK IN FRONT OF CROWD

The trained animal turns and looks at Larry, then
suddenly withdraws backwards, slowly, as if in fear.
The gypsy, amazed, tries to prod the bear forward
toward Larry, who steps up to it, fists clenched like
a boxer.

> LARRY
> (beginning to
> look cruel)
> Come on, you brown beggar!

He dances lightly around the bear, taunting it. The
crowd murmurs in surprise and disappointment at the
unwilling bear. Gwen and Frank exchange looks.

> CUT TO:

156   EXT. - SQUARE - CLOSE ON GWEN AND FRANK

Frank says scornfully:

> FRANK
> Why, the bear's so old,
> there's no life left in him!

But Gwen isn't so sure... She shakes her head doubt-
fully.

> CUT BACK TO:

157

EXT. - SQUARE - BACK TO LARRY AND CROWD

The crowd is murmuring angrily as the bear continues
to disappoint them by trying to draw back from Larry
who continues to tease it. The gypsy, embarrassed,
gets hold of the chain and yanks the bear forcibly
toward Larry. And the animal, reluctantly following
the chain which hurts his nose, suddenly stands on his
hind legs and in desperation tries to grab hold of Larry.
Larry quickly side-steps and hits the bear - who finds
himself embracing the empty air.

158   EXT. - SQUARE - FLASH - THE CROWD

as it howls in delight. Gwen grabs Frank's arm in
tension and fear.

159   EXT. - SQUARE - BACK TO LARRY AND BEAR

The bear, furious now, turns and tries to attack Larry
who, side-stepping again, hits him hard on the head.
The bear turns away for a moment, hurt.

160   EXT. - SQUARE - CLOSE - LARRY'S FACE

His expression becomes ferocious, his teeth bared in a
cruel grin, his eyes wild with the lust to kill. He
looks more like an animal than a man.

161   EXT. - SQUARE - BACK TO LARRY AND BEAR - MED. CLOSE

Larry rushes at the bear in a furious attack, hitting
him, stepping back light-footedly, then charging in
again. The bear, too plump to move fast, and seeming
to be strangely frightened too, tries to defend himself,
clumsily, growlingly...

It is a one-sided battle, and the crowd senses there's
something unnatural about it. The people are quiet,
tense...

The bear is never able to reach Larry, who, always faster
and more elusive, hits the animal with powerful blows...
The helpless beast finally stops defending himself -
and a last walloping blow topples him over. Larry rushes
in to hit him again.

(Inter-cut above scene with close shots of Larry, the
bear, the crowd, Gwen and Frank, and the gypsy, who is
afraid for his animal.)

162   EXT. - SQUARE - CLOSE TWO SHOT - GWEN AND FRANK
IN FRONT OF CROWD

Frank watches Gwen, who is biting her fist to keep
from crying out in her excitement and strain. She
is appalled at the way Larry looks and acts - but she
never takes her eyes off him. Frank's face shows his
jealousy and bitterness.
Gwen suddenly can't stand the strain any longer. She
cries out:

GWEN

Larry...!

163   EXT. - SQUARE - MED. CLOSE - GWEN, FRANK & THE CROWD

Before Frank can hold her back, Gwen dashes forward,
while the crowd howls with excitement.

164   EXT. - SQUARE - MED. CLOSE - THE BEAR AND LARRY & GWEN

The bear is sitting helplessly on the ground, and Larry
is bending over him, looking as if he's ready to finish
him off -- but Gwen rushes in between Larry and the
animal, to stop the fight.

165   EXT. - SQUARE - CLOSE - LARRY AND GWEN

His fists ready to strike out, Larry stares at Gwen,
glassy-eyed, as if about to hit her, too.

GWEN
(in despair)
Larry!

He stops, petrified.

166   EXT. - SQUARE - FULL SHOT - CROWD IN B.G.

The crowd, scared now, is suddenly silent. Larry,
seeming to come back to himself, drops his arms, and
suddenly pale and weak, whispers:

LARRY
I'm sorry...

CONTINUED

166   CONTINUED

The gypsy rushes in to take the bear away, while Larry
turns, walking back with Gwen to Frank. The crowd
silently steps back and slowly disperses, as if in
fright.

167   EXT. - SQUARE - MED. CLOSE - LARRY, GWEN AND FRANK

Larry and Gwen reach Frank. Gwen takes Larry's coat
and picks up his stick, which he had dropped. Larry
tries to recover his self-possession. He says apologetically, ashamed:

                    LARRY
                (slightly dazed)
            I don't know what came over me.
            I hope I didn't hurt that poor
            thing!

and, with a wan smile to Gwen:

                    LARRY (cont'd.)
            You saved his life...

Gwen looks at him, puzzled. But Frank does not see
anything unnatural in Larry's behavior. In a sudden
fit of envy and jealousy, Frank says:

                    FRANK
                (sarcastically)
            I don't think he was in that
            much danger, old man!

and to Gwen:

                    FRANK (cont'd.)
            Fun's over, Gwen...
            Let's go.

But Larry looks only at Gwen and says softly:

                    LARRY
                (to Gwen)
            Thank you...

Before Gwen can answer, Frank takes her arm and pulls
her around.

                                        CONTINUED

167   CONTINUED

                         FRANK
                        (rudely)
           Come on...

                         GWEN
                        (submissively,
                         her thoughts
                         far away)
           Yes, Frank...

Then, realizing the situation, she nods sadly to Larry
and walks off with Frank.

168   EXT. - SQUARE - CLOSE - LARRY

He looks after Gwen and Frank, sadly, wearily. He
passes his hand over his forehead, upset by all the
turmoil of the day's emotions.
Then, taking a firm hold on his walking-stick, he
starts off in the opposite direction to that taken by
Gwen and Frank.

                                        CUT TO:

169   EXT. - SQUARE - TRAVELING SHOT - GWEN AND FRANK & CROWD

They are walking through the crowd. They are having a
lovers' quarrel and look very unhappy.

                         GWEN
           But you were the one who
           invited him...

                         FRANK
           So I was. But that's no reason
           why you should run after him
           and make a spectacle of yourself!

Gwen looks at him resentfully.

                         GWEN
           You needn't have been so rude.

                         FRANK
           To him? He wouldn't know the
           difference. Did you see him
           when he was fighting that bear?
           He looked like a wild animal!

                                        CONTINUED

> GWEN
> (appalled)
> An animal...

> FRANK
> (furiously)
> Yes! - His eyes - his mouth -
> the way he jumped when he
> attacked - it was uncanny!
> He looked like a - wolf!

As Gwen looks at him, we know that she does not for
a moment believe anything against Larry and resents
Frank talking this way.

                                    CUT TO:

170   EXT. - SQUARE - NEAR ROW OF TENTS - DAY - MED. CLOSE

It is late afternoon. Larry walks along slowly, lost
in dark thoughts, when suddenly he hears a woman's voice:

> MALEVA'S VOICE (O.S.)
> You've been a long while
> coming...

He wheels around and sees:

171   EXT. - SQUARE - CLOSE - MALEVA AT DOOR OF HER TENT

The old gypsy woman is looking toward Larry (O.S.)
with a somber expression. She continues:

> MALEVA
> I expected you sooner...
> Come in...

She motions him to enter the tent.

172   EXT. - TENT - LARRY AND MALEVA

He looks at her, surprised and annoyed. Wearily, he
answers:

> LARRY
> I'm not buying anything...

                                    CONTINUED

He turns to go on. Maleva says nothing but just stares
at him compellingly. Larry turns back, suddenly recog-
nizing her.

>   LARRY
>   I've seen you before -
>   that night - and in the crypt --

Maleva nods solemnly. Again she motions him inside the
tent. Larry enters apprehensively.

173   INT. - MALEVA'S TENT - MED. CLOSE - <u>DUSK</u>

An oil lamp throws a flickering light on a small table,
on which silversmith tools are spread out, parts of a
chain on which Maleva has worked, and some half-finished
jewelry. On another table are finished pieces of silver
- hand-made rings, bracelets, charms, trinkets...

Larry enters, followed by Maleva. He looks around uneasily, then looks at her. She seats herself behind the
table with the silversmith tools.

174   INT. - MALEVA'S TENT - CLOSE - MALEVA AND LARRY

Her wrinkled face is sad and quiet, but her eyes burn
with strange knowledge. She leans toward Larry and says
in an awful whisper:

>   MALEVA
>   You killed the wolf...!

>   LARRY
>   (defensively)
>   Well? That's no crime, is it?

He turns away impatiently - but Maleva stops him with:

>   MALEVA
>   The wolf - was - Bela!

Larry stops dead. The woman looks at him silently.
He turns back toward her. Troubled and upset, he says
with a half-derisive laugh:

>   LARRY
>   D'ya think I can't tell the
>   difference between a wolf
>   and a man?

174   CONTINUED

But Maleva disregards his outburst, and goes on, like
one reciting a chant:

                    MALEVA
          Bela became a wolf - and you
          killed him... A werewolf can
          be killed only with a silver
          bullet, or a silver knife, or --

She points to the stick Larry is holding.

                    MALEVA (Cont'd.)
          -- a stick with a silver handle!

Larry looks down at his stick, as if it were a snake.
Horrified, he wonders if it's possible that this stick
had actually killed a man... a man who could assume
the shape of a wolf... Then he suddenly bursts out:

                    LARRY
          You're insane! What I hit was
          a wolf - a plain ordinary wolf!

Maleva pays no attention to his words. She turns to
the table and picks up a chain with a dangling silver
coin.

                    MALEVA
          Take this chain...

She hands it to Larry. He looks at it.

175   INT. - MALEVA'S TENT - CLOSE - THE CHAIN IN LARRY'S
       HAND

On the chain hangs a round silver coin, engraved with
a pentagram. In the middle of the five-pointed star,
a flower is engraved - the wolfbane.

                    MALEVA'S VOICE
          The pentagram!
          The sign of the wolf!

176   INT. - TENT - LARRY AND MALEVA - MED. CLOSE

Larry stares at the chain, as Maleva continues:

                                        CONTINUED

                     MALEVA
       The flower - the wolfbane -
       can break the evil spell...

Larry flings away in a rage:

                     LARRY
       'Evil spell'! 'Pentagram!'
       'Wolfbane'! I've had enough
       of this rot - I'm getting out
       of here!!

But Maleva goes on implacably:

                     MALEVA
             (chanting
              fearfully)
       Whoever is bitten by a
       werewolf - and lives -
       becomes a werewolf himself!

Larry drops his hands, stunned, shaken in spite of
himself. He laughs almost hysterically:

                     LARRY
       Quit handing me that!
       You're wasting your time!

But he is trembling. Maleva continues to stare at him
with hypnotic dread.

                     MALEVA
       The wolf bit you, didn't he?

She comes close to him, her gaze holding his.

                     LARRY
             (nodding
              slowly)
       Yeah - yeah, he did...

The old woman steps still closer.

                     MALEVA
       Wear the chain over your
       heart - always...

Larry decides to accept the chain. In order not to
give the impression that he is afraid, he pretends to
like the chain.

                                      CONTINUED

                          LARRY
                    All right, all right...
                    It's not bad-looking...
                    How much do you want for it?

Maleva shrugs.

                          LARRY (cont'd.)
                    I'll give you a couple of
                    shillings for it...
                              (tossing some
                              money on the
                              table)

Maleva pays no attention to the money.

                          MALEVA
                    Do you dare to show me the
                    wound?

Under the spell of her hypnotic glance, he opens his
shirt. Maleva looks at his chest, and gasps.

177   INT. - MALEVA'S TENT - CLOSE - LARRY'S CHEST

Larry looks down at Maleva, as she stares at his chest
with terrified expression. He looks at his chest.
Clearly we see a mark over his heart - a pentagram -
where the faint scar had been before. It is like an
imprint. He stares at it - then at Maleva, who stares
back at him and says, in a voice of doom:

                          MALEVA
                    Go - now - and God help you!

Larry wants to deny the implications of this but feels
it's useless. He turns to go, feeling that if he stays
another moment, his nerves will break...

178   INT. - MALEVA'S TENT - MED. CLOSE

Larry turns and runs out of the tent. Maleva stands
for a moment, motionless. Then she picks up a shawl,
throws it around her shoulders, and leaves.

179   EXT. - MALEVA'S TENT AND MARKET STREET - <u>NIGHT</u>

THE MUSIC IS STILL HEARD (as it has been continuously
since the beginning of the gypsy fair sequence, playing various gypsy tunes, gay and somber, loud and soft...)

Maleva leaves her tent. It is dark by now, and the
passage between the tents is lighted by oil lamps.

CAMERA FOLLOWS Maleva, as she hurries to a neighboring
tent in front of which a big gypsy stands beside his
pile of hand-made rugs. Maleva talks to him in a
language we don't understand. He steps back in alarm,
and Maleva hastens away. The gypsy at once takes his
rugs inside the tent, preparing to depart.

CUT TO:

180   **EXT.** - ANOTHER TENT - MED. CLOSE - <u>NIGHT</u>

Maleva is talking now to a gypsy woman, who is sitting
in front of her tent. She is a fortune-teller. As
soon as she has heard Maleva's warning (about Larry
being a werewolf), she too jumps up and takes her chair
inside the tent.

CUT TO:

181   EXT. - NEAR TENTS - MED. CLOSE - LARRY - <u>NIGHT</u>

Larry walks along, quickly, on his way home. His head
is down, his hand clutching the pentagram over his heart.

He almost stumbles over a bench. A white figure jumps
up from the bench. It is Gwen. She looks as if she
had been having a good quiet cry.

182   EXT. - NEAR TENTS - CLOSE TWO SHOT - LARRY AND GWEN - <u>NIGHT</u>

Larry is suddenly flooded with relief and happiness at
this chance to be alone with Gwen - and she seems glad
of this unexpected meeting also.

                         LARRY
               Gwen: Gee, it's good to
               see you...

                                   CONTINUED

182   CONTINUED

                              GWEN
              Larry...

                              LARRY
              I thought Frank took you home...

                              GWEN
                          (embarrassed)
              We - had - an argument...
              I ran away from him.

       Larry frowns. He senses he has been the cause of dis-
       sention between Gwen and Frank. He has promised not
       to come between them - he has said he was going away
       and would not see her any more. Yet Fate continues to
       throw them together. Well, he must just see that she
       gets home safely now, and try to forget her.

                              LARRY
                          (softly)
              I'll see you home...

       He offers her his arm and Gwen takes it happily.

183   EXT. - NEAR TENTS - LARRY AND GWEN - MED. CLOSE - <u>NIGHT</u>

       They begin to walk in the direction leading to Conliffe's
       shop.
       CAMERA DOLLIES: Larry and Gwen walk along the crowded
       square. Groups of people elbow past them. Pushed this
       way and that, they stop between two tents, behind which
       a horse and carriage are standing.

                              LARRY
              Let's go through here before
              they stampede us.

       CAMERA PANS: Larry steps between the tents, taking her
       with him. Gwen suddenly sees the charm he is still
       holding in his hand.

                              GWEN
              What's that...?

                              OTHER
184   EXT. - NEAR/TENTS - LARRY AND GWEN - MED. CLOSE - <u>NIGHT</u>

       Larry and Gwen stop. The tent hides them from the crowd.
       THE MUSIC IS HEARD FROM AFAR, and the noise of the throng
       pushing its way through the market street. An oil lamp
       stands on the carriage and lights their faces.

                                                  CONTINUED

Larry opens his hand, displaying the chain.

> LARRY
> (with forced
> casualness)
> Oh - just a charm... I met
> that old gypsy dame again...
> They sure hand you a sales-talk!

He laughs hollowly.

> GWEN
> (eagerly)
> Let me see...

She takes it in her hands and holds it close to the
oil lamp.

185   EXT. - TENTS - LARRY AND GWEN - CLOSE - <u>NIGHT</u>

As Gwen looks at the charm, Larry says in a mock-
solemn voice:

> LARRY
> 'The pentagram... the sign
> of the wolf....'!

> GWEN
> (her express-
> ion serious)
> - And the wolfbane...

She stares at him in uncomfortable surprise, and hands
the charm back to him.

> LARRY
> Yes... and she told me I was
> a werewolf, too!
> (he laughs derisively,
> but not quite convincingly)

> GWEN
> (with slight
> apprehension)
> But surely - you don't believe - ?

Larry doesn't answer for a moment. A cloud passes over
his face as he remembers the strange inexplicable things
that have happened to him lately... But as he looks into
her limpid eyes, the shadow passes... He thinks only how
lovely she is and he answers:

CONTINUED

<pre>
                        LARRY
                   (with a shy
                    smile)
               Could a werewolf fall in love
               with a beautiful girl?

                        GWEN
                   (laughing)
               I don't know...

                        LARRY
                   (tenderly)
               I know...

He holds out the charm to her.

                        LARRY (Cont'ing)
               I won't need this now.
               Take it, Gwen. It will
               protect you ---

                        GWEN
                   (flirtatiously)
               Protect me? From what...?

She looks up at him and he answers, half-playful,
half-serious:

                        LARRY
               From me.

He puts the chain around her neck, carefully, so as
not to touch her or offend her, and withdraws his hands
at once. Gwen looks at him gratefully, then at the chain.

                        GWEN
               In Wales, we never accept
               a present without giving
               something in return...

She opens her small handbag and searches among its
dainty contents.

                        GWEN
               Here's a penny...

She wants to hand him the coin but Larry shakes his head.

                        LARRY
               It's worth more than that...
</pre>

CONTINUED

THE MUSIC STOPS SUDDENLY. SHOUTS AND THE SHUFFLING
OF HUNDREDS OF FEET ARE HEARD. But Gwen and Larry
pay no attention. They are looking deep into each
other's eyes. He bends down, wanting to kiss her.
Quickly, shyly, she reaches up and gives him a peck
on the cheek. With a soft laugh to hide her emotion,
she steps back. Larry is disappointed by this unsatis-
factory counterfeit of a kiss.

                    LARRY
          I should have taken the penny!

                    GWEN
          You drive a hard bargain for
          your present...

Larry suddenly sweeps her into his arms and kisses her
full on the mouth. She resists at first, then returns
his embrace, forgetting self-control, forgetting that
she is engaged to Frank...

Suddenly the tent behind them collapses - and they break
apart in shock and alarm.

186   EXT. - TENT - LARRY AND GWEN - MED. CLOSE - NIGHT

The tent collapses - Larry and Gwen look around in alarm.
Three gypsies are folding the tent, hurrying to get away.
Larry and Gwen look out of scene.

187   EXT. - MARKET SQUARE - FROM LARRY'S ANGLE - WIDE - NIGHT

The market square can be seen, looking like a beehive,
with gypsies all folding their tents, harnessing horses
to their carriages, while a crowd of townspeople stare,
surprised at the sudden preparations for flight. Why
are the gypsies hurrying away all of a sudden?

188   EXT. - BACK TO LARRY AND GWEN - MED. CLOSE - NIGHT

Larry looks at Gwen and starts to speak:

                    LARRY
          Everyone's pulling out...

But Gwen has suddenly realized what she has done - and
she is ashamed to look at him or stay with him. She
turns and says hurriedly, anxiously:

                                        CONTINUED

188   CONTINUED

                         GWEN
          I must go too... Goodnight!

She runs off. Larry calls after her:

                         LARRY
              Gwen! Wait!

But the girl has disappeared. Larry runs after her.

189   EXT. - ANOTHER SPOT IN MARKET SQUARE - MED. CLOSE -
       NIGHT

       Larry comes running in -- he can't find Gwen. A gypsy
       approaches, leading his horse and carriage. Larry asks:

                         LARRY
              What's the rush?
              Where's the fire?

                              GYPSY (might be the bear-trainer)
              There's a werewolf in town!

       The gypsy's face is distorted with fear. Hurriedly
       he pulls his horse out of scene.
       Larry stares after him, terrified...

                                        FADE OUT

       FADE IN

190   EXT. - MARKET STREET - LONG SHOT - NIGHT (JUST BEFORE DAWN)

       The street is deserted. A gust of wind blows papers and
       colored streamers into the air,- souvenirs of the gypsies'
       visit.

       SUDDENLY A LOW HOWL emerges, rises piercingly to a high
       pitch, then repeats again, shattering the quiet of the
       night. It is topped by a blood-curdling HUMAN CRY OF
       TERROR - which subsides at once.

       Silence - for a moment - as if the whole town holds its
       breath. THEN DOGS BEGIN TO BARK, HORSES NEIGH, in fear.
       And lights appear in the windows.

191   EXT. - OUTSIDE TWIDDLE'S HOUSE - MED. CLOSE - EARLY DAWN

It is a narrow-chested building, cramped between two
similar houses - Phillips' Tailor Shop and Mr. Wykes',
the baker's. Light appears in Phillips' show window.

Twiddle, the policeman, emerges from his house, hastily
buttoning his coat and donning his helmet.

PHILLIPS appears, opening the door of his shop.

WYKES looks out of his window. His wife, in her night-
gown, peeps behind his back, frightened.

                    PHILLIPS
          Did you hear that, Mr. Twiddle?

                    TWIDDLE
                 (curtly)
          Of course... or I'd still be
          snug and warm in my bed.

                    WYKES
                 (from his
                 window)
          It sounded like a wild
          animal to me...

                    PHILLIPS
          Maybe some beast the gypsies
          left behind...

                    MRS. WYKES
          It seemed to come from the
          church yard...

                    TWIDDLE
                 (resolutely)
          Let's go and see!

He takes a firm grip on his truncheon and starts to
hurry off, followed by Phillips.

                                        DISSOLVE TO:

192   EXT. - THE CHURCHYARD - SEEN FROM THE MAIN STREET -
        LONG SHOT - EARLY DAWN

The church towers over the small grave yard. It is
just before dawn, when the first pale hint of light
touches the night sky. All seems quiet in the town still
- except where a few lights (lamps) are grouped around
a grave.

                                        CONTINUED

192   CONTINUED

THE HUM OF A MOTOR CAR COMES CLOSER, stops, and a man,
(Dr. Lloyd) gets out, carrying a flashlight. He passes
the CAMERA and walks toward the other lights.

193   EXT. - GRAVE YARD - THE GROUP - MED. CLOSE - <u>EARLY DAWN</u>

Twiddle, the policeman, is holding a lamp which illuminates the black shadow of a gravestone thrown toward the
CAMERA.
A body is lying behind the tombstone, which only reveals
the body's heavy, muddy shoes. A shovel lies nearby.

Near the body stands Kendall, chief of police, and not
far from him, Cotton, his assistant, who, in his thin
coat, shivers in the chill of dawn.

Dr. Lloyd enters the scene.

                    DR. LLOYD
          Good morning, Mr. Kendall...

                    KENDALL
          It could be a better one,
          Doctor...

He points toward the hidden body. Lloyd steps closer.

194   EXT. - GRAVE YARD - ANOTHER ANGLE - THE GROUP

                    DR. LLOYD
                 (looking down
                  at the body)
          Isn't it Richardson, the
          grave-digger...?

                    KENDALL
          Yes. He was working last
          night... digging Jenny
          Williams' grave...

Lloyd moves his flashlight over the body (hidden by the
tombstone).

                    LLOYD
                 (surprised)
          Severed jugular!

                                        CONTINUED

                         KENDALL
            Isn't that the way Jenny died?

The men look at each other in consternation.

196   EXT. - GRAVEYARD - ANOTHER ANGLE - KENDALL FEATURED

         Kendall turns and plays the flashlight on the broken
         twigs of a rosebush.

                         KENDALL
            Look! Somebody - something -
            must have jumped through
            this rosebush...

He lowers the flashlight, and Lloyd looks at the circle
of light thrown on the ground by the flashlight.

197 -   EXT. - GRAVEYARD - THE CIRCLE OF LIGHT ON THE GROUND - CLOSE

         revealing animal tracks.

                         KENDALL'S VOICE (OVER)
               Wolf tracks!...

                                             DISSOLVE TO:

198   EXT. - THE MOOR - SHOOTING TOWARD TALBOT CASTLE - LONG -
         DAWN

         The sky is overcast; a heavy wind is blowing over the
         desolate moor. The dark castle can be seen in the B.G.

                                             DISSOLVE TO:

199   INT. - LARRY'S ROOM - THE WINDOW SILL - CLOSE - DAWN

         CAMERA PANS from the window sill to Larry's bed.

         The sill is littered with particles of earth, in the
         form of foot-tracks, and there are the same tracks on
         the rug covering the floor of the room.

                                             CONTINUED

199   CONTINUED

        CAMERA PANS, following the earthy tracks, until they
        end at the bed, where a broken twig of roses lies.

        CAMERA PANS UP - to Larry's feet. They are bare -
        and there are bits of earth on them.

        CAMERA PANS UP to show Larry, lying prone on his bed,
        his face deep in the pillow, his arms limp...

        PEOPLE ARE HEARD RUSHING BY THE DOOR (O.S.) - VOICES
        MURMUR indistinctly. THE WIND IS BANGING the window-
        shades.

        Larry turns and wakes up. He listens to the voices,
        sits up, and sees his bare feet. He stares at them,
        astonished,- then at his crumpled suit - and his dirty
        hands. He turns and looks into the mirror.

        CAMERA PANS BEHIND HIM, shooting into the mirror.

        Larry gets up - CAMERA MOVES INTO:

200   INT. - LARRY'S ROOM - CLOSE-UP - LARRY AT MIRROR

        A pale, dirty face stares at him, the hair disheveled,
        the eyes wild. From the corners of his mouth, a small
        trickle of dried blood has run toward his chin. Larry
        wipes his mouth with the back of his hand and stares
        at his hand with terror. He pushes his hair away from
        his eyes - and a few rose leaves fall into his hands.
        He looks at them, bewildered, and drops them to the
        ground. He turns, like a man in a dream. CAMERA PANS:

201   INT. - LARRY'S ROOM - MED. CLOSE

        The bed he has slept on has not been turned down. His
        shoes lie near the window, as if torn off in a hurry.
        The window is open and the curtains blowing inward.

        Larry comes to the edge of the bed, sees the twig of
        roses, bends down and picks it up, staring at it in-
        credulously. Then he moves to the window, throws the
        twig out, and closes the window.

        On the window sill, clearly marked, are the tracks of a
        wolf.

202   INT. - LARRY'S ROOM - CLOSE - THE TRACKS ON THE WINDOW-
       SILL

       CAMERA PULLS BACK:

203   INT. - LARRY'S ROOM - CLOSE - ON LARRY AT WINDOW

       Larry looks down at the wolf tracks on the window-sill,
       his face distorted with anguish and fear. Then he
       quickly begins to rub the tracks away with his hand.

                                        DISSOLVE TO:

204   INT. - LIBRARY - MED. CLOSE - LARRYXX SIR JOHN - EARLY
       MORNING

       Sir John, in his dressing-gown, is opening a gun-case.
       He takes out a rifle, breaks it open, puts in a cart-
       ridge. The DOOR IS HEARD TO OPEN. Sir John looks up.

                         SIR JOHN
                  Oh, good morning, Mr. Gill.
                  Did the commotion arouse you?

205   INT. - LIBRARY - LARRY & SIR JOHN - MED. CLOSE

       Larry enters the room, closing the door behind him.
       He has washed and changed his clothes, but his face still
       shows his awful bewilderment.

                         LARRY
                  I thought I heard a lot of
                  people running down the
                  corridor... Something wrong?

       He steps closer to Sir John, who puts down the gun.

                         SIR JOHN
                         (gravely)
                  Richardson was killed last night.
                  He was our grave-digger....The
                  tracks lead toward this house!

                         LARRY
                         (hoarsely)
                  Foot prints?

                                        CONTINUED

                              SIR JOHN
                    No... animal tracks...
                    a wolf's...

Larry leans his head back against the book-shelves to
steady himself a moment. Then he looks at Sir John,
his face a mask. Forcing himself to be matter-of-fact,
he says:

                              LARRY
                    But where could it have
                    come from - this wolf?

                              SIR JOHN
                    Inspector Kendall thinks it
                    might have escaped from a
                    circus - or a zoo -

Larry nods and asks, casually, to hide his emotions:

                              LARRY
                    Tell me, Sir John, do you think
                    there's any truth in that story
                    they tell around here... about
                    a man changing into a wolf?

He turns and looks at the books, as if he were interested in them. Sir John looks at him, surprised at this
question.

                              SIR JOHN
                    You mean - the werewolf?

Larry picks out a book at random but does not open it.

                              LARRY
                    Yeah - that's what they call it.

                              SIR JOHN
                           (with scientific
                            relish)
                    It's an old legend... you'll find
                    something like it in the folk-
                    lore of nearly every nation. The
                    scientific name for it is LYCANTHROPIA.
                    It's a variety of SCHIZOPHRENIA...

Larry puts back the book without having looked at it.

                                        CONTINUED

205   CONTINUED
                        LARRY
                That's Greek to me...

Sir John smiles and steps over to the bookshelves.

206   INT. LIBRARY - CLOSE - LARRY AND SIR JOHN

                        SIR JOHN
                It is Greek! But it's only a
                technical expression for some-
                thing very simple: the good and
                the evil in every man's soul.
                And the evil takes the shape of
                an animal...

Larry shakes his head, baffled, as he looks at his
big hands. He says:

                        LARRY
                There's nothing I can't figure
                out, if you give me wires and
                tubes and electric current...
                but when it comes to things you
                can't even touch...
                        (he shakes his head;
                        then anxiously)
                Do you believe in these yarns,
                Sir John?

Sir John considers a moment. He sees the young man's
bewilderment, and though rather surprised at it, he
tries to answer sympathetically:

                        SIR JOHN
                        (lightly)
                As an astronomer, I've learned
                to accept the improbable. How
                else could I approach the
                miracle of the Universe?

From afar, the CHURCH BELLS START RINGING.

Sir John's expression becomes more serious, as he says:

                        SIR JOHN
                Sunday... Time for church...
                Belief in God is a healthy
                counterbalance to all the
                conflicting doubts we poor
                scientists are prey to...
                Would you like to go with me?

                        LARRY
                        (softly)
                Yes, Sir John...

                                        DISSOLVE TO

207   EXT. - THE SQUARE BEFORE THE CHURCH - LONG SHOT

The CHIMES PLAY A HYMN. The church door is open and
the people cross the square and enter slowly.

At one side of the square, a horse-drawn carriage
stands, loaded with chicken coops. A dog wanders
about. At the church door, a few people are talking
together.

208   EXT. - THE CHURCH DOOR - MED. CLOSE - GROUP

Mrs. Williams, dressed in mourning; Miss Bally;
Phillips, the tailor; Wykes, the baker; and Twiddle,
the policeman, comprise one of the groups outside the
church. The townspeople are all upset about the
recent killings.

                    WYKES
                  (solemnly)
          Aye...Last night it caught
          up with Richardson...

                    PHILLIPS
                  (with veiled
                   satisfaction)
          Many's the grave he dug for
          others...now they're digging
          one for him...

                    MISS BALLY
                  (shuddering)
          I don't dare open my door any
          more, for fear of that beast...

                    MRS. WILLIAMS
                  (scornfully)
          'That beast'! Has anybody
          seen it? I don't believe it
          even exists!
                  (then
                   insinuatingly)
          It's very strange... There
          were no murders here before
          that American arrived! I
          wonder if...

                    TWIDDLE
                  (sternly)
          Hold your tongue, Mrs. Williams!
          That's slander!

CONTINUED

208   CONTINUED

                              MRS. WILLIAMS
                           (venomously)
               I know what I know! You didn't
               see him when he looked at me
               in Conliffe's shop...like a
               wild animal - with murder in
               his eyes!

                              PHILLIPS
               Shh...Here he comes...

The people turn.

                                             CUT TO

209   EXT. - THE CHURCH WALK - LONG SHOT - SIR JOHN AND LARRY -
        THE CAMERA TRAVELS IN FRONT OF THEM

        Larry's steps are faltering, his face pale from lack
        of sleep and his mental turmoil. Sir John walks be-
        side him, trying to make conversation, but getting
        little response, he casts a sidelong glance at Larry,
        beginning to feel concerned about the young man's
        state of mind.

        As they come closer, they pass the dog, which suddenly
        turns and runs away, yelping, its tail between its legs.

        Larry does not seem to be aware of the dog. When he
        and Sir John pass the car with the chickens, the fowl
        suddenly begin to cackle excitedly in fright, as if a
        fox had invaded their coops.

                                             CUT TO

210   EXT. - THE GROUP IN FRONT OF THE CHURCH DOOR - MED. CLOSE

        They are narrowly watching Larry approaching (o.s.)
        Miss Bally says breathlessly:

                              MISS BALLY
               Do you see...? The animals
               are afraid of him!

                                             CONTINUED

210   CONTINUED

Sir John and Larry appear in the SHOT, and the townspeople quickly turn and walk into the church.

At the door, Larry and Sir John stop, as Gwen and her
father walk into the picture. Conliffe is dressed in
his Sunday suit. Around Gwen's neck hangs the charm
Larry gave her; it glitters blindingly in the sun.
She carries herself stiffly, knowing that people's
eyes are focussed on herself and Larry.

                    SIR JOHN
                    (formally)
          Mr. Conliffe...

                    CONLIFFE
                    (stiffly, not
                    looking at Larry)
          It's a pleasure to see you,
          Sir John.

                    GWEN
                    (with suppressed
                    excitement)
          How do you do, Mr. Gill...

                    LARRY
                    (with difficulty)
          How do you do, Miss Conliffe...

Sir John and Conliffe's greetings are simultaneous
with the greetings of Gwen and Larry. There is an
embarrassed pause after these formalities, while Gwen
and Larry continue to look into one another's eyes.
Sir John coughs. The next moment, Conliffe, sensing
the bond between the young people, takes his daughter's
arm and leads her into the church. Sir John follows,
taking for granted that Larry will also enter. But
Larry pauses in the doorway.

211   INT. CHURCH - FROM LARRY'S ANGLE - MED. LONG

The church is half dark - no sunshine illumines the
stained glass windows (the sun is behind a cloud for
the moment. THE ORGAN IS PLAYING, LOUDER NOW. Gwen
is just sitting down in her pew, looking toward the
altar. But the other people slowly turn and gaze
toward CAMERA (Larry). They stare at him, rigidly;
distrust, suspicion, fear of him in their eyes.

212   INT. CHURCH - LARRY AT CHURCH DOOR - MED. CLOSE

He looks at the people inside, his face showing his
uncertainty and apprehension, as he feels their
hostility.

213   INT. CHURCH - FROM LARRY'S ANGLE - MED. CLOSE

The people still stare at him - this stranger in their
midst, to whom such peculiar things have happened lately.

Suddenly a gust of wind causes the lights on the altar
to begin flickering, bending their flame toward him;
and through the stained glass window behind the altar
a bright beam of sunshine appears. It throws the shadow
of the high Cross toward the door. The shadow ends at
Larry's feet, as if barring his way.

214   INT. CHURCH - LARRY - AT DOOR - CLOSE

He stares at the shadow of the Cross - (symbol of the
Savior's sacrifice for the evil in man). He feels
horribly unworthy to enter this holy place - thoughts
of his guilt unnerve him. He looks up and sees the
hostile people still observing him. He suddenly turns -

215   INT. CHURCH - CAMERA NEAR ALTAR - FACING TOWARDS DOOR -
       MED. CLOSE

Larry hurries away from the church. The people stare
after him, relieved that he has gone, but morbidly
curious about his strange behavior. Gwen has not turned.

The ORGAN CHANGES ITS TUNE and the people turn toward
the altar, as the Reverend Norman steps out of the
sacristy and the service begins.

                                        DISSOLVE TO

216   EXT. JENNY'S GRAVE IN THE CHURCH YARD - CLOSE

The rose-bush, where the wolf jumped through, is in
the foreground.
The SINGING VOICES of the congregation are HEARD from
the church.

CAMERA PANS AND PULLS BACK:

216   CONTINUED

Larry stands near the rose-bush, looking at the
hole dug by the animal, the broken twigs...His features
express his painful bewilderment. He bends down and
breaks off one of the twigs, which, cracked the night
before, is already withering. Larry stares at the
twig, in fear...Was it really he who broke it...in
the dead of the night..in the shape of a wolf?   His
left hand clasps the spot where the pentagram is hidden
below his coat and shirt. THE VOICES AND THE ORGAN STOP.

                                        DISSOLVE TO

217   INT. CHURCH - SACRISTY - MED. CLOSE

THE CHIMES OF THE CHURCH STRIKE THE ELEVENTH HOUR and
play "THE SELF-BANISHED." The door leading into the
church opens and Reverend Norman enters, still in his
surplice. The Reverend walks to a cupboard where his
coat is hanging, and opens it, then suddenly sees Larry.

218   INT. CHURCH - SACRISTY - MED. CLOSE - LARRY

Larry has been sitting in the half-darkness of the
sacristy, waiting for the Rev. Norman. He gets up
now, as Norman walks toward him and says in a friendly
voice:

                    REV. NORMAN
          There you are, Mr. Gill!
          I had hoped to see you at
          the service.

                    LARRY
                  (hesitantly)
          I - sort of felt I wasn't
          welcome...

                    REV. NORMAN
                  (surprised)
          Not welcome? But my dear
          Mr. Gill... Our Welch church
          may not have the same rites
          as your own, but we pray to
          the same God...

                                        CONTINUED

218   CONTINUED

                        LARRY
                   (with a weary
                    half-smile)
          It isn't that I was afraid
          of God...

                        NORMAN
                   (laughs good-
                    humoredly)
          But of his sheep! Well,
          you shouldn't be. But now
          you've come all the same...

He motions Larry to sit down and takes a chair himself,
looking at the young man in a friendly, fatherly manner.

219   INT. SACRISTY - ANOTHER ANGLE - LARRY AND REV. NORMAN

Larry sits down, encouraged by Norman's kind attitude.
He says apologetically.

                        LARRY
          I had to talk to you alone,
          sir...

                        NORMAN
                   (smiling)
          Speak freely. He who listens
          here, keeps our secrets...

Larry hesitates, then blurts out in a tortured whisper:

                        LARRY
          I killed a man...

But Norman does not seem shocked.

                        NORMAN
                   (gravely)
          Bela? It was an accident that
          happened in the dark of the night.
          You didn't mean to kill him.

                        LARRY
                   (desperately)
          But that's not all! Something's
          happening to me! When I woke up
          this morning, I found I'd left
          Talbot Castle during the night
          without knowing it...

                                        CONTINUED

219   CONTINUED

Norman looks puzzled, serious, nods for him to go on.

                    LARRY
                 (in terror)
          And - another man was killed
          last night!

                    NORMAN
                 (quietly)
          Richardson was killed by an
          animal, not a human being.

                    LARRY
                 (wildly)
          No! It was me - ! At night
          I change shape... I run on
          all fours! - I murdered Richard-
          son!

The Rev. Norman looks at him aghast.

                    REV. NORMAN
                 (distantly)
          What you are saying is beyond
          the bounds of reason! You
          should see a doctor at once.

                    LARRY
                 (almost
                  hysterically)
          But I know! I know!

He buries his face in his hands in horror and despair.
Norman, baffled, looks at him in amazement. Then he
says, compassionately.

                    REV. NORMAN
          You must stop these dark
          imaginings, my son. It's all
          in your mind. God does not
          punish the innocent...

                                        CONTINUED

:B

219   CONTINUED - 2

Norman smiles and puts his hand on Larry's knee,
looking into his eyes reassuringly. But Larry gets
up abruptly - in despair that he cannot make anybody
understand. He feels as if he is butting against a
stone wall - the wall of incomprehension between him
and the normal world.

220   INT. SACRISTY - MED. CLOSE - ANOTHER ANGLE

Larry has risen and turned away in despair. Then he
turns back to Norman, flinging at him:

                    LARRY
          You don't understand!...
          I found a twig in my room,
          a rose twig - the same kind
          of roses that grow in the
          church yard...where Richardson
          was found dead!

                    NORMAN
              (reassuringly)
          Roses grow everywhere...

Larry looks at him, wondering. Is he losing his mind?
He shudders with fear.

                    LARRY
              (whispering)
          I'm scared...

Norman gets up and puts an arm around Larry
consolingly.

                    NORMAN
          Your soul is yearning for
          peace, my son.

He smiles encouragingly as he leads Larry toward
the church.

                    NORMAN
          Come with me...   Let us pray.

221   INT. CHURCH - <u>DAY</u> - MED. CLOSE

The church is empty as Larry and Rev. Norman enter.
Norman walks to the altar, Larry following hesitatingly.
It is half dark and the expressions on their faces can-
not be clearly seen.

222   INT. CHURCH - CLOSE - NEAR THE ALTAR

with the stained glass window above it. Norman says
quietly:

                    REV. NORMAN
          I shall pray for you.   But you
          must pray too. God is as close
          to you as you are to Him...

Larry does not answer. He stands there stiffly, trying to hide his emotion. Norman walks away. Larry
looks at the altar, then lifts his unhappy face.

223   INT. CHURCH - CLOSE - TOWARD ALTAR - FROM LARRY'S ANGLE

Through the stained glass window, the sun shines bright-
ly. The window depicts the "Temptation of St. Anthony."
The Saint is kneeling, about to be attacked by fiendish
creatures with dragon tails and animal heads. In front
of the helpless Saint, a huge wolf rears its head, about
to sink its teeth into Anthony's chest. The wolf's head
is crowned with a pentagram.

224   INT. CHURCH - CLOSE - LARRY'S FACE

staring at the wolf, he feels terror grip him again and
his forehead breaks out into a sweat. He sways weakly.

225   INT. CHURCH - CLOSE - THE STAINED GLASS WINDOW - THE WOLF

with the pentagram. The wolf's fiery tongue seems to
move.

226   INT. CHURCH - MED. CLOSE - NEAR ALTAR - FACING LARRY

He starts, unable to bear his fear. His hand is clutch-
ed over the spot where the wolf has bit him. He suddenly turns and runs out of the church.

                                        DISSOLVE TO:

227   INT. LIBRARY - CLOSE - A PLASTER CAST ON A TABLE

showing the tracks of a wolf.

> KENDALL'S VOICE
> This is a cast of the animal's
> tracks. I'm sending it to the
> expert at Scotland Yard -

While he is talking, the CAMERA PULLS BACK and reveals
the LIBRARY at Talbot Castle. On the table is the
plaster cast and grouped around it are Inspector Kendall,
Sir John, Dr. Lloyd, and Frank Andrews, the game-keeper.
They are discussing the case of the wolf and the murder
of Richardson.

Frank picks up the cast and looks at it:

> FRANK
> There's no question about it.
> It _is_ a wolf...

Putting the cast down, Frank continues:

> FRANK (cont'd)
> He must be hiding somewhere out
> in the woods... quiet enough by
> day when he's satisfied - but by
> night, when he wakes...

There is a silence; the men look at Frank.

> FRANK
> (determined)
> I'm going to lay traps!

> KENDALL
> Why not take a hundred men,
> chase him out and kill him?

> SIR JOHN
> An excellent idea, Inspector. You
> shall have all the assistance you
> need. Let's arrange a hunt!

> KENDALL
> (with a good-humored
> smile)
> Listen to Sir John, always the
> Nimrod! You've always been
> keen on hunting, eh, Sir?

CONTINUED

Q

227   CONTINUED

        Kendall looks at Sir John, who smiles back, pleased,
        as the Inspector points to the walls.

        CAMERA PANS, showing the walls on which stuffed heads
        of boars, antelopes, etc., stare down at the people
        in the room.

228   INT. - THE LIBRARY - MED. CLOSE - GROUP

        The men, except Dr. Lloyd, are looking at the stuffed
        animals admiringly. Dr. Lloyd has turned to the book-
        shelves, taking out a book, looking at it with inter-
        est, and putting it back. He turns and says:

                        DR. LLOYD
                Let's hold the hunt at once --
                before the town becomes com-
                letely hysterical.

                        KENDALL
                We'll round up the men and do it
                tomorrow. Isn't it strange, by
                the way, that nobody has ever
                actually seen the beast? I wonder
                what he looks like ...

        He looks up as the door opens. The others look in the
        same direction.

229   INT. - CLOSE - NEAR LIBRARY DOOR

        In the doorway stands Larry. He is still under fearful
        tension, but he is determined not to let these men see
        he is afraid. His eyes look cunning. He closes the
        door behind him quietly and enters the room noiselessly.

230   INT. LIBRARY - BACK TO SCENE - MED. CLOSE - THE GROUP

        They feel an unpleasant atmosphere as Larry enters the
        room. But Sir John, trying to be friendly and natural,
        says:

                        SIR JOHN
                Mr. Gill can tell us.
                He saw the wolf!

                                        CONTINUED

230   CONTINUED

Larry tenses himself for another ordeal. Always this
wolf -- nowhere can he escape it! He walks over to the
fireplace, looking down at the men. Suddenly they seem
little and pitifully human to him -- he feels a strange
reckless strength as he looks at them.   Deliberately
scornful, he answers:

                    LARRY
          Sure, I'll tell you. It isn't
          a wolf at all! It's a werewolf - !

The men look at him astonished. Can he be serious?
Frank is the first to recover. With a short sarcastic
laugh, he says:

                    FRANK
          A werewolf! Listen to the
          American. He believes in
          werewolves!

Larry looks at him with hatred - there is almost a mad
glint in his eyes as he goes on:

                    LARRY
          The only way you can kill it
          is with a silver bullet!

The others feel decidedly uneasy. Kendall puffs at his
cigar and tries to laugh off the strain:

                    KENDALL
          That would be quite an addition to
          your collection of animals, Sir John!
          Just imagine having a stuffed werewolf
          staring at you from that wall there...
          The British Museum would be green with
          envy, indeed!

Dr. Lloyd, at the bookshelves, turns to Kendall and says
gravely:

                    DR. LLOYD
          I wouldn't joke about it, Kendall.

                                        CONTINUED

Q

230   CONTINUED - 2

Larry wheels around and stares at the doctor. Here is
an intelligent man who knows this is no laughing matter!

                    LARRY
                (pathetically)
          Dr. Lloyd... do you believe
          in werewolves?

Dr. Lloyd walks toward the fireplace and speaks solemnly:

                    DR. LLOYD
          Of course...

The men look at him in amazement. Dr. Lloyd sits down
and continues:

                    DR. LLOYD (cont'd)
          Wolf-madness -- Lycanthropia --
          is nothing new in medical history.
          It's a recognized form of insanity.
          A man, lost in the mazes of his
          brain, may imagine he is anything...

                    KENDALL
          Just as some people imagine they're
          Napoleon -- a man might think he's
          a wolf?

                    DR. LLOYD
          Precisely. They're sick people...

231   INT. LIBRARY - MED. CLOSE - THE GROUP - ANOTHER ANGLE

Larry realizes the dreadful implications of what Dr.
Lloyd is saying. He is stunned, despairing. Sir John
asks:

                    SIR JOHN
          Did you ever meet a --
          lycanthrope, Doctor?

                    DR. LLOYD
          Not that I've known of... They're
          difficult to diagnose. Ordinarily,
          their behavior seems normal. It's
          only when the madness comes over
          them that they become dangerous...
          I'd rather meet a real wolf than a
          man who imagines he's a wolf!

                                        CONTINUED

231   CONTINUED

                        LARRY
                  (with yearning)
         Can they be cured -- these
         sick people?

                      DR. LLOYD
         Not they -- it's hopeless! An
         asylum is the only safe place
         for them. Their sick brain
         keeps reverting to the idea of
         the werewolf and they end up --
         inevitably -- by killing what
         they love most!

                      LARRY
                  (aghast)
         ... what they love most?

He looks so shaken that Dr. Lloyd peers at him sharply
and a gleam of suspicion comes into his eyes. The other
men look at Larry uneasily too. Dr. Lloyd thinks the
conversation has gone far enough and decides to end
it for the time being.

                      DR. LLOYD
                  (more lightly)
         Well, don't take me literally,
         Mr. Gill... We doctors don't
         pretend to know everything...

He tries to smile and nod -- the other men's features
also start to relax -- they are glad to ease the tension. But Larry is in turmoil. He bursts out:

                      LARRY
                (almost hysterical)
         You know nothing - nothing!

Almost screaming, he dashes out of the room. The men
are stupified by this unexpected outburst.

232   INT. LIBRARY - FULL SHOT -

Larry dashes out of the room, leaving the men aghast.
As the door bangs behind him, Frank makes a sudden
decision and dashes after him.

                                    DISSOLVE TO

JS

233   INT. OBSERVATORY - MED. CLOSE - LARRY - DAY

Larry comes in, panting, his face still showing the
emotion of his outburst in the library. He opens his
tool chest and starts to put his tools back in their
proper places. In spite of his panic, he automatically handles his tools carefully like a good mechanic,
polishing each instrument with a bit of soft chamois.
But his mind is not on what he is doing.
The door is HEARD TO OPEN behind him - but he does not
look up.

                        FRANK'S VOICE
                          (o.s.)
                    Are you leaving soon?

234   INT. OBSERVATORY - MED. CLOSE - ANOTHER ANGLE - LARRY
        AND FRANK

Frank stands in the doorway, then closes the door, his
eyes on Larry. Larry only looks over his shoulder in-
differently, then turns back to his job of packing.

                        LARRY
                    I'm taking the first train
                    out in the morning.

Frank steps forward, his face lighting up.

                        FRANK
                    And you're going all the
                    way back to America...?

                        LARRY (without turning)
                    I'm going home.

Frank comes nearer to Larry. There is a pause while
Larry goes on with his tools, and Frank tries to find
words for what he has to say.

                        LARRY
                         (gruffly, over
                          his shoulder)
                    Want something?

                        FRANK
                         (sharply)
                    Yes - and you know what it is!

Larry turns slowly, feeling the compulsion of Frank's
will.

235   INT. OBSERVATORY - CLOSE - LARRY AND FRANK

                    LARRY
                 (tired)
            No - I don't.

Frank steps closer to him and asks with suppressed
excitement and fear:

                    FRANK
            I want to know what's happened
            between you and Gwen!

Larry looks at him with hostility.

                    LARRY
            What makes you think any-
            thing's happened?

                    FRANK
                 (with quiet
                  rage)
            I want an answer - not a
            question!

Larry puts down his tools; his face becomes more surly
and animal-like.

                    LARRY
            Why don't you ask Gwen?
            Or maybe you're afraid she
            might like to go with me?

                    FRANK
                 (furious)
            D'you mean to say - ?

                    LARRY
                 (cruelly)
            Nothing - to you.

And his eyes light up with a fierce joy at the thought
that Frank has given him. Yes, why not take Gwen along?

Frank suddenly almost breaks down. He says, half-
brokenly:

                    FRANK
            You know I'm in love with
            her. I want to marry her.
            Everything was all right -
            till you came here -

                                        CONTINUED

235   CONTINUED

                         LARRY
                      (scornfully)
              It's up to her to decide.

Larry turns back to his work table. Frank makes an
effort to control himself.

                         FRANK
                    (with intensity)
              I swear to you, if you hurt her,
              I'll shoot you down like a dog
              ...like I'd shoot that wolf -
                    (Larry wheels around)
              - that kills people in the dark!

He turns and starts out.

236   INT. OBSERVATORY - CLOSE - LARRY

He has wheeled around at the word "wolf" - his face
almost wolf-like in its fury. He looks at Frank's re-
treating back, trembling. THE DOOR SLAMS.

                                        FADE OUT

FADE IN

237   EXT. - FRANK ANDREWS' HUNTING LODGE IN THE WOODS -
       LONG SHOT - DAY

The lodge is built in the style of Henry Vth, overgrown with vines, and surrounded by a small garden.
Peter, the dog, has his little dog-house in the garden.

In front of the lodge stands a horse-drawn carriage.
Three men are loading it with animal traps (Frank,
Wykes and Phillips). The clanging of steel is HEARD.

238   EXT. - LODGE - MED. CLOSE - NEAR THE CARRIAGE

Frank, Wykes and Phillips are carrying the traps from
the lodge to the carriage. They are rather big traps,
with two sharp iron bars which snap tight when an
animal steps between them.
When the traps are loaded, Frank gets up on the driver's
seat, the other two men climb up in back, and the
carriage drives off.

                                        DISSOLVE TO:

239   EXT. - ANOTHER PART OF THE WOODS - MED. CLOSE - FRANK
AND MEN

The men have dug a hole - then Frank sinks the first
trap, fastening the anchor and chain. The men pick
up their shovels. The carriage stands in the background.

240   EXT. - SAME AS 239 - CLOSE - THE TRAP

as it sinks into the ground, the earth falls on it and
begins to cover it.

241   EXT. - SAME AS 239 - MED. CLOSE

Frank steps toward the carriage, to leave, Wykes and
Phillips following him with their shovels.

                                     DISSOLVE TO:

242   EXT. - ANOTHER PART OF THE WOODS - NEAR WHERE JENNY WAS
KILLED - MED. CLOSE

The carriage stands nearby. Frank is carrying the last
trap to the hole that Wykes and Phillips are digging.

243   EXT. - SAME AS 242 - CLOSE - THE TRAP HOLE

Frank dumps the trap, wearily.

                          FRANK
                The last one...

He pushes the iron bars with his boot.

                          FRANK
                   (continued)
            That'll hold him.

As the men start shoveling dirt over it.

                                       DISSOLVE TO:

244   EXT. - THE MOOR - <u>NIGHT</u> - LONG SHOT

Low-hanging mist. The moon pierces through racing
clouds, shedding its white light on Talbot Castle.
From afar is HEARD THE HOWLING OF A WOLF.

                                     DISSOLVE TO:

JS

245   EXT. - PART OF THE WOODS - <u>NIGHT</u> - LONG SHOT

The HOWL OF A WOLF IS HEARD - nearer now.

DISSOLVE TO:

246   EXT. - THE MOOR - ANOTHER ANGLE - <u>NIGHT</u> - LONG

OVER the moor the BARKING OF DOGS IS HEARD.
Out of the fog, four men emerge.

247   EXT. - THE MOOR - MEN AND DOGS - <u>NIGHT</u> - MED. CLOSE

The dogs, their noses to the ground, pull the men along.
Suddenly the dogs stop, and sniffing, run around in
circles. The men are Frank, and Wykes and Phillips.
Frank plays a flashlight over the ground.

                    FRANK
                 (excitedly)
        Here... he passed by here...

His flashlight is focussed on a certain place.

248   EXT. - MOOR - THE GROUND - IN THE GLARE OF THE FLASH-
LIGHT - <u>NIGHT</u> - CLOSE

The light shows the muddy ground, on which heavy marks
of big animal claws are seen.   THE CAMERA PANS following the tracks, as the flashlight moves along. But the
tracks end suddenly in front of a muddy pool.

249   EXT. - MOOR - NEAR THE POOL- <u>NIGHT</u> - MED. CLOSE

The dogs, whining and sniffing the ground, are unable
to go further.

                    WYKES
        They've lost the scent...

                    FRANK
                 (angrily)
        He can't have disappeared
         into thin air! Let's search
        systematically. Go on -
        every one take a dog...

The men eachgrab the leash of a dog and lead them
away in different directions.

JS

250   EXT. - THE MOOR - NIGHT - LONG SHOT

The men, pulled by the dogs into different directions,
disappear in the mist...

SLOW DISSOLVE TO:

251   EXT. - PART OF THE WOODS - NIGHT - MED. CLOSE

The bright moonlight thins the dark shadows of the
night.
Under a big oak tree lies a man, hunched, motionless.
Small clouds of mist drift through the trees.

252   EXT. - WOODS - NIGHT - CRANE SHOT

Slowly, into the picture walks a woman (Maleva), wrapped
in a shawl. Twigs crackle under her feet as she walks
toward the unconscious figure (Larry).

As she approaches him, CAMERA SWINGS through the
branches of the trees, and down CLOSE on the two figures.

Maleva stares down at the body. It is Larry, lying
hunched up on the ground, his arms limp, his head sunk
to one side. His face is contorted in pain. His right
leg is caught in a wolf trap.

CAMERA MOVES STILL CLOSER: His feet are bare, and the
sharp teeth of the trap have bitten deeply into the
flesh of his ankle.

CAMERA PULLS BACK: Maleva gasps and bends down. With
her old, weak hands, she tries to open the trap.

FROM AFAR THE BARKING OF A DOG IS HEARD.

Maleva labours in vain to open the trap. Suddenly Larry
groans. Maleva looks up, moves closer to him, and taking
his head in one hand, wipes his face with some leaves
she picks up from the bush nearby.

253   EXT. - WOODS - LARRY AND MALEVA - NIGHT - ANOTHER ANGLE -
CLOSE

Larry opens his eyes. He stares at Maleva, still half
conscious, not realizing where he is. Suddenly his face

CONTINUED

253   CONTINUED

distorts in pain and he sits up, staring at his foot,
caught in the trap.

                    LARRY
                  (hoarsely)
              What happened...?

The old woman does not reply, but again tries to open
the trap, her fingers vainly pulling at the iron clamps.

Larry suddenly snarls like an animal and, in a fit of
fury, he bends down. Exerting his powerful muscles,
he unbends the thick iron prongs. Quickly he pulls out
his leg - and the trap snaps back.

Painfully,-swaying, he gets up and looks down at the
still kneeling woman.

The barking of the dog is HEARD - CLOSER.

254   EXT. - WOODS - LARRY AND MALEVA - NIGHT - MED. CLOSE

                    LARRY
                  (bewildered,
                   desperate)
              What am I doing here?

He looks around and cries out in fear:

                    LARRY (cont'd)
              How did I get here?

Suddenly he realizes his situation and a wild, ferocious
expression comes over his face.

                    LARRY
                  (snarls)
              And how did you get here?

He steps toward her, as if he wanted to kill her, his
hands outstretched. Maleva does not move - she does
not seem to be afraid. He drops his hands.

                    LARRY
                  (hoarsely,
                   weakly)
              I'm getting away from
              this place -

                                        CONTINUED

254   CONTINUED

He turns, but Maleva's voice stops him:

>   MALEVA
>   (as if
>   incanting)
>   There's no escape...

Larry turns again and stares at her, petrified, his
last hope fading.

>   MALEVA (cont'd)
>   Bela wouldn't believe it
>   at first - but he couldn't
>   escape either.

She looks at him with pity.

The barking of the dog is HEARD STILL CLOSER, other
dogs bark from afar.

Maleva hurries off as quickly as her old legs can
carry her.

CAMERA PANS to Larry as he stares after her bent form,
disappearing in the mist. He feels lost, desolate.

>   LARRY
>
>   Wait...!

He limps off after her.

255   EXT. - THE WOODS - LARRY - TWO MEN AND DOGS - NIGHT - LONG

Through the fog walk two men, pulled by their dogs
towards Larry. As they come closer, the barking of
the dogs crescendos into a furious HOWL.

256   EXT. - THE WOODS - NIGHT - MED. CLOSE

Larry is limping along. The dogs pull toward him.
One of the men, Wykes, calls to him:

>   WYKES
>   Hello, there... You... Stop!

                                        CONTINUED

256   CONTINUED

Larry limps on - he does not turn.

> WYKES
> Stop - or I'll turn the
> dogs loose!

One dog suddenly tears himself free and runs to Larry.

257   MED. CLOSE - WOODS - NEAR LARRY - NIGHT

Larry stops and turns. The dog suddenly gets frightened.
It halts before him, cringes in fear, and baring its
teeth, HOWLS, terrified.

> LARRY
> (furiously)
> Call off your dog!

The men enter the shot, and one grabs the leash and
pulls the dog back. Wykes looks at Larry, astonished.

> WYKES
> The American..!

The dogs continue their furious HOWLING

> PHILLIPS
> (to the dogs)
> Quiet..!

He hits them with the whip he carries. The dogs begin
to WHIMPER. Wykes plays the flashlight on Larry's face.

> WYKES
> What are you doing here,
> Mr. Gill...?

> LARRY
> (laughing
> insanely)
> Hunting - ! The same as you!

He turns and limps away.

CAMERA PANS, showing him disappearing in the mist.

258   EXT. - THE WOODS - WHITE AND PHILLIPS - NIGHT -MED. CLOSE

The two men stare after Larry, then turn and look at
each other, bewildered, fearful... while the dogs
begin to HOWL AGAIN.

DISSOLVE TO:

259   EXT. - TALBOT CASTLE - JUST BEFORE DAWN - LONG

It begins to rain, and soon the castle is veiled by a
curtain of rain.

SLOW DISSOLVE TO:

260   INT. LARRY'S ROOM - MED. CLOSE

Larry stands at the open cupboard. He has thrown his
clothes into a suitcase, and he takes up his hat and
coat hurriedly. He is dripping wet and his hair hangs
dankly over his pale face. He is in a desperate hurry
to get out of this place as soon as possible. He closes
the suitcase, pressing the cover down with all his
strength, then he picks it up, walks to the door (still
limping a bit from the wolf-trap), opens it and peers out.

261   INT. - THE CORRIDOR - THROUGH THE HALF-OPEN DOOR - MED. LONG

The corridor is empty. Larry steps out and noiselessly,
like an animal, he limps down the hall with his suitcase.

DISSOLVE TO:

262   EXT. - MARKET STREET - EARLY MORNING - LONG

It is early morning and the first glimpse of the new day
battles with the night. A yellow street lamp burns in
front of Conliffe's shop. The street is deserted.

Limping close to the house walls, Larry runs down the
street, and stops in front of Conliffe's antique shop.

263   EXT. - THE ANTIQUE SHOP - LARRY - MED. CLOSE

The rain drips from Larry's hat into his eyes, as he
looks up at the dark house-front.

264   EXT. - THE HOUSE-FRONT, WITH GWEN'S WINDOW - FROM
LARRY'S POINT OF VIEW BELOW - MED. CLOSE

265   EXT. - LARRY ON SIDEWALK - MED. CLOSE

He picks up a pebble and throws it against the window.
He waits, in tension, picks up another pebble and
throws it against the window. Faintly now, Gwen can
be seen behind the window, her face distorted by the
wet glass. She signals to him.

Larry turns and walks to the shop window, hiding there
in the doorway, so as not to be seen by any passerby.

266   INT. - ~~SHOP INTERIOR~~ Gwen's room - GWEN - MED. CLOSE

Gwen, fastening her dressing gown, which she has
thrown over her night dress, noiselessly and quickly
passes through the room to the entrance door.

267   INT. SHOP - MED. CLOSE - GWEN AND LARRY

Gwen quickly enters the shop, carrying an old-fashioned
frosted glass shaded lamp. She puts the lamp on a
table, noiselessly, so as not to wake her father, then
hurries to the door. With her left hand she holds the
chimes, to prevent them from ringing, then opens the
door a crack.
Larry enters, water dripping from hat and coat. He
takes off his hat and pushes the hair away from his
forehead.
Gwen sees the suitcase in his hand, and at once understands.

                    GWEN
          Larry...

Larry does not even put the suitcase down. He has made
up his mind to go at once.

                    LARRY
          I'm going away...

He looks at her intently, as if to fix her face in his
memory for the rest of his days. The girl suddenly
loses control, realizing she loves him deeply and can't
bear the thought of his leaving.

                    GWEN
                    (shocked)
          Away?
                    (trying to
                    understand)
          But why...?

                    LARRY
          I can't stay here any longer.

                    GWEN
                    (feverishly)
          Let me go with you!

But Larry does not move.

                    GWEN (cont'd)
          I'll fetch a few things
          and be back in a minute.

She turns to go upstairs, then realizes he has not asked
her to go with him. She is suddenly afraid; she needs
to feel that he wants her.

                                        CONTINUED

267   CONTINUED

> GWEN
> (urgently)
> Larry...

He puts down the suitcase and wipes his face with
his sleeve. He says with difficulty:

> LARRY
> I'm going alone.

> GWEN
> (stunned)
> But - you -- I --

Larry sits down, weary, his strength deserting him.

268   INT. SHOP - CLOSE - TWO SHOT

Larry makes a last effort to do what is right:

> LARRY
> (harshly)
> You wouldn't run off with
> a murderer!

Gwen steps close to him. She thinks he is still
suffering over the killing of Bela.

> GWEN
> Larry - you're not!
> You know you're not!...

> LARRY
> (looking at her
> hopelessly)
> I killed Bela. I killed
> Richardson -

> GWEN
> (horrified)
> You didn't...!

> LARRY
> (getting up,
> miserably)
> If I stay here, God knows
> who'll be next!

He walks toward the door.

269   INT. SHOP - CLOSE - AT DOOR

As if with a premonition, Larry says:

> LARRY
> It may be you...!

He opens the door - THE CHIMES RING.

> GWEN
> Larry!

She runs to him, trying to hold him back. She takes
his arms and turns him around, but he avoids her eyes.

> GWEN (cont'd)
> Look at me...

Larry slowly turns his head and looks into her eyes.

Suddenly she embraces and kisses him. And as if her
kiss had broken the evil spell, he embraces her too,
with desperate longing, as if he could find salvation
through her.

STEPS ARE HEARD - and Gwen breaks away from Larry.
As she does so, the charm she had been wearing around
her neck falls to the floor.

270   INT. SHOP - CLOSE - THE CHARM ON THE FLOOR

It has fallen near their feet. The chain is broken.
Larry's hand bends down and picks it up.

271   INT. SHOP - NEAR DOOR - MED. CLOSE

Larry picks up the charm, as the girl turns toward the
living-room door.
CAMERA PANS TO:

272   INT. SHOP - LIVING-ROOM DOOR - MED. CLOSE - CONLIFFE

In the doorway Conliffe appears, in his dressing gown.
His face is strained and indignant as he sees Larry
and Gwen. He goes toward them quickly.

> CONLIFFE
> (sharply)
> Mr. Gill!

CAMERA PANS BACK TO:

273   INT. SHOP - NEAR STREET DOOR - CLOSE

Larry looks as if he is waking up from a dream.
Gwen is saying to her father:

                        GWEN
                     (urgently)
          I'm going with Larry, Father...

Conliffe is aghast. But Larry suddenly seems to come
to his senses. He bends down and picks up his suitcase.

                        LARRY
          It's no use, Gwen.
                     (to Conliffe,
                     hoarsely)
          Take care of her, Mr.
          Conliffe. I - I can't -

And suddenly, as if afraid to be swayed again to stay
and endanger Gwen, he turns and runs out of the shop.
(THE CHIMES TINKLE).
The girl stares at the door - then suddenly runs after
him. The father stands rooted to the spot, his mouth
open with astonishment.
The glancing headlights of a car sweep through the door.

                                        CUT TO:

274   EXT. MARKET STREET - RAIN - MED. CLOSE - KENDALL AND LARRY

A chauffeur-driven Rolls Royce pulls up in front of the
antique shop. Kendall looks through the car window and
addresses Larry:

                        KENDALL
          I say, Gill - !

Larry stops and turns toward the car in surprise.

                        KENDALL (cont'd)
                     (friendly)
          Step inside - I'll give
          you a lift!

Larry shakes his head.

                        LARRY
          No, thanks...

                                        CONTINUED

274   CONTINUED

                    KENDALL
                 (urgently)
         Don't fuss, old man...
         I don't want to see you drown...

Larry steps into the car, after a slight hesitation.
The car door closes, and the car begins to turn, its
lights shining into the shop window.

275   INT. SHOP - NEAR WINDOW - CLOSE - GWEN AND FATHER

The car is seen turning away from Gwen's view. She
turns to her father and says desolately:

                    GWEN
         They've arrested him!

                    CONLIFFE
                 (coming to her,
                  taking her arm)
         Come to bed, child.
         They won't harm him -
         if he's innocent.

                                        CUT TO:

276   INT. CAR - PROCESS - LARRY AND KENDALL

Kendall picks up the speaking tube and says to the
chauffeur:

                    KENDALL
         To Talbot Castle...

Larry starts.

                    LARRY
                 (flaring up)
         I'm going to the station!

                    KENDALL
                 (politely)
         It's too early for the train.

                    LARRY
         I can wait there.

                                        CONTINUED

mc

276   CONTINUED

                        KENDALL
               Your train will leave when
               Scotland Yard closes your case,
               Mr. Gill - not before.

Larry stares at him, then looks at his left hand.

                        KENDALL (cont'd.)
               Sorry, old man...
               No use running away...

277   INT. CAR - CLOSE - LARRY'S HAND

It opens - he is still holding the charm - and we see
the pentagram enclosing the engraved wolfbane.

                        LARRY'S VOICE
                     (repeating,
                      defeatedly)
               No use running away...

                                        DISSOLVE TO:

278   CLOSE - THE CHARM - LYING ON A TABLE IN THE OBSERVATORY
       at Talbot Castle.
       CAMERA PULLS BACK INTO:

279   INT. THE OBSERVATORY - MED. CLOSE - LARRY

Larry has changed his wet clothes and stands at a work
table in the observatory. On the table, near the silver
charm, stands a Bunsen burner, its flame heating a small
melting pot. CAMERA MOVES CLOSER:

Larry picks up the charm and CAMERA MOVES INTO A CLOSEUP.
He drops the chain and charm into the small pot. CAMERA
focusses on the charm until it melts.

                                        DISSOLVE TO:

280   INT. OBSERVATORY - MED. CLOSE - LARRY

Larry picks up the pot and pours the molten metal into a
small plaster mold. He then takes the form over to the
water-tap, turns on the water over the mold, which fumes
and cracks. A silver bullet falls out. Larry picks it up.

281   INT. OBSERVATORY - CLOSE - THE SILVER BULLET

in Larry's hand. He looks at it gravely, as we

                                        FADE OUT

FADE IN

282   EXT. HUNTING LODGE - DAY - LARRY, FRANK, DOG -

A score of men, wooden flails over their shoulders,
pass the hunting lodge. They are beaters, ready to
chase the animals out of their lairs, toward the high
stand where the hunters will shoot from.

Frank, with his dog Peter at his side, watches them
pass. His gun hangs over his shoulder. Suddenly
Peter begins to bark furiously. Frank turns and sees
Larry.

CAMERA PANS to include Larry, who stands in front of
the dog, staring at Peter, his walking stick upheld
as if to beat the animal.

                    LARRY
                  (snarls)
          Keep your dog quiet!

                    FRANK
                  (hostile)
          I thought you'd left town...

Larry walks toward him, while the dog retreats in fear.
Frank steps back and Larry walks past him into the
house. Frank turns to follow him.

                    LARRY
                (as he passes
                    Frank)
          I want to talk to you, Andrews...

He disappears into the house without waiting for Frank's
reply.

283   INT. HUNTING LODGE - WIDE VIEW - LARRY AND FRANK

It is a well-furnished place, with a staircase leading
to the upper floor. A broad comfortable couch stands
near the wall; above it, a wooden board with a picture
of Christ. A few easy chairs are grouped around the
big fireplace.

                                        CONTINUED

283   CONTINUED

Larry enters and throws his stick on the couch.
Frank follows him and pauses in the doorway. He
watches Larry with hostility.

                    FRANK
          What about?

284   MED. CLOSE - INT. LODGE - LARRY & FRANK

Larry turns and his wild expression suddenly vanishes,
and becomes weary, unhappy. Frank steps closer, as
Larry looks at him with obvious desperation. Frank
is moved by the man's distress.

                    FRANK
                  (softly)
          Sit down.

                    LARRY
          Thank you, Frank...

He sits down, tiredly, as if all fight had left him.
Frank takes a seat opposite and waits for Larry to talk.

                    LARRY
          The hunt's starting...

                    FRANK
          Surely you didn't stay for
          that?

                    LARRY
                  (quietly)
          I had to stay.

                    FRANK
                  (friendly)
          Well, what's on your mind?

                    LARRY
                  (shakes his head)
          Watch out for Gwen.
          Promise me you'll do that!

                    FRANK
                  (with sudden hope)
          Then... she's not leaving
          with you?

                                        CONTINUED

284   CONTINUED

                    LARRY
        No.

They look at each other. Frank is overwhelmed with
joy to know that Gwen is not going with Larry.

                    FRANK
                (embarrassed)
                (but gratified)
        I - I didn't know...

                    LARRY
        You've got to look after her.
        The wolf is still loose.
        If it attacks Gwen -

                    FRANK
                (surprised)
        Gwen...?

Larry takes the silver bullet out of his pocket and
holds it out to Frank.

                    LARRY
        - then shoot him with -
        this.

                    FRANK
                (astonished)
        What's that?

                    LARRY
                (gravely)
        A silver bullet.

Frank is aghast. Does Larry really believe in the
werewolf? But he takes the bullet.

                    FRANK
                (shrugs shoulders)
        My gun can digest silver
        as well as lead...

                    LARRY
        You promise to use it?

                    FRANK
                (solemnly)
        Yes.

                                        CONTINUED

me

284   CONTINUED - 2

Larry gets up and leaves without another word.

285   INT. LODGE - MED. CLOSE - ANOTHER ANGLE

Larry leaves. The dog outside is HEARD HOWLING as
Larry walks by. CAMERA MOVES INTO A CLOSE SHOT:

Frank looks after Larry, shaking his head in bewilderment. Then he looks at the silver bullet in his
hand. With sudden decision, Frank takes his gun,
breaks it open, and after a moment's hesitation, re-
moves the bullet from the barrel, and puts the silver
bullet in its place.

                                        DISSOLVE TO:

286   EXT. THE WOODS - LONG SHOT - GWEN - DAY

The path where Larry and Gwen walked the first night
they met.

Gwen is walking along, quickly, hurrying to cross the
woods and reach the castle. From the other side, a
horse-drawn carriage comes along.

287   EXT. THE WOODS - MED. CLOSE - GWEN AND MALEVA

The carriage and the girl meet. On the carriage seat
sits Maleva, wrapped up in her shawl, hunched and bent.
She stops the carriage. The girl looks up, recognizes
her and stops, unpleasantly surprised.

288   EXT. WOODS - MED. CLOSE - ANOTHER ANGLE - MALEVA & GWEN

                        MALEVA
            Don't go through the woods.

Gwen is visibly afraid of her - she wants to hasten on
- but driven by her fear, she asks:

                        GWEN
            Why...?

                                        CONTINUED

me

288   CONTINUED

                        MALEVA
              Listen!

From afar comes the NOISE OF THE BEATERS, SHOUTING
AND HITTING the bushes and trees with their flails.

                        MALEVA (cont'd)
              The hunt is on...

Gwen starts to hurry on, but Maleva calls after her:

                        MALEVA
              You won't find him at the
              castle... you'd better come with me --

The girl stops at once, astonished.

                        GWEN
              No - I must find him.

                        MALEVA
              Come with me, or he will find you...

The girl shakes her head and runs off. Maleva looks
after her, then pulls the reins and the horse begins
to move.

                        DISSOLVE TO:

289   EXT. A CLEARING IN THE WOODS - LONG SHOT--DAY

        A shooting stand has been built into a huge oak tree.

        Faintly from afar, the SHOUTS OF THE BEATERS and the
        monotonous NOISE OF THEIR WOODEN FLAILS hitting the
        bushes and trees, are heard.

290   EXT. THE SHOOTING STAND IN THE WOODS - MED. LONG -
        THE HUNTERS

        A wooden ladder leads up to the stand. The hunters,
        Sir John, Kendall, Dr. Lloyd, are waiting for the
        wolf to appear.

me

291   EXT. WOODS - THE STAND - MED. CLOSE - HUNTERS

Sir John is fixing the telescopic sight to his rifle.
Kendall is sitting down, his rifle across his knees.
Dr. Lloyd, a curious spectator, is not armed at all.

                    DR. LLOYD
          Suppose the beast doesn't pass
          here?

                    SIR JOHN
          If he's in the woods, he must
          pass this stand. The beaters
          are driving toward this point.

                    KENDALL
                  (with irony)
          If he's not in Devonshire by
          now...

Suddenly, louder than the NOISE OF THE BEATERS, but
still very distant, the long-drawn-cut HOWL OF A
WOLF is heard, rising to a crescendo, then stopping.

The men stare at one another; Kendall jumps up.

                                        CUT TO:

292   EXT. WOODS - MED. CLOSE - GWEN

Gwen, on her way, stops, listens, petrified. The
HOWL is repeated. Gwen begins to run.

                                        CUT TO:

293   EXT. WOODS * A HUGE TREE NEAR A DARK POOL OF WATER -
        MED. CLOSE - LARRY

CRANE SHOT - Larry is leaning against the tree. His
face is tense, the muscles of his cheeks clearly marked,
his teeth bite his lips, as if he had just uttered the
frightful wolfish howl and were aghast at himself.
Suddenly his hands clasp his mouth, as if to suppress
another howl. He turns and sits down on a fallen tree,
which stretches its barren limbs over the water.
CAMERA shows Larry from behind, bending down, as if in
terror.

294   EXT. WOODS - SHOOTING INTO THE CLEAR SURFACE OF THE
        WATER - CLOSE - AS SEEN WITH LARRY'S EYES - (SUPERIMPOSE)

        Larry's face writhes in agony, his hands are clasped
        around his throat. And now: his forehead seems to
        become overgrown with fulvous grey hair - it sprouts
        on his cheeks - his arms become wolfishly long and
        thin - his teeth grow pointed and wolfish. The wolf-
        headed creature stares at himself, then stretches out
        a hairy, claw-like hand, touching the surface of the
        clear forest pool. The water, disturbed, obfuscates
        the picture.

295   EXT. WOODS - NEAR THE POOL - MED. CLOSE

        The creature has turned around and we only see his
        back. He looks like Larry from this angle, but he
        walks like an animal, soft-footed, wary. NOTE: The
        wolf-man's face is never seen - ONLY IN THE MIRROR
        OF THE WATER - AS SEEN THROUGH LARRY'S EYES - AS HE
        IMAGINES HIMSELF.
        The monster dashes into the bushes and disappears.

                                                CUT TO:

296   EXT. WOODS - OTHER SIDE OF THE BUSHES - MED. CLOSE

        Out of the bushes breaks a wolf! He pauses, listening.

                                                CUT TO:

297   EXT. WOODS - THE WOODS - THE BEATERS - MED. CLOSE

        The noise of their flails is LOUDER NOW.

                                                CUT TO:

298   EXT. WOODS - MED. CLOSE - GWEN

        running along. Suddenly she stops - as the wolf comes
        running into scene.

299   EXT. WOODS - CLOSE - GWEN

       seeing the wolf, she stares, unable to move.

300   EXT. WOODS - CLOSE - THE WOLF

       as seen by Gwen.

301   EXT. WOODS - CLOSE - GWEN

       as seen with the wolf's eyes. She suddenly turns
       to run in the opposite direction, leaving the path.

       THE NOISE OF THE BEATERS continues, like an accompany-
       ing music; their wooden sticks hitting the trees have
       the same impression on the listener as the drums in
       "Emperor Jones".

                                                WIPE TO:

302   EXT. THE WOODS - MED. CLOSE - FRANK

       and his dog, walking along, Frank moving warily, his
       gun in hand, ready to shoot. The dog is close at his
       heels, as if afraid.

       THE HOWL OF THE WOLF IS HEARD AGAIN. Frank stops.
       Then comes a cry for help.

                          GWEN'S VOICE (O.S.)
                Help! Larry... Larry!

       Frank starts, then runs out of scene, the dog following.

                                                CUT TO:

303   EXT. THE SHOOTING STAND IN THE WOODS - MED. CLOSE

       The hunters, their rifles ready to shoot, look down
       at the clearing.

304   EXT. WOODS - MED. CLOSE - CAMERA ON THE STAND

       Animals rush by, frightened out of their lairs by the
       beaters, - rabbits, a deer, a fox, squirrels... They
       run toward the darker part of the woods, where they
       think they may be safer.

305   EXT. WOODS - THE STAND - MED. CLOSE - HUNTERS

Kendall is about to leave the stand in a hurry, to
rescue the girl. But Sir John, rifle ready to shoot,
stares at the clearing, determined to let nothing get
in the way of killing the wolf. As Kendall climbs
down, Dr. Lloyd, not knowing what to do, looks after
him, then joins Sir John, who suddenly calls out:

                    SIR JOHN
          Here he comes!

He lifts his gun to his shoulder.

306   EXT. WOODS - THE CLEARING - MED. LONG - GWEN AND WOLF

Gwen runs across the clearing, not seeing the stand.
A second later, after she has disappeared into the
woods again, the wolf crosses the clearing, in long,
powerful strides.

                                        CUT TO:

307   EXT. WOODS - FLASH - SIR JOHN ON THE STAND

as he points his gun toward the wolf -

                                        CUT TO:

308   EXT. WOODS - FLASH - AS SEEN THROUGH HIS GUN TELESCOPE SIGHT

In the cross, the wolf is seen - WE HEAR THE GUN
REPORT - but the wolf runs away.

                                        CUT TO:

309   EXT. WOODS - THE STAND - MED. CLOSE

Dr. Lloyd exclaims in dismay:

                    DR. LLOYD
          You missed!

                    SIR JOHN
          Impossible! I'm sure I
          stained him -

He turns to follow Kendall, who has climbed down.

                                        CUT TO:

310   EXT. - OTHER PART OF THE WOODS - MED. LONG - GWEN AND WOLF

Gwen is running for her life. But now the wolf,
with a powerful jump, overtakes and leaps upon her.
She collapses under his weight.

311   EXT. WOODS - THE WOLF - MED. CLOSE - GWEN AND WOLF

standing over Gwen's motionless body. He lifts his
head and HOWLS as if in triumph.

Then the BARKING OF A DOG IS HEARD. The wolf turns.

312   EXT. WOODS - FRANK - MED. CLOSE

his gun pointing at the wolf. Peter the dog rushes
toward the camera. Frank's gun REPORTS. He shoots
the silver bullet.

                                        CUT TO:

313   EXT. WOODS - THE WOLF - MED. LONG - SEEN FROM FRANK'S VIEW

the wolf suddenly rears as if hit. Turning, it runs
away, brokenly, and disappears through the bushes.

314   EXT. WOODS - GWEN - MED. CLOSE

Frank runs into the picture and bends over Gwen.
Peter the dog has run up too and stands in front of
the girl, as if to protect her against the wolf's return.

315   EXT. WOODS - FRANK AND GWEN - CLOSE

Frank bends down, takes the girl's head into his arms.
Gwen opens her eyes, their expression full of terror
at first, but her fear fades as she sees Frank's face,
smiling consolingly.

                         FRANK
                      (comfortingly)
                No danger any more...
                no danger...

The girl hides her face against his chest.

                                        CUT TO:

316   EXT. WOODS - THE WOLF - CLOSE

wounded, it crawls into some bushes.

DISSOLVE TO:

317   EXT. WOODS - THE MONSTER - NEAR THE POOL - MED. CLOSE

seen from the back. Groaning, his hands pressed
against his chest, he limps along toward the pool,
then collapses at the fallen tree. (His FACE SHOULD
NOT BE SEEN.)

CUT TO:

318   EXT. WOODS - THE POOL - CLOSE

CAMERA BEHIND THE MONSTER as it looks into the pool.
ITS GROANING IS HEARD.

THE NOISE OF THE BEATERS SUDDENLY STOPS - BUT THE
BARKING OF THE HUNTING DOGS IS STILL HEARD.

The monster bends, dying, over the tree and sees himself in the water. His hairy, claw-like hands are
presses against his chest; blood pours through his
hairy fingers and drips on to the ground. He stares
at his reflection in agony. Then his eyes droop and
his ugly head sinks forward.

CUT TO:

319   EXT. - WOODS - MED. CLOSE

Sir John and Kendall are running through the bushes,
followed by Dr. Lloyd, who, older and heavier, has
difficulty in keeping up with them.

CUT TO:

os

320   EXT. WOODS - THE BEATERS - FLASH

        running toward the wolf with their sticks.

                                                CUT TO:

321   EXT. WOODS - WYKES AND PHILLIPS - FLASH

        Leading two dogs, who, yelping, pull the men forward.

                                                CUT BACK TO:

322   EXT WOODS - AT POOL - MED. LONG

        In the foreground (dimly out of focus) lies the
        monster, hanging over the dead tree. In the background,
        Wykes and Phillips break through the bushes and hasten
        toward the pool with their dogs barking and howling.

        As they approach the monster,

                                                CUT TO:

323   EXT. WOODS - NEAR POOL - MED. CLOSE

        Wykes points to the spot where the monster is lying.

                            WYKES
                There it is!

        CAMERA PANS As they move close to the monster.

                            WYKES
                Hold the dogs...

        He gives the leash to Phillips and dashes forward.
        The dogs suddenly stop barking and WHINE as if in fear.

                            WYKES
                It's a man!

                            PHILLIPS
                Who is it?

                                                CONTINUED

323   CONTINUED

                              WYKES
                    I don't know...

                              PHILLIPS
                         (excitedly)
                    Turn him over!

324   EXT. WOODS - AT POOL - CLOSE

       Wykes turns over the monster... It is Larry.

                              WYKES
                         (amazed)
                    Why... it's the American!

325   EXT. WOODS - LARRY'S FACE - CLOSEUP

       It is distorted in a fiendish grin... the same con-
       tortion Bela showed after he was killed, the eyes half-
       open, the mouth fixed in a crooked smile.

       FROM HERE TO THE END OF THE PICTURE, THE SCENE IS
       PHOTOGRAPHED IN ONE CAMERA ANGLE - AS SEEN THROUGH
       LARRY'S EYES.

326   EXT. WOODS - SHOOTING UPWARD - FROM LARRY'S ANGLE -
       WIDE VIEW

       The sky can be seen, with massed clouds wildly flying
       by. The tops of the trees are swaying stormily.
       CAMERA PANS DOWN - Phillips' frightened and bewildered
       face bends over Larry (Larry not shown).

                              PHILLIPS
                    Somebody shot him!

                              WYKES
                         (coming into view)
                    He's dead...

       They move out of the shot. OTHER VOICES COME CLOSER -
       people out of scene.

                              WYKES (O.S.)
                    Dr. Lloyd! Quick - there's
                    been an accident..!

                                               CONTINUED

                         DR. LLOYD (O.S.)

        Coming...

Into the shot comes Dr. Lloyd. He bends down to ex-
amine Larry's body (not seen by us). His face is
 bewildered, then grave. Behind him, Sir John's anxious
face comes into view.

                         SIR JOHN
                         (shocked)
        Gill...!

                         DR. LLOYD
                         (gravely)
        Shot through the heart.

He and Sir John disappear out of the shot.

                         DR. LLOYD (O.S.)
        Mr. Andrews...

                         FRANK (O.S.)
        Who's that?

                         SIR JOHN (O.S.)
        Gill. He's been shot.

Suddenly Gwen's voice IS HEARD, in terror and grief:

                         GWEN (O.S.)
                         (crying out)
        Larry!

Gwen's face appears in the shot, desperately unhappy,
her eyes overflowing in terror and grief.

                         GWEN
                         (softly)
        Larry...

For a moment, the CAMERA HOLDS her face, quietly.

THE WIND IS HEARD - the howl of the wind should slowly
mingle with the church chimes coming over faintly from the
town, playing "Now, O Now I Needs Must Part". The music
gradually drowns out the wind. At the end of the picture, only
a hymn is heard, accompanied by angelic voices.

Now behind Gwen, Maleva's face appears, old, withered, but
peaceful.

                                        CONTINUED

                          MALEVA
                        (murmurs)
              As the rain enters the soil,
              as the river enters the sea,
              so tears run to a predestined end...

Gwen turns and looks at her. Maleva says:

                          MALEVA
              Take this flower...

She gives a flower to the girl - who takes it (the
wolfbane).

Maleva disappears out of the shot - only Gwen is seen
- her face slowly over-run with tears.

                          MALEVA'S VOICE (O.S.)
              Touch his heart...

Gwen's hand moves as she puts the wolfbane on Larry's
heart.

                          MALEVA'S VOICE
              Touch his cheeks...

The flower, moved by Gwen, comes into the picture,
where Larry's cheeks would be.

                          MALEVA'S VOICE
              His lips...
              His eyes...

The flower moves, stopping where Larry's lips would
be.

                          GWEN
                        (smiling through
                        her tears)
              Look!... He's smiling...!

The girl lifts the wolfbane, and as it moves toward
Larry's eyes, the flower blacks out the camera, and
the picture fades out as THE MUSIC RISES TO A MAJESTIC
HYMN - and the scene

                          ENDS.

On the following pages we present
the original pressbook
as distributed to theater owners in 1941

THE WOLF MAN

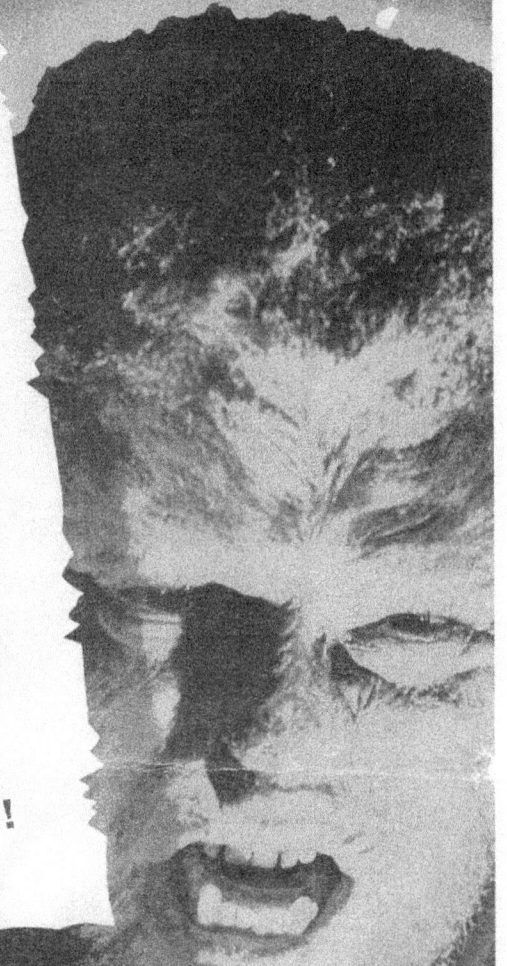

Eerie Legend Enacted In 'Wolf Man'

CREDITS

Universal Pictures
Presents
"THE WOLF MAN"
with
CLAUDE RAINS
WARREN WILLIAM
RALPH BELLAMY
PATRIC KNOWLES
BELA LUGOSI
MARIA OUSPENSKAYA
EVELYN ANKERS
and
LON CHANEY as THE WOLF MAN
Cameraman..........Joseph Valentine
Art Director ....Jack Otterson
Gowns.............................Vera West
Sound Director...Bernard B. Brown
Musical Director........Charles Previn
Associate Producer-Director........
..............................George Waggner

SYNOPSIS

(Not for publication)

Sir John Talbot (Claude Rains) welcomes his son Larry (Lon Chaney) when the latter returns to ancient Talbot castle in Wales after an 18-year absence.

Larry takes Gwen Conliffe (Evelyn Ankers) and her girl-friend, Jenny (Fay Helm) to a Gypsy carnival. While Bela (Bela Lugosi), Gypsy fortune-teller, reads Jenny's palm, Larry and Gwen wander off together.

Jenny's screams attract Larry, who returns in time to see a giant wolf making his kill. Larry beats the wolf to death with his cane, but is badly bitten.

Next day Larry finds himself recovered, except for the faint mark of a wolf's head and pentagram over his heart. According to the legend, this is the sign of a were-wolf's victim.

Capt. Montford (Ralph Bellamy) and Dr. Lloyd (Warren William) insist that there hasn't been a wolf in the vicinity for years. And villagers find the body of Bela—not that of an animal.

When Larry learns that Gwen is engaged to Frank Andrews (Patric Knowles), he decides not to intrude. But he sees Gwen after she has quarreled with Frank, and Larry and Gwen are strangely drawn toward one another.

Maleva (Madame Maria Ouspenskaya), Bela's mother, tells Larry that, having been bitten by a were-wolf, he has become one himself.

Larry scoffs feebly, but the turbulence within him grows when he awakens to find wolf tracks in his room, and learns that there has been another murder.

He decides to leave, but in saying goodbye to Gwen he sees the werewolf sign upon her.

In desperation Larry confesses everything to Sir John. The latter dismisses it as all in Larry's mind, but he straps Larry to a chair before going to join the villagers in a hunt for the four-footed killer.

A wolf-cry pierces the night, and Sir John finds the beast about to make Gwen his victim.

Sir John kills the wolf, and Maleva arrives to repeat Gypsy ministrations over the body.

The werewolf reassumes human shape, and villagers see that it was Larry Talbot.

THE CAST

Sir John Talbot..........Claude Rains
Dr. Lloyd................Warren William
Capt. Paul Montford..Ralph Bellamy
Frank Andrews.......Patric Knowles
Bela................................Bela Lugosi
Maleva ....Maria Ouspenskaya
Gwen Conliffe............Evelyn Ankers
Larry Talbot.................Lon Chaney

Appearing in Universal's horror drama, "The Wolf Man," are Claude Rains (top L), Warren William, Ralph Bellamy (center L), Patric Knowles, Bela Lugosi, Maria Ouspenskaya and Evelyn Ankers.
(Mat 11)

Weird Film Has Ralph Bellamy

(Advance)

Earliest ambition of Ralph Bellamy was to become a minion of the law. His father wanted Ralph to be an advertising man.

So Bellamy became an actor.

In one respect, Bellamy has achieved his first aim. He has scored some of his biggest successes as "cops." In Universal's "The Wolf Man," horror drama, coming....................to the................ Theatre, he is seen as a constable of police, whose thankless task it is to track an elusive four-footed "wolf man" killer.

Title role in the weird shocker is played by Lon Chaney, while leading players include Claude Rains, Warren William, Patric Knowles, Bela Lugosi, Maria Ouspenskaya and Evelyn Ankers.

"The Wolf Man," regarded as one of the most eerie pictures to come from Hollywood, is based on the "werewolf" legend, spooky tale of the European countryside. For the screen, the story is intensified by special photography and weird backgrounds.

George Waggner was associate producer-director.

Assemble Talented Cast For Amazing Chill-Drama

(Advance)

Spectacular horror dramas of the past almost without exception have been exceptional successes, although most of the horror hits have presented but a single star.

The "Frankenstein" films featured Boris Karloff, "Dracula" starred Bela Lugosi, and the late Lon Chaney, Sr., was virtually the only star to appear in "The Phantom of the Opera," the original "Hunchback of Notre Dame" and his other successes.

Monster Introduced

Now Universal studios, creator of all the above-mentioned thrillers, not only brings a new horror star to the screen in "The Wolf Man," but the drama opening at the ....Theatre also features seven other prominent players.

Young Lon Chaney is seen in the title role, a hair-raising characterization said to out-do all of the previous horror creations of the screen.

The cast is headed by Claude Rains, now recognized as one of the movies' most distinguished actors, who was introduced in another thrill-filled film of 1933, "The Invisible Man."

Prominent Players

The other featured roles are filled by Warren William and Ralph Bellamy, the "Lone Wolf" and "Ellery Queen," respectively, of two series of mystery films.

Bela Lugosi, the original "Dracula" of stage and screen, has a comparable role in the new film. Maria Ouspenskaya, outstanding character actress of many dramas, is seen as Lugosi's mother.

In romantic assignments are Patric Knowles, leading man of several mystery films, and Evelyn Ankers, young leading lady of another recent mystery on the comedy side, Abbott and Costello's "Hold That Ghost."

Terrifying Tale

Directed by George Waggner, who also served as associate producer, "The Wolf Man" traces the terrifying tale of a young man who returns to his family's ancient castle in Wales, after a lengthy absence.

Attempting to rescue a girl who is attacked by a werewolf, the young man is bitten severely and, as the legend dictates, later becomes a werewolf himself. The transformation of man to savage beast is said to provide some of the most astonishing scenes ever filmed.

◆ ◆ ◆

Unseen Actors

(Current)

Both Claude Rains and Lon Chaney, who play father and son in Universal's horror drama, "The Wolf Man," now at the .... Theatre, made invisible film debuts.

Rains was introduced in the title role of "The Invisible Man," Universal thrill film of 1933.

Young Chaney was also unseen in his first picture, "Girl Crazy," in 1932. He was on the end of the chorus line unseen behind a pillar.

Evelyn Ankers and Patric Knowles in Universal's latest and most imposing horror drama, "The Wolf Man." (Mat 12)

Make-Up Turns Man Into Wolf

(Current)

Five years of research, five months' preparation and almost five hours of daily work were required by Jack Pierce, Universal studio make-up chief, in making a werewolf of Lon Chaney for the horror drama, "The Wolf Man," now at the .... Theatre.

Horror Manufactured

Creator of the "Frankenstein" monster, "The Mummy" and other movie horror make-ups, Pierce was originally taught the make-up art by Lon Chaney, Sr., late character star known as "the man with a thousand faces."

Pierce spent five years combing countless histories of England in a vain attempt to find a description or illustration of a werewolf.

Finally, Pierce decided merely to create a make-up combining human features with those of a wolf.

As title player in "The Wolf Man," young Chaney is said to become one of the most blood-curdling horror characters of all time. It took four hours for Pierce to apply the make-up on Chaney.

Players Listed

Claude Rains heads the cast of "The Wolf Man," with featured players also including Warren William, Ralph Bellamy, Patric Knowles, Bela Lugosi, Maria Ouspenskaya, Evelyn Ankers and Chaney.

Directed by George Waggner, who was also associate producer, the thrilling film traces the weird story of a young man who is bitten by a werewolf, and later becomes one himself.

Horror Movies Pay Dividends

(Advance)

There can't be too much of a bad thing, agree Boris Karloff, Bela Lugosi and others who have made horror pay.

What may become the first star-director "team" of horror pictures consists of Lon Chaney and George Waggner. The former is among featured players and the latter was associate producer-director of "The Wolf Man," hair-raising Universal drama coming................. to the..........................Theatre.

Waggner was the director and Chaney a star of the recent shocker, "Man Made Monster."

On the basis of this film, Universal signed Chaney and Waggner to long-term contracts.

Claude Rains, Warren William, Ralph Bellamy, Patric Knowles, Bela Lugosi, Maria Ouspenskaya, Evelyn Ankers and Chaney have leading roles in the current film.

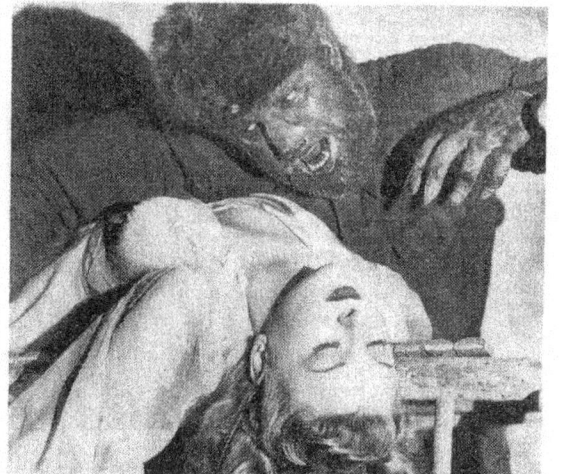

The werewolf's victim. Lon Chaney is the monster and Evelyn Ankers his prey in Universal's spine-chilling horror drama, "The Wolf Man." (Mat 21)

'Wolf Man' Shuddery Film Has Outstanding Players

(Review)

Crying wolf is a mistake, according to the legend, but Universal studios made no mistake in creating "The Wolf Man," horror drama which opened yesterday at the.............Theatre.

Universal is the home of "Frankenstein," "Dracula," "The Mummy," "The Invisible Man" and other shockers, as well as the early horror hits of Lon Chaney, Sr. Films of this type have always been successful and the new offering will be no exception.

Audiences Shudder

Opening day audiences who shuddered at the more eerie passages from the current picture will not forget the terrifying "wolf man" for a long time.

Nor will young Lon Chaney be forgotten. His performance as title player is one which expertly combines "straight" dramatics and the emotional stress which horror roles entail.

What is perhaps the finest cast ever assembled for a horror film furnishes expert portrayals in all departments.

The story of the new chiller finds a young man (Chaney) returning to his family's ancient castle in Wales after a lengthy absence. Attempting to save a village girl from an attack by a wolf, the young man is bitten.

Legend Re-Enacted

A legend of ancient days comes to life when it turns out that the savage beast was actually a werewolf and, having been bitten by a werewolf, the young man later becomes one himself.

All this, including the weird and horrifying transformation from man to werewolf, is told thrillingly and believably. The screenplay is written so that the subsequent ravaging of the werewolf might have taken place in the victim's

mind—although it is unfolded vividly in the action.

Claude Rains portrays Chaney's father, head of a 500-year old Welsh family, with his customary finesse. Outstanding in another leading role is Warren William, as a physician who understands the working of the werewolf victim's mind.

Sturdy Performance

Ralph Bellamy gives a sturdy performance as a police constable and Patric Knowles is a stand-out in a romantic assignment. Bela Lugosi of "Dracula" fame is right at home in his role as a menace. Madame Maria Ouspenskaya adds another brilliant character role as an old Gypsy woman. Evelyn Ankers gives additional promise of future stardom as a girl strangely drawn to the "wolf man."

A diverting and colorful interlude is provided in the Gypsy festival sequence. Staged in an enormous forest setting, the picturesque affair is highlighted by the striking performance of La Riana, noted Gypsy dancer. Chico de Verdi, violin leader and his Hungarian Gypsy orchestra provide vivid musical accompaniment.

Eerie Mood Established

Associate Producer-Director George Waggner establishes an eerie mood for his story, and has injected all possible action and drama into the film. Photography by Joseph Valentine, particularly in the scenes in the fog, and sets by Jack Otterson are other highlights.

Film Producing Is Actor's Goal

(Current)

Talented Patric Knowles added another to his long list of ambitions while appearing in "The Wolf Man," Universal's horror drama now playing at the................. Theatre with Claude Rains, Warren William, Ralph Bellamy and others in the cast.

Although he started out as an actor, and now is rated one of the screen's most popular leading men, Knowles has always wanted to be a director. And he has already made his mark as a writer, having a published book, "With the Wandering Players in Ireland," to his credit.

Now Knowles has decided to aim at a producer-director-writer post.

The actor took his cue from George Waggner, associate producer-director of "The Wolf Man" and holder of one of the new producer-director-writer studio contracts.

Featured players in "The Wolf Man" also include Bela Lugosi, Maria Ouspenskaya and Lon Chaney, the latter playing the important title role.

"The Wolf Man," Universal's latest horror film, features Lon Chaney as the werewolf. Others prominent in the cast are (top L) Claude Rains and Evelyn Ankers; (center L to R) Ralph Bellamy, Bela Lugosi and Warren William; (lower L) Patric Knowles; (lower R) Maria Ouspenskaya. (Mat 22)

Claude Rains, Notorious Screen Villain 'Reforms'

(Advance)

Mild-mannered Claude Rains, the worst sort of heel in his early stage and screen roles, now seems destined to be a good guy for the remainder of his career.

As title player in "Here Comes Mr. Jordan," Rains shed so much sweetness and light that his fan mail multiplied from fans who thanked him for restoring faith in mankind.

Fickle Memories

Those same fans must have forgotten that Rains has done his share of tearing down that faith. For the actor was not always as sympathetic a character as he portrays in Universal's "The Wolf Man," horror drama coming .... to the.....................Theatre with Warren William, Ralph Bellamy, Patric Knowles, Bela Lugosi, Maria Ouspenskaya, Evelyn Ankers and Lon Chaney.

Rains' career as a bad man clashes with his background, because he started out in public as a church choir boy.

As an adult, however, Rains turned "heel" professionally and played bad man in almost all of his stage plays. He came to the screen as "The Invisible Man," a strange cinema killer of 1933. Then he followed with "Crime Without Passion," in which he was another villainous party.

Known as "Jordan"

Now Rains is best known as the kindly "Mr. Jordan."

In "The Wolf Man" Rains plays Chaney's father. The young man becomes bitten by a werewolf, and, as the legend has it, later becomes one himself. The tragedy places Rains in the position of hunting down his own son.

George Waggner was associate producer-director of the new hair-raising drama.

Actress Famed For Sad Roles

(Current)

Hollywood, like life, keeps handing out the grief to Madame Maria Ouspenskaya, but she takes it and comes back for more.

The distinguished actress has another anguishing role in Universal's horror drama, "The Wolf Man," now at the............................. Theatre. In the new film, Ouspenskaya sees her son, Bela Lugosi, die with the curse of the werewolf.

As Greta Garbo's mother in "Conquest," Mme. Ouspenskaya was driven insane. In "Love Affair" as Charles Boyer's grandmother, she was driven to her grave by his escapades.

As a Chinese crone in "The Shanghai Gesture" Mme. Ouspenskaya says not a word. She just suffers. And in "King's Row" she is an 84-year-old grandmother who finally dies.

Ouspenskaya's film roles might well have been inspired by her real life story. During her 54 years she has lived through two revolutions and has suffered the cold and hunger of a famine that took almost every friend she had.

But her success of the past few years has more than made up for the human suffering she has seen and experienced, Mme. Ouspenskaya insists.

Featured players in "The Wolf Man" include Claude Rains, Warren William, Ralph Bellamy, Patric Knowles, Evelyn Ankers and Lon Chaney.

Nightmares Are Promised By 'The Wolf Man'

(Advance)

New nightmares are forecast for fans who will shudder at the sight of "The Wolf Man" when the horror drama opens at the............ Theatre on.............................

Creators of the "Frankenstein" films, "Dracula," "The Mummy" and other horror hits, Universal studios is said to out-do all previous efforts in the field with the new "wolf man" shocker.

Potential Star

A potential star is uncovered in the person of Lon Chaney, whose father, the late Lon Chaney, Sr., appeared in "The Phantom of the Opera," the original "Hunchback of Notre Dame" and other early horror successes at the same studio.

In addition, the most imposing cast yet assigned to a horror drama finds eight important players in featured roles.

The distinguished actor Claude Rains heads a cast which also includes Warren William, Ralph Bellamy, Patric Knowles, Bela Lugosi, Maria Ouspenskaya, Evelyn Ankers and Chaney.

With George Waggner as associate producer-director, "The Wolf Man" traces the tragic career of a young man who returns to his home in Wales after an 18-year absence, and who is bitten by a werewolf.

Legend Is Spooky

According to the legend, whoever is bitten by a werewolf becomes one himself. The blood-curdling story of "The Wolf Man" shows this weird transformation of man to a werewolf, who finally turns even on the beautiful girl he loves, to climax a series of mysterious killings.

♦ ♦ ♦

Horrendous Film

(Current)

Most pretentious horror film since "Son of Frankenstein" is presented in Universal's "The Wolf Man," with Claude Rains, Warren William, Ralph Bellamy and others, now playing at the .... Theatre.

Others in the horrendous drama of a man turned werewolf are Lon Chaney, playing the title role; Patric Knowles, Bela Lugosi, Maria Ouspenskaya and Evelyn Ankers. George Waggner was associate producer-director.

♦ ♦ ♦

Sinister Star

(Advance)

A new star is expected to emerge from the grim proceedings in "The Wolf Man," Universal horror drama opening.....................at the................ Theatre.

Marked for immediate stardom, according to advance word, is Lon Chaney, sinister title player in the eerie offering.

Claude Rains, Warren William, Ralph Bellamy, Patric Knowles, Bela Lugosi, Maria Ouspenskaya and Evelyn Ankers are well-known players who appear in the film, directed by George Waggner.

Trapped by the werewolf. Lon Chaney is the monster and Evelyn Ankers one of his many victims in Universal's horror drama, "The Wolf Man." (Mat 13)

"The Wolf Man," Universal's latest horror movie, features Claude Rains (upper L), Evelyn Ankers, Warren William (lower L), and Lon Chaney in a cast which includes Ralph Bellamy, Patric Knowles, Bela Lugosi and Maria Ouspenskaya.
(Mat 23)

Young Lon Chaney Dispells Myth About Famous Father

(Advance)

Since the death of Lon Chaney, countless actors have claimed they once shared the character star's dressing room and many make-up experts have taken credit for his uncanny disguises.

Evelyn Ankers Near Stardom

(Current)

Evelyn Ankers has traveled more than 150,000 miles during her short lifetime and she is destined to "go far" as a star, too.

Critics of at least three countries have predicted stardom for the young actress.

Miss Ankers progresses further with what is perhaps her most rigorous role to date, as leading lady in Universal's horror drama, "The Wolf Man."

The new movie chiller is now playing at the....................Theatre with Claude Rains, Warren William, Ralph Bellamy, Patric Knowles, Bela Lugosi, Maria Ouspenskaya and Lon Chaney, the latter in the title role.

Although she is British, Miss Ankers was born in Valparaiso, Chile. She made her film debut in a Colombian picture, "La Hija De La Dolores," and later appeared in several British films. Following her success in the Broadway version of "Ladies In Retirement," Miss Ankers was signed by Universal.

In "The Wolf Man" Miss Ankers is seen as a Welsh village girl who is strangely drawn toward a man who later turns werewolf.

George Waggner directed the drama, and also was associate producer.

Fact is that Chaney never shared his dressing room with anyone, and he always was his own make-up man.

Stardom For Son

Authority for that is another Lon Chaney, the late star's son, who himself emerges a star of horror dramas as title player in "The Wolf Man."

The Universal horror spectacle opens....................at the....................Theatre with a cast that includes Claude Rains, Warren William, Ralph Bellamy, Patric Knowles, Bela Lugosi, Maria Ouspenskaya and Evelyn Ankers.

Young Chaney was the only actor who ever shared his father's dressing room. He was literally born between curtain calls in Oklahoma City, where his parents were playing a stock engagement. At six months of age the son made his stage debut, as a "prop" in a balancing act with his father.

Has Horror Role

In "The Wolf Man" Chaney has his first big horror role, and is said to possess the same ability to portray believable horror characterizations his father displayed.

Story of the new drama presents Chaney as a young Welshman who is bitten by a werewolf, and, in an amazing and terrifying transformation, becomes one himself.

Remarkable new camera effects, devised to intensify the eerie atmosphere of "The Wolf Man," were created by Joseph Valentine, one of Hollywood's best known cinematographers.

George Waggner was associate producer-director.

Warren William Scores In Big Cast Of 'Wolf Man'

(Advance)

Presumably a John Barrymore profile and voice would be enviable assets to an aspiring actor, but not for Warren William.

For years Broadway producers slammed their doors in William's face, saying, "You look too much like Barrymore."

Now William has licked the jinx. He has been a screen star for years, and has his latest important role in "The Wolf Man," Universal horror drama coming....................to the....................Theatre with Claude Rains, Ralph Bellamy, Patric Knowles, Bela Lugosi, Maria Ouspenskaya, Evelyn Ankers and Lon Chaney.

Was Newspaper Scribe

Before he overcame the Barrymore obstacle, William served two years as a newspaper reporter and a similar period in the World War. Finally, however, he obtained his "break" in "Expressing Willie."

Alexander Woollcott reported, "Warren William has a Barrymore accent, looks the very image of the young John Drew." But William went on to achieve success on the stage, and then on the screen.

The jinx pursued William to this day, despite his success. When a portable dressing room arrived for him on the set of "The Wolf Man," the name John Barrymore was on the door. It was explained that Barrymore had used the same dressing room while appearing in "The Invisible Woman" for Universal, and the name had not yet been changed.

Portrays Doctor

William portrays a doctor in "The Wolf Man," story of a young Welshman who is bitten by a werewolf, and later becomes one himself in a terrifying transformation. Chaney plays the title role, and George Waggner was associate producer-director.

♦ ♦ ♦

Mythical Menace

(Advance)

A new and savage horror creation, half-man and half-beast, is introduced in "The Wolf Man," Universal drama coming....................to the....................Theatre.

For the first time, a spectacular horror film has been devised with a werewolf, mythical menace of the Welsh countryside, as the killer.

Lon Chaney plays the title role and the cast includes Claude Rains, Warren William, Ralph Bellamy, Patric Knowles, Bela Lugosi, Maria Ouspenskaya and Evelyn Ankers. George Waggner was associate producer-director.

♦ ♦ ♦

Cinema Chiller

(Advance)

Most important cast ever assembled for a horror drama comes to the....................Theatre on.................... when Universal's "The Wolf Man" begins its local run.

Claude Rains of "Mr. Jordan" fame is a headliner in the cinema chiller which also features Warren William, Ralph Bellamy, Patric Knowles, Bela Lugosi and Lon Chaney, the latter in the title role.

Bela Lugosi Is 'Slain' Again In 'Wolf Man'

(Advance)

Every actor lives to die.

Long, lingering death scenes offer an actor more opportunities to emote than any other type of scene.

But the thespic thrill of professionally passing on has begun to pall for Bela Lugosi.

Lugosi has died in more than 100 stage and screenplays, and he adds one more to his private obituary list in Universal's horror drama, "The Wolf Man," coming....................to the....................Theatre, with Claude Rains, Warren William, Ralph Bellamy, Patric Knowles, Maria Ouspenskaya, Evelyn Ankers and Lon Chaney in the cast.

Perhaps Lugosi's most notable death took place in "Dracula," when a wooden stake was driven through his heart. He has been killed in almost every conceivable way, and is clubbed to death by Chaney in the new shocker.

Later, Chaney turns into a werewolf himself, having been bitten by the legendary creature.

Although Lugosi is condemned to a lifetime of dying, he really doesn't mind.

"It's a living," he says.

"The Wolf Man," based on one of the most eerie of European legends, was directed by George Waggner who also presided as associate producer.

Lon Chaney as the werewolf in Universal's "The Wolf Man."
(Mat 14)

Historic Castle Is Movie Locale

(Advance)

Interiors and exteriors of an ancient historic Welsh castle are features of the grim settings designed by Jack Otterson for Universal's hair-raising horror drama, "The Wolf Man," coming....................to the....................Theatre.

Claude Rains heads the cast as head of the family which owns the castle and Lon Chaney portrays his son, a werewolf victim. Featured players include Warren William, Ralph Bellamy, Patric Knowles, Bela Lugosi, Maria Ouspenskaya and Evelyn Ankers.

Lavish forest settings are other backgrounds for the terrifying story, which is relieved only by scenes of a gala Gypsy festival which takes place in the forest.

George Waggner was the associate producer and director of the spine-chilling drama.

Ralph Bellamy (L), Claude Rains, Evelyn Ankers and Lon Chaney, in one of the terror-striking dramatic sequences of Universal's horror film, "The Wolf Man."
(Mat 24)

SHOWMANSHIP

FIRST AID BOOTH

The illustration conveys the details of this stunt. Provide everything necessary for those who suffer "thrill-shock" when they see "The Wolf Man." But do it with a humorous twist. The copy and illustration indicates how. Place booth near entrance with nurse in white on hand . . . also possibly an ambulance parked at curb with sign: RESERVED FOR THOSE "THE WOLF MAN" GETS.

LOBBY

"The Wolf Man" is tops for building an exciting lobby. It brings showmanship into the lobby on a scope that is limited only by your ingenuity. Anything goes that is bold, striking, different. Here are a few suggestions to get you started:

Use fantastic shaped trees and foliage as background with receptacles of dry ice and water covered with leaves at base. This will give off the fog effect of the moors. Cover floor of lobby with imitation ground covering to tie-in the effect.

Hang dim, smoky gypsy and hunter's lanterns at advantageous spots for weird effect. Bathe marquee and lobby in green lights.

Use life-sized cut-outs of the wolf man and girl among trees, over box office, wherever possible to spot them. Try for shadow effects in lighting them.

Huge cut-out from 24-sheet should be on top of your marquee, lit by green spots.

Use gypsy iron pot on triangle suspension with dry ice and water combination to give off vapors.

Play siren slowly for howl effect, or secure atmospheric sound records of animals, frogs, woman's scream, siren, etc., from Thomas J. Valentino, Inc., 1600 Broadway, New York.

Easels should be made in tree and bush form with wolf's head cut-out on each, and stills mounted under green cellophane.

Much can be done for effectiveness by red and amber baby spots highlighting and giving shadow effect to your displays.

●

WALKING BALLY

A man heavily armed with two bloodhounds on chains walking the street wearing the following sign will get over your picture's message:

"The Wolf Man" baffles all hunters . . . a citizen by day, he prowls at night. See him at the Rivoli this week.

Banner the dogs: We're looking for (picture of the Wolf Man).

STRONG NERVES GAG

Station a nurse in white uniform at small table in lobby. In back of her have huge medical poster of man showing nerve and artery diagrams. Large sign reads: TEST YOUR NERVES. Nurse takes pulse and copy of handwriting as patron enters, and again when patron exits. Gives them their readings on a card with theatre and picture copy. Where handwriting shows nervousness on exiting, patron should get "caution" mark, otherwise card should read flattering message of "strong" nerves so patron will proudly show card to others . . . a vest-pocket ad as well as lobby novelty.

●

IS HE FACT OR FICTION?

Legends of wild men that might be "wolf men" abound in America. They were brought to public notice in the American Weekly, Sunday newspaper magazine, in their publication of Nov. 16, 1941. Among the localities listed as having "wild man" hunts and legends are: the hill country of Arkansas near Benton; The Long Island woods near Mattituck; the town of Pine Hill, Massachusetts; around Mullica Hill not far from Atlantic City and another near Milville in New Jersey; also another case in that state near Keyport; and the outlying districts of Brewton, Alabama.

With these stories rife, and of recent national attention, you can capitalize with a search for local residents who have seen a "Wolf Man" or know of specific incidents, hunts, captures, etc., etc.

If your paper issues copies of The American Weekly try for reprints of this article with underline information about your picture. (Center article Page 2.)

Passes to see "Wolf Man" should be all the inducement needed to bring forth the tales of those who have seen or know about any of these legendary persons.

Make a "Believe It Or Not" type of lobby display using clipping from this American Weekly surrounded by rogues gallery of wild looking men (borrow from newspaper or police morgue) and accent with horror heads of "The Wolf Man" plus fright stills from your Exchange set.

HORROR CONTEST

Horror attracts certain types of persons whom the psychologists call the "hyper-sensitive." These people are always relating their nightmares to anyone who will listen. Here is their chance to reach print and really tell a good one. Through your newspaper or radio offer an autographed photo of the Wolf Man as prize for the most fantastic nightmare related in a letter of not over 200 words. Autograph can be a wolf's track dabbed on the corner of photo . . . your artist can do this.

●

GYPSY WAGON BALLY

A wagon similar to the gypsy covered camp wagon can be cheaply simulated out of wood and plyboard, with barred windows and cut-out heads from posters of "The Wolf Man" peering out behind the bars. Banner with ad lines and have driven by a couple in gypsy costumes.

SHOWMANSHIP

SPECIAL LOBBY BOARD

You can bring home the terror of the Wolf Man most realistically by a special lobby board in which you show how the human elements of man turn into those of a beast. With drawings and art to illustrate the following changes show:

WHEN "THE WOLF MAN" TURNS FROM MAN TO BEAST —

Hair grows on his hands
His fingers become claws
His eyes grow wild
His teeth sharpen to fangs
His heart turns to ice
His face becomes a beast's
(Ad lines . . . cast . . . credits)

Illustrate this change as shown in the accompanying drawing . . . or use wax models and dummy articles borrowed from taxidermist and costumer.

•

FOOT MARKS

Use as snipes . . . stencils . . . etc., four foot prints, two of them human, two of them Wolf's tracks. Copy: "The 'Wolf Man' is coming. Is it man or beast?" (Front two tracks should be one human hand and one paw . . . back two should be one human foot and one paw.)

•

FORTUNE TELLER

Bela Lugosi's weird role as a gypsy seer gives you a striking model for duplication in your fore-court or foyer. Garb either a man or woman as a gypsy, supply them with the colorful nomad's tent and atmosphere. Include in the "fortune" a "Mystic Message" that sells the attraction. This message should be in writing, with a few strange signs of the zodiac, mystic symbols, etc. . . . and then the line "He who is bitten by a werewolf — becomes a werewolf. Watch yourself! I see a strange attraction for you in THE WOLF MAN!"

LIVE LOBBY DISPLAY

You can play on the dual angle of your lead character in a novel display attraction by having a live wolf in a cage in your lobby (borrowed from your zoo) . . . and beside it a cage holding a young man dressed in the height of fashion. Signs on cage read—MAN BY DAY—BEAST BY NIGHT. SEE THE MOST TERRIFYING MASTERPIECE OF IMAGINATIVE HORROR THE SCREEN HAS EVER REVEALED.

SCARE LINE TIE-UPS

Cash in on the fear and horror angle of "The Wolf Man" with these tie-ups:

★ **HARDWARE STORES.** Display guns . . . locks . . . door-chains . . . bolts . . . window guards . . . etc. . . . with copy: "Keep your doors and windows bolted while 'The Wolf Man' is in town."

★ **ELECTRICAL STORES.** Display flash-lights, electric lanterns . . . burglar alarms . . . etc. . . . with copy: "Don't be taken by surprise. Don't go in dark places without a light while 'The Wolf Man' is in town."

★ **INSURANCE AGENCIES.** Tie-up with life and accident policies . . . copy: "You never know what may happen to YOU while 'The Wolf Man' is in town. Be prepared."

★ **DRUG STORES.** Display first-aid equipment and remedies. Copy: "Take no chances. A bite is a dangerous thing. 'The Wolf Man' is on the prowl. Beware!"

•

EXTRA TIE-UPS

★ **BOOKS.** Library and book store displays with mystery novels . . . also magazine racks and spot announcements after mystery yarns over the air.

★ **HANGERS.** Pastboard padlocks on milk bottles, as doorhangers on telephone booths, office doors, etc. Copy: "Lock your doors, 'The Wolf Man' is coming."

★ **LETTERS.** To members of the medical profession asking, "How would you treat a werewolf bite? Do you believe in the powers of wolfbane treatment? See 'The Wolf Man!'"

★ **QUIZ.** Cards handed out to girls in shops, stores and offices showing The Wolf Man with the girl and question: "Can a girl tame a man . . . or does she set him wild? See 'The Wolf Man' at the Rivoli."

•

GIVE-AWAYS

Pass out in glassine envelopes a small amount of some powdered herb. Call it wolfbane . . . the magic plant which kills the venom of a werewolf's bite. Under art of the vicious head of the Wolf Man print the following:
PRESCRIPTION: He who is bitten by a werewolf . . . becomes a werewolf . . . unless within the hour he applies a poultice of this wolfbane powder mixed with two spoonsful of boiling water. Carry this for your protection during the week of (date) while "The Wolf Man" is at the Rivoli.

MIDNIGHT OPENING

There are two ways you can capitalize on the weird and powerful selling possibilities of "The Wolf Man" with a midnight show.
(1) Offer a premiere presentation exactly at midnight the night before regular opening . . . inviting the dignitaries from your city as guests . . . these should especially include scientists who might doubt the existence of werewolves . . . the police officials who might have to hunt one sometime . . . the psychologists of local importance . . . and any others who could augment your campaign with statements about the show for the press and for your lobby.
(2) Offer $25 cash to any girl who will be the only person in your theatre for a midnight performance. This could be ballyed to the skies, with nurse and ambulance in front of theatre . . . ad and publicity campaign to find the girl . . . doctor's test of her heart . . . psychologist's warnings . . . art strip of her horror reactions with reporter's interview . . . etc. . . . etc.

•

MAGIC MIRROR

Build a "magic mirror" as shown in the illustration. Plate glass has back covered by dark, fine mesh scrim that gives appearance of mirror till patron steps in front on concealed platform that trips off spot light and shows up large head of "The Wolf Man" instead of patron's reflection.

•

CATCH LINES

A living horror . . . its body a twitching tomb of strange desires. See it—if you dare.

•

A prowling . . . killing . . . night monster! Terrifying a countryside. Is he man—or unholy beast?

His howl a dirge of death! A mortal man by day . . . by night an unearthly monster.

The most terrifying masterpiece of imaginative horror the screen has ever revealed.

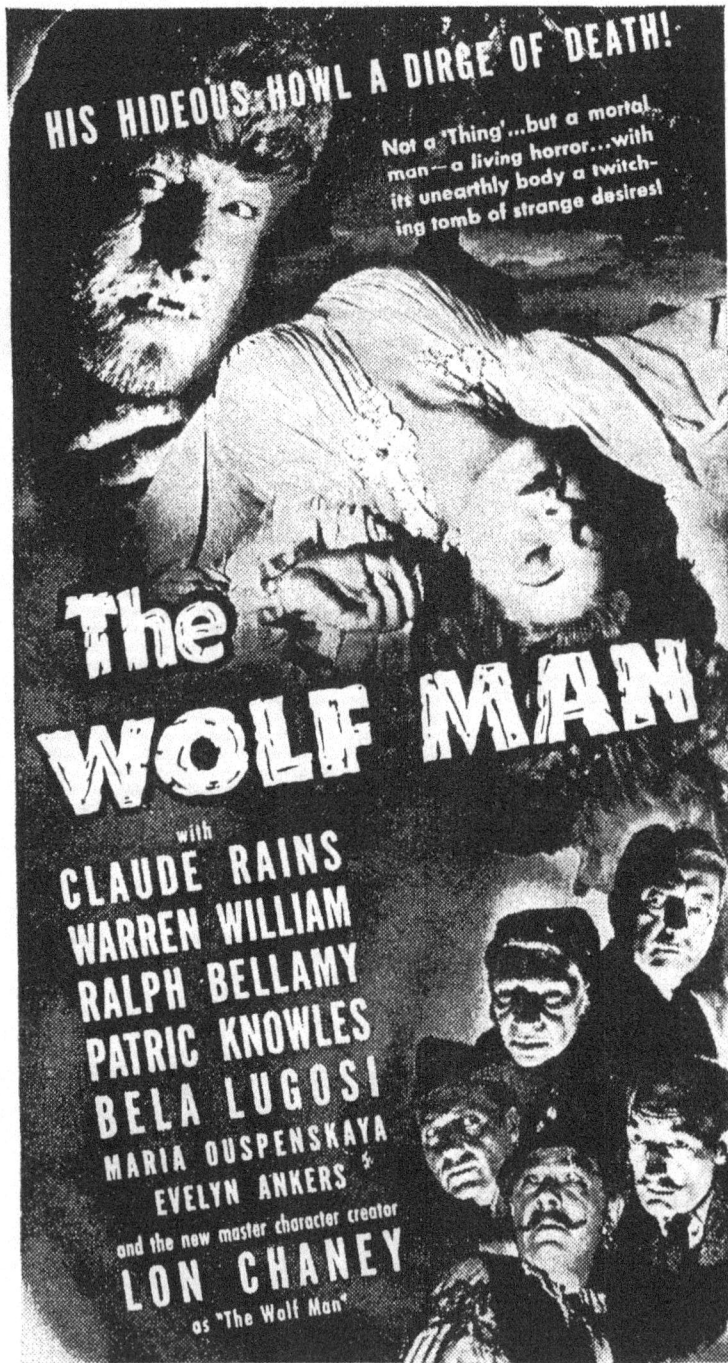

HIS HIDEOUS HOWL A DIRGE OF DEATH!

Not a 'Thing'...but a mortal man—a living horror...with its unearthly body a twitching tomb of strange desires!

The WOLF MAN

with
CLAUDE RAINS
WARREN WILLIAM
RALPH BELLAMY
PATRIC KNOWLES
BELA LUGOSI
MARIA OUSPENSKAYA
EVELYN ANKERS
and the new master character creator
LON CHANEY
as "The Wolf Man"

Directed by GEORGE WAGGNER • A UNIVERSAL PICTURE • Associate Producer, GEORGE WAGGNER

2B

1G

Is he MAN or UNHOLY BEAST?

The WOLF MAN

with
CLAUDE RAINS
WARREN WILLIAM
RALPH BELLAMY
PATRIC KNOWLES
BELA LUGOSI
MARIA OUSPENSKAYA
EVELYN ANKERS
LON CHANEY
as "The Wolf Man"

Directed by GEORGE WAGGNER
Associate Producer, GEORGE WAGGNER
A UNIVERSAL PICTURE

1D

MAN TURNED BEAST...
his unearthly body a twitching tomb of strange desires!

The WOLF MAN

with
CLAUDE RAINS
WARREN WILLIAM
RALPH BELLAMY
PATRIC KNOWLES
BELA LUGOSI
MARIA OUSPENSKAYA
EVELYN ANKERS
and
LON CHANEY
as "The Wolf Man"

Directed by GEORGE WAGGNER
Associate Producer, GEORGE WAGGNER
A UNIVERSAL PICTURE

1A

MAN TURNED BEAST...
his unearthly body
a twitching tomb of
strange desires!

The WOLF MAN

with Claude RAINS Warren WILLIAM
Ralph BELLAMY Patric KNOWLES Bela LUGOSI
MARIA OUSPENSKAYA EVELYN ANKERS
and the new master character creator
Lon CHANEY
as 'The Wolf Man'

Directed by GEORGE WAGGNER · Associate Producer, GEORGE WAGGNER
A UNIVERSAL PICTURE

2C

Ad. No. 2C—2col.—Mat 30c

The Legend of the Damned!

When the full moon wanes...
the deadly wolfbane blooms...its
pale stench cursing this strange
mortal man...with the hair and
fangs of an unearthly beast...his
hideous howl becoming a dirge
of death...his unholy heart a
twitching tomb of strange desires!
Beware!

The WOLF MAN

with
Claude RAINS Warren WILLIAM
Ralph BELLAMY Patric KNOWLES Bela LUGOSI
MARIA OUSPENSKAYA EVELYN ANKERS
and the new master character creator
Lon CHANEY
as 'The Wolf Man'

Directed by GEORGE WAGGNER · Associate Producer, GEORGE WAGGNER
A UNIVERSAL PICTURE

2D

Ad. No. 2D—2 col.—Mat 30c

Is he MAN
or
UNHOLY
BEAST?

The WOLF MAN

with
CLAUDE RAINS
WARREN WILLIAM
RALPH BELLAMY
PATRIC KNOWLES
BELA LUGOSI
MARIA OUSPENSKAYA
EVELYN ANKERS
LON CHANEY
as 'The Wolf Man'

Directed by GEORGE WAGGNER
Associate Producer, GEORGE WAGGNER
A UNIVERSAL PICTURE

1D

Ad. No. 1D—1 col.—Mat 15c

HIS HIDEOUS HOWL
A DIRGE OF DEATH!

His unholy heart
a twitching tomb
of strange desires!

The
WOLF
MAN

with
Claude RAINS   Warren WILLIAM
Ralph BELLAMY   Patric KNOWLES
Bela LUGOSI
MARIA OUSPENSKAYA
EVELYN ANKERS
and the new master character creator
Lon CHANEY
as "The Wolf Man"

ADDED ATTRACTIONS

A UNIVERSAL PICTURE

Ad. No. 1E—1 col.—Mat 15c

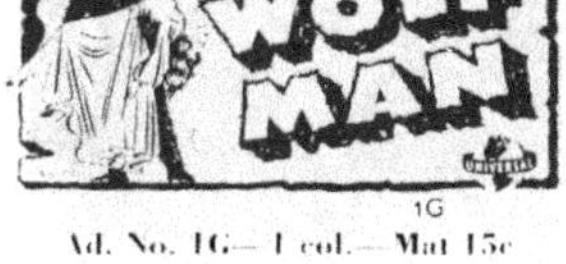

The WOLF MAN

Ad. No. 1G—1 col.—Mat 15c

with
CLAUDE RAINS
WARREN WILLIAM
RALPH BELLAMY
PATRIC KNOWLES
BELA LUGOSI
MARIA OUSPENSKAYA
EVELYN ANKERS
and the new master character creator
LON CHANEY
as "The Wolf Man"

THE WOLF MAN

with
Claude RAINS   Warren WILLIAM
Ralph BELLAMY   Patric KNOWLES
Bela LUGOSI   Maria OUSPENSKAYA
Evelyn ANKERS
and Lon CHANEY as "The Wolf Man"

The
WOLF
MAN

HELD
OVER

The
WOLF
MAN

with
CLAUDE RAINS
WARREN WILLIAM
RALPH BELLAMY
PATRIC KNOWLES
BELA LUGOSI
MARIA OUSPENSKAYA
EVELYN ANKERS
and the new master character creator
LON CHANEY
as "The Wolf Man"

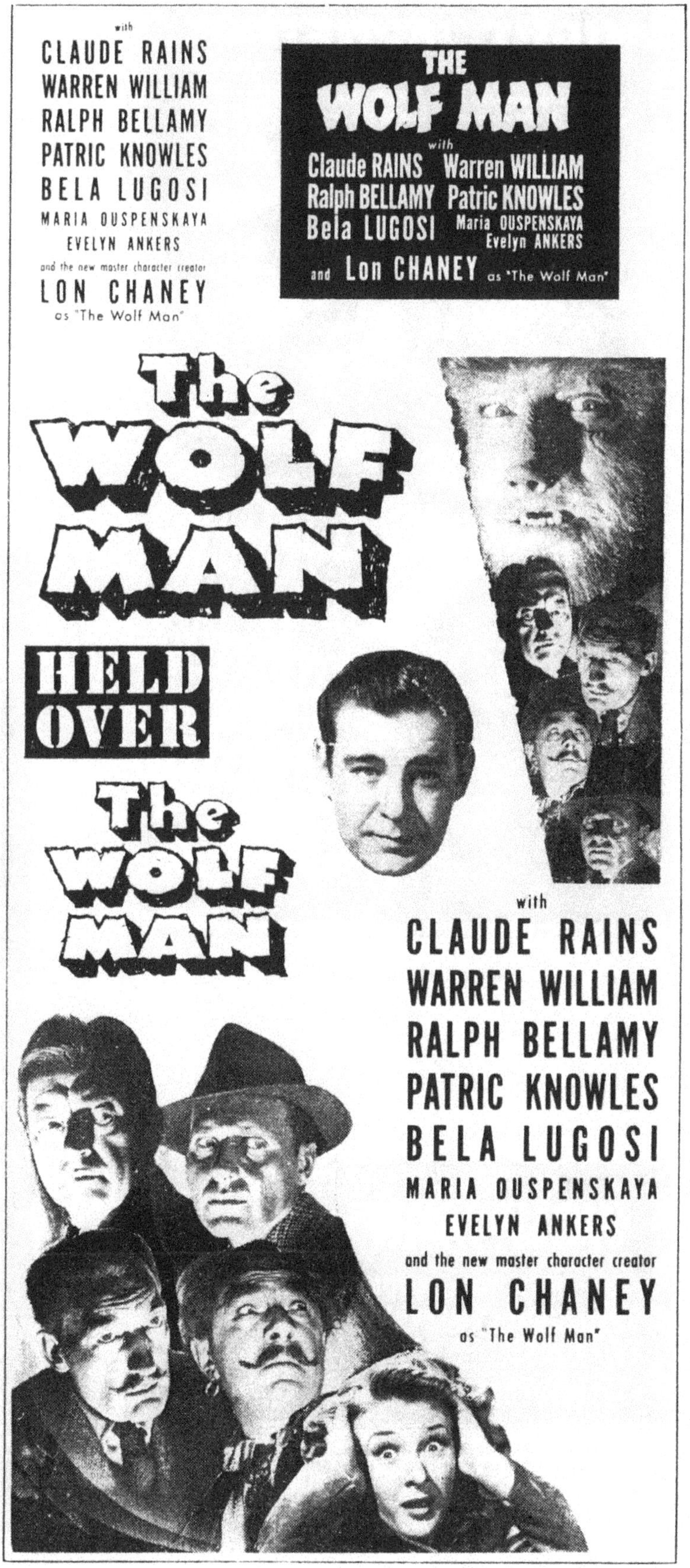

Ad. No. Util. No. 1—3 col.—Mat 45c

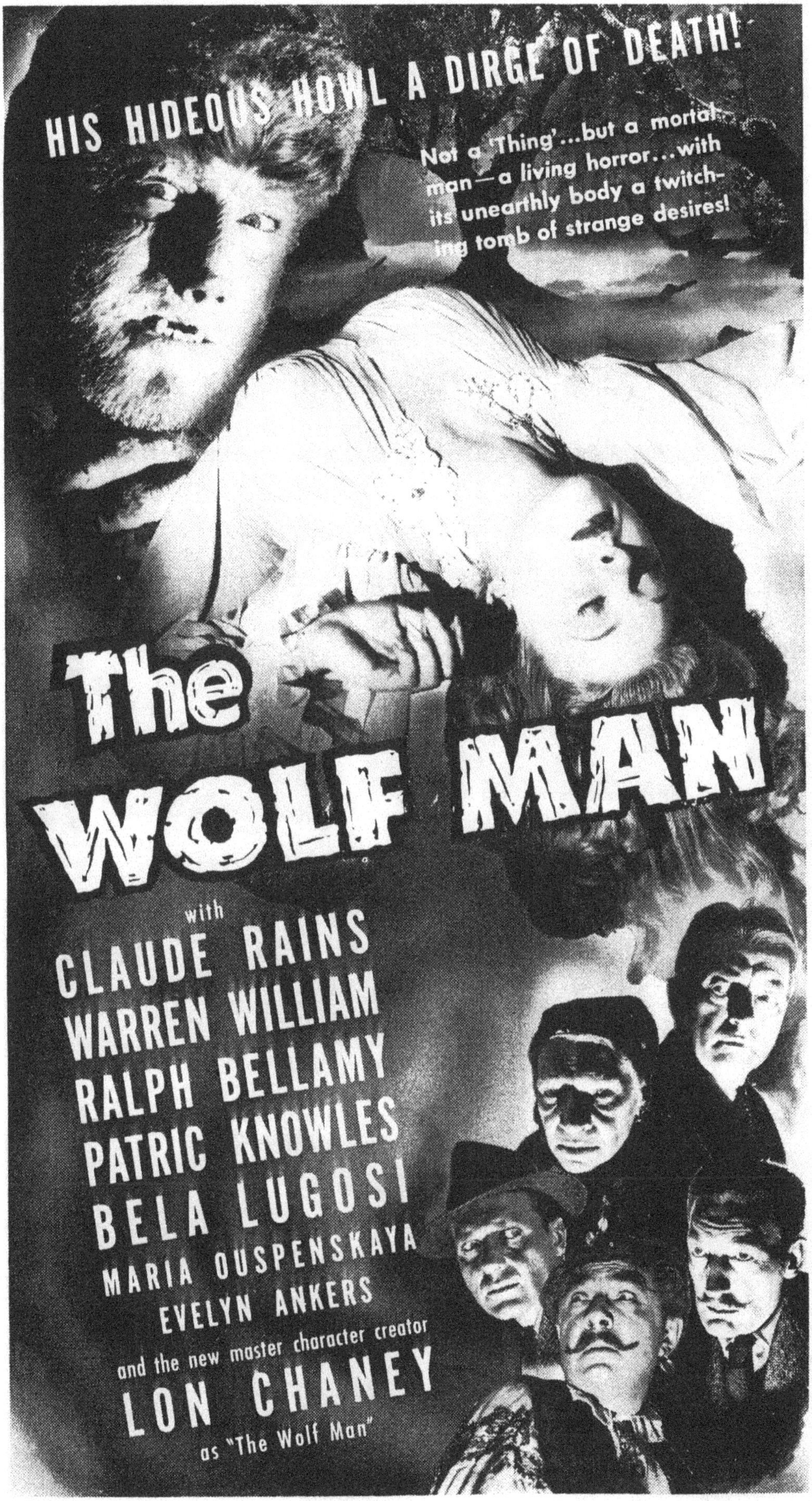

HIS HIDEOUS HOWL A DIRGE OF DEATH!

Not a 'Thing'...but a mortal man—a living horror...with its unearthly body a twitching tomb of strange desires!

The WOLF MAN

with

CLAUDE RAINS
WARREN WILLIAM
RALPH BELLAMY
PATRIC KNOWLES
BELA LUGOSI
MARIA OUSPENSKAYA
EVELYN ANKERS

and the new master character creator

LON CHANEY

as "The Wolf Man"

Directed by GEORGE WAGGNER • A UNIVERSAL PICTURE • Associate Producer, GEORGE WAGGNER

3B

Ad. No. 3B—3 col.—Mat 45c

POSTERS and ACCESSORIES

24 SHEET Face and background in weird reds, green and black, title in yellow, cast white on black.

3 SHEET

ONE SHEET

22 x 28

WINDOW CARDS

IMPRINT SPACE

ADDED ATTRACTIONS

Regular

IMPRINT SPACE

Midget

14 x 36

SET OF EIGHT 11 x 14's

SIX SHEET

6 x 9 HERALD $2.25 PER M.

Continuity script for the Wolf Man trailer - 1941

Page (Title)

T R A I L E R

"T H E   W O L F   M A N"

With

L O N   C H A N E Y

and

A N   A L L   S T A R   C A S T

PICTURE NO. 1195
DIRECTOR - WAGGNER

DECEMBER 15, 1941

Page One

PICTURE NO. 1195
DIRECTOR - WAGGNER
PAGE ONE

CONTINUITY & DIALOGUE

T R A I L E R

ON

"T H E   W O L F   M A N"

With

L O N   C H A N E Y

and

A N   A L L   S T A R   C A S T

1.   IN MIST-FILLED WOOD
     Words come on - move up -   MUSIC

     The Legend of the Damned

     In many a distant village
     there exists the Legend
     of the Werewolf or Wolf
     Man ... a legend of a
     strange mortal man with the
     hair and fangs of an un-
     earthly beast ... his
     hideous howl a dirge of
     death -   HOWL OF WOLF

     Background changes to

     DIFFERENT SHOT OF WOODS
     Wolf Man in f.g. by graves
     - howling over body of man -

     ...SWINGING DIAGONAL WIPE

     MED. CLOSE SHOT IN VILLAGE
     Lamp-post in f.g. - words   MUSIC
     come on -

     (Continued)

Page Two

PAGE TWO

1.   (Continued)
     UNIVERSAL Presents

              A
     MASTERPIECE
     OF HORROR   MUSIC

     Words exit - man running
     - other words come on -

     "THE WOLF MAN"

     Words exit -

     ...OPENING CIRCLE TO

     LARGE CLOSE UP SIR JOHN TALBOT
     Words come on -   "

          With
          Claude RAINS

     Words exit -
     ...SCALLOPED HORIZONTAL WIPE

     CLOSE UP IN CHURCH
     Dr. Lloyd and Colonel Montford
     seated in pew back of Sir John   "
     and old man - two men looking
     around - words come on -

          Warren WILLIAM

     Words exit -
     ...SCALLOPED HORIZONTAL WIPE

     CLOSE VIEW IN WOODS
     Col. Montford in f.g. - words
     come on - gypsies in b.g. -   "
          Ralph BELLAMY

     Words exit -

     ...SCALLOPED HORIZONTAL WIPE

Page Three

PAGE THREE

1.   (Continued)
     CLOSE UP IN ROOM
     Frank Andrews crossing -   MUSIC
     name comes on -

          Patric KNOWLES

     Name exits -
     ...RISING SCALLOPED WIPE

     CLOSE UP GYPSY
     Startled - name comes on -   "

          Bela LUGOSI

     Name exits -
     ...RISING SCALLOPED WIPE

     CLOSE UP MALEVA THE GYPSY
     Old woman looking off - name   "
     comes on -

          Maria OUSPENSKAYA

     Name exits -
     ...RISING SCALLOPED WIPE

     CLOSE UP GWEN CONLIFFE
     Frightened - name comes on -   "

          Evelyn ANKERS

     Name exits -
     ...OPENING CIRCLE WIPE

     CLOSE UP IN GYPSY CAMP
     Larry Talbot looking off -   "
     name comes on -

          and LON CHANEY

     Name exits
     ...DISSOLVES INTO

1. (Continued)
   LARGE CLOSE UP WOLF MAN
   Words come on -   MUSIC

   - as
     THE WOLF MAN

   Words exit -
   ...OPENING TRIANGLE WIPE

   IN THE GRAVEYARD
   Man with lanterns - body in
   f.g. by open grave -   "
                                           WOLF'S HOWL

                MAN'S VOICE - Isn't that the way
                     Johnny Williams was killed?

                DOCTOR - Yes. Find something?

                MONTFORD - Animal tracks.

   ...OPENING DIAGONAL CROSS

   CLOSE VIEW IN CARAVAN
   Woman seated in f.g. - Bela
   turns and faces f.g. -   MUSIC

                JENNY - What did you see?
                     Something evil?

                BELA - No, no!

2. CLOSE UP IN DOORWAY
   Bela frightened - speaks   MUSIC

                BELA - Go quickly! GO!

   ...CLOSING ANGLE WIPE

---

2. (Continued)
   CLOSE SHOT INT. BEDROOM
   Larry seated on bed - Sir   MUSIC
   John, Dr. Lloyd and Col.
   Montford standing - talking -

                SIR JOHN - Paul wants to ques-
                     tion him. Go ahead.

                LARRY - Yeah. But don't try
                     to tell me that I killed
                     a man when I know I killed
                     a wolf.

   ...OPENING SLANTED HOLE

   CLOSE UP IN TENT
   Maleva seated - Larry stand-   MUSIC
   ing - she talks - he comes
   forward -

                MALEVA - Whoever is bitten by a
                     werewolf - and lives - be-
                     comes a werewolf himself.

                LARRY - Aw, don't hand me that!
                     You're just wasting your
                     time.

                MALEVA - The wolf bit you,
                     didn't he?

                LARRY - Yeah! Yeah, he did!

   ...OPENING VERTICAL WIPE

   CLOSE UP BEFORE FIREPLACE
   Sir John and Dr. Lloyd stand-   MUSIC
   ing - talking -

                DOCTOR - Your son is a sick man
                     He has received a shock that
                     has caused definite psychic
                     maladjustment. You must
                     send him out of this village.

                SIR JOHN - You're talking like a
                     witch doctor.

   ...RISING SQUARE WIPE

---

2. (Continued)
   CLOSE UP INT. SHOT   MUSIC
   Larry and Gwen talking -

                LARRY - You wouldn't want to run
                     away with a murderer, would
                     you?

                GWEN - Oh, Larry! You're not!
                     You know you're not!

                LARRY - I killed Bela. I killed
                     Richardson! If I stay here
                     any longer you can't tell
                     who'll be next!

   ...BROKEN DIAGONAL WIPE

   CLOSE SHOT IN WOODS
   Larry passes back of large   MUSIC
   tree in f.g. - looks off

   IN THE WOODS
   Searching party with flares   "
   etc -

4. ANOTHER SHOT IN WOODS   "
   Gwen running across clearing
   to f.g. -

5. LARGE CLOSE UP WOLF MAN   "
   Peering through branches

                WOLF MAN - Howls

6. CLOSE SHOT IN WOODS
   Gwen startled - stops -
   Larry runs on - attacks   MUSIC - HOWLING
   her -

                GWEN - Screams

---

7. CLOSE UP IN WOODS
   Larry howling - comes forward
   - words on -

                NIGHT MONSTER   MUSIC - HOWLING

   Words exit -

   ...OPENING DIAGONAL WIPE

   IN THE WOODS
   Man crosses in f.g. with blazing   "
   torch - others moving about in
   b.g. - words on -

                PROWLING ...
                     KILLING ...
                          TERRIFYING
                     A COUNTRYSIDE ...

   Words exit - others come on -

                - WITH THE
                     BLOOD LUST OF A SAVAGE   "
                          BEAST!

   Words exit -

   ...OPENING DIAGONAL DIAMOND WIPE

   CLOSE UP WOLF MAN   "
   Words over it -

                "THE WOLF MAN"

                A UNIVERSAL HORROR HIT!

Appendix

On June 11, 1590, a man was brought to trial having been accused of being a Werewolf. The transcript, translated from Dutch into English by E. Venge, is reproduced in Old English - exactly as entered on June 22, 1590 (The trial took place in the present area of Holland which was then considered upper or high Germany):

A True Discourse Declaring the Damnable Life and Death of One
Stubbe Peeter,
A most Wicked Sorcerer, Who in the Likeness of a Wolf
Committed Many Murders, Continuing This Devilish Practise 25
Years, Killing and Devouring Men, Women, and Children.
Who for the Same Fact Was, Taken and Executed
the 31st of October Last Past
in the Town of Bedbur, Near the City of Collin in Germany

In the towns of Cperadt and Bedbur near Collin in high Germany there was continually brought up and nourished one Stubbe Peeter, who from his youth was greatly inclined to evil and practising of wicked arts, surfeiting in the damnable desire of magic, necromancy and sorcery, acquainting himself with many infernal spirits and fiends. The Devil, who hath a ready ear to listen to the lewd motions of cursed men, promised to give him whatsoever his heart desired during his mortal life; whereupon this vile wretch, having a tyrannical heart and a most cruel bloody mind, requested that at his pleasure he might work his malice on men, women, and children, in the shape of some beast, whereby he might live without dread or danger of life, and unknown to be the executor of any bloody enterprise which he meant to commit. The Devil gave him a girdle which, being put around him, he was transformed into the likeness of a greedy, devouring wolf, strong and mighty, with eyes great and large, which in the night sparkled like brands of fire, a mouth great and wide, with most sharp and cruel teeth, a huge body and mighty paws. And no sooner should he put off the same girdle, but presently he should appear in his former shape, according to the proportion of a man, as if he had never been changed.

Stubbe Peeter herewith was exceedingly well pleased, and the shape fitted his fancy and agreed best with his nature, being inclined to blood and cruelty. Therefore, satisfied with this strange and devilish gift (for it was not troublesome but might be hidden in a small room, he proceeded to the execution of heinous and vile murders, for if any person displeased him, he would thirst for revenge, and no sooner should they or any of theirs walk in the fields or the city, but in the shape of a wolf he would presently encounter them and never rest till he had plucked out their throats and torn their joints asunder. And after he had gotten a taste hereof, he took such pleasure and delight in shedding of blood, that he would night and day walk the fields and work extreme cruelties. And sundry times he would go though the streets of Collin, Bedbur and Cperadt, in comely habit, and very civilly, as one well known to all the inhabitants thereabout, and often-times was he saluted of those whose friends and children he had butchered, though nothing suspected for the same. In these places, I say, he would walk up and down, and if he could spy either maid, wife, or child that his eyes liked or his heart lusted after, he would wait their issuing out of the city or town. If he could by any means get them alone, he would in the fields, ravish them and after in his wolvish likeness cruelly murder them. Often it came to pass that as he walked abroad in the fields, if he chanced to spy a company of maidens playing together or else milking their kine, in his wolvish shape he would run among them, and while the rest escaped by flight, he would be sure to lay hold of one, and after his filthy lust fulfilled, he would murder her presently. Besides, if he had like or known any of them, her he would pursue, such was his swiftness of foot while he continued a wolf that he would outrun the swiftest greyhound in the country; and so much he had

practised this wickedness that the whole province was frightened by the cruelty of this bloody and devouring wolf. Thus continuing his devilish and damnable deeds, with the compass of a few years, he had murdered thirteen young children, and two goodly young women bit with child, tearing the children out of thei wombs, in most bloody and savage sort, and after ate their hearts panting, hot and raw, which he accounted dainty morsels and best agreeing to his appetite.

Moreover, he used many times to kill lambs an kids and such like beasts, feeding on the same most usually raw and bloody, as if he had been a natural wolf indeed.

He had at that time living a fair young daughter, after whom he also lusted most unnaturally, and cruelly committed most wicked incest with her, a most gross and vile sin, far surmounting adultery or fornication, though the last of the three doth drive the soul into hell fire, except hearty repentance, and the great mercy of God. This daughter of his he begot when he was not altogether so wickedly given, who was called by the name of Stubbe Beell, who beauty and good grace was such as deserved commendations of all those that knew her. And such was his inordinate lust and filthy desire toward her, that he begat a child by her, daily using her as his concubine, but as an insatiate and filthy beast, given over to work evil, with greediness he also lay by his own sister, frequenting her company long time. Moreover, being on a ere he thence departed he so won the woman by his fair and flattering speech, and so much prevailed, that ere he departed the house, he lay by her, and ever after had her company at his command, this woman exceeding good favour and one that was well esteemed among her neighbours. But his lewd and inordinate lust being not satisfied with the company of many concubines, nor his wicked fancy contented with the beauty of any woman, at length the Devil sent unto him a wicked spirit in the similitude and likeness of a woman, so fair of face and comely of personage, that she resembled rather some heavenly sort of women, and with her, as with his hear's delight, he kept company the space of seven years, though in the end she proved and was found indeed no other than a she-Devil. Notwithstanding, this lewd sin of lechery did not any thing assuage his cruel and bloody mind, but continuing an insatiable bloodsucker, so great was the joy he took therein, that he accounted no day spent in pleasure wherein he had not shed some blood, not respecting so much who he did murder as how to murder and destroy them, as the matter ensuing doth manifest, which may stand for a special note of a cruel and hard heart. For, having a proper youth to his son, begotten in the flower and strength of his age, the first fruit of his body, in whom he took such joy that he did commonly call him his heart's ease, yet so far his delight in murder exceeded the joy he took in his son, that thirsting after his blood, on a time he enticed him into the fields, and from thence into a forest hard by, where, making excuse to stay about the necessaries of nature, while the young man went forward, in the shape and likeness of a wolf he encountered his own son and there most cruelly slew him, which done, he presently ate the brains out of his head as a most savory and dainty delicious means to stanch his greedy appetite: the most monstrous act that ever man heard of, for never was known a wretch from nature so far degenerate.

Long time he continued his vile and villainous life, sometime in the likeness of a wolf, sometime in the habit of a man, sometime in the towns and cities, and sometime in the woods and thickets to them adjoining, whereas the Dutch copy maketh mention, he on a time met with two men and one woman, whom he greatly desired to murder. In subtle sort he conveyed himself far before them in their way and craftily couched out of their sight, but as soon as they approached near the place where he lay, he called one of them by his name, supposing it was some familiar friend that in jesting sort stood out of his sight, went from his company toward the place from whence the voice proceeded, of purpose to see who it was, but he was no sooner entered within the danger of this transformed man, but he was murdered in that place, the rest of his company staying for him, expecting still his return, but finding his stay over long, the other man left the woman and went to look for him, by which means the second man was also murdered. The woman then seeing neither of both return again, in heart unsuspected that some evil had fallen upon them, and therefore, with all the power she had, she sought to save herself by flight, though it nothing prevailed, for, good soul, she was also soon overtaken by this light-footed wolf, who, when he had first deflowered, he after most cruelly murdered. The men were after found mangled in the wood, but the woman's body was never after seen, for she he had most ravenously devoured, whose flesh he esteemed by sweet and dainty in taste.

Thus this damnable Stubbe Peeter lived the term of five and twenty years, unsuspected to be author of so many cruel and unnatural murders, in which time he had destroyed and spoiled an unknown number of men, women and children, sheep, lambs, and goats and other cattle, for, when he could not through the wariness of people draw men, women, or children in his danger, then, like a cruel and tyrannous beast, he would work his cruelty on brute beasts in most savage sort, and did act more mischief and cruelty than would be credible, although high Germany hath been forced to taste the truth thereof.

By which means the inhabitants of Collin, Bedbur, and Cperadt seeing themselves so grievously endangered, plagued, and molested by this greedy and cruel wolf, insomuch that few or none durst travel to or from those places without good provision of defence, and all for fear of this devouring and fierce wolf, for oftentimes the inhabitants found the arms and legs of dead men, women and children scattered up and down the fields to the great grief and vexation of heart, knowing the same to be done by that strange and cruel wolf, whom by no means they could take or overcome, so that if any man or woman missed their child, they were out of hope ever to see it again alive and here is to be noted a most strange thing which setteth forth the great power and merciful providence of God to the comfort of each Christian heart. There were not long ago certain small children playing in a meadow together hard by the town, where also some store of kine were feeding, many of them having young calves sucking upon them. And suddenly among these children come this vile wolf running and caught a pretty fine girl by the collar, with intent to pull out her throat, but such was the will of God, that the wolf could not pierce the collar of the child's coat, being high and very well stiffened and close clasped about her neck, and therewithal the sudden great cry of the rest of the children which escaped so amazed the cattle feeding by, that being fearful to be robbed of their young, they altogether came running against the wolf with such force tha he was presently compelled to let go his hold and to run away to escape the danger of their horns, by which means the child was preserved from death, and, God be thanked, remains living at this day.

And that this thing is true, Master Tice Artine, a brewer dwelling at Puddlewarfe in London, being a man of that country born, and one of good reputation and account, is able to justify, who is near kinsman to this child, and hath from thence twice received letters, concerning the same, and for that the first letter did rather drive him into wondering at the act then yielding credit thereunto, he had shortly after, at request of his writing, another letter sent to him, whereby he was more fully satisfied, and divers other persons of great credit in London hath in like sort received letters from their friends to the like effect.

Likewise in the towns of Germany aforesaid continual prayer was used unto God that it would please Him to deliver them from the danger of this greedy wolf.

And, although they had practised all the means that men could devise to take the ravenous beast, ye until the Lord had determined his fall, they could not in any wise prevail, notwithstanding they daily sought to entrap him and for the intent continually maintained great mastiffs, and dogs of much strength to hunt and chase the beast. In the end, it pleased God, as they were in readiness and proved to meet with him, that they should espy him in his wolvish likeness at what time they beset him round about, and most circumspectly set their dogs upon him, in such sort that here was no means of escape, at which advantage they never could get him before, but as the Lord delivered Goliath into the hands

of David, so was this wolf brought in danger of these men, who, seeing as I said before, no easy way to escape the imminent danger, being hardly pursued at the heals, presently slipped his girdle from about him, whereby the shape of a wolf clean avoided, and he appeared presently in his true shape and likeness, having in his hand a staff as one walking toward the city, but the hunters, whose eyes were steadfastly bent upon the beast, and seeing him in the same place metamorphosed contrary to the expectations, it wrought a wonderful amazement to their minds, and, had it not been that they knew the man so soon as they saw him, they had surely taken the same to have been some Devil in man's likeness, but forasmuch as they knew him to be an ancient dweller in the town, they came unto him, and talking with him, they brought him home to his own house, and finding him to be the man indeed, and no delusion or phantastical motion, they had him before the magistrates to be examined.

Thus being apprehended he was shortly after put to the rack in the town of Bedbur, but fearing the torture, he voluntarily confessed his whole life, and made know the villainies which he had committed for the space of twenty-five years, also he confessed how by sorcery he procured of the Devil a girdle, which being put on, he forthwith became a wolf, which girdle at his apprehension he confessed he cast it off in a certain valley and ther left it , which, when the magistrates heard, they sent to the valley for it, but at their coming found nothing at all, for it may be supposed that it was gone to the Devil from whence it came, so that it was not to be found. For the Devil having brought the wretch to all the shame he could, left him to endure the torments which his deeds deserved.

After he had some space been imprisoned, the magistrates found out through due examination of the matter, that his daughter Stubbe Beell and his Gossip Katherine Trompin, were both accessory to diverse, murders committed, were arraigned, and with Stubbe Peeter condemned, and their several judgements pronounced the 29th of October 1589, in this manner, that is to say: Stubbe Peeter as principal malefactor, was judged first to have his body laid on a wheel, and with red hot burning pincers in ten places to have the flesh pulled off from the bones, after that, his legs and arms to be broken with a wooden axe or hatchet, afterward to have his head struck from his body, then to have his carcase burned to ashes.

Also his daughter and his Gossip were judged to be burned quick to ashes, the same time and day with the carcase of the aforesaid Stubbe Peeter. And on the 31st of the same month, they suffered death accordingly in the town of Bedbur in the presence of many peers and princes of Germany.

Thus Gentle Reader, have I set down the true discourse of this wicked man Stubbe Peeter, which I desire to be a warning to all sorcerers and witches, which unlawfully follow their own devilish imagination to the utter ruin and destruction of their souls eternally, from which wicked and damnable practice, I beseech God keep all good men, and from the cruelty of their wicked hears. Amen

After the execution, there was by the advice of the magistrates of the town of Bedbur a high pole set up and strongly framed, which first went through the wheel whereon he was broken, whereunto also it was fastened, after that a little above the wheel the likeness of a wolf was framed in wood to show unto all men the shape wherein he executed those cruelties. Over that on the top of the stake the sorcerer's head itself was set up, and round about he wheel there hung as it were sixteen pieces of week about a yard in length which represented the sixteen person that were perfectly known to be murdered by him. And the same ordained to stand there for a continual monument to all ensuing ages, what murders by Stubbe Peeter were committed, with the order of his judgement, as this picture doth more plainly express.

Witnesses that this is true: Tyse Artyne, William Bewwar, Adolf Staedt, George Bores. With divers others that have seen the same:

Trial transcript STC 23375, f. E. Venge: Entered June 1590

www.ingramcontent.com/pod-product-compliance
Lightning Source LLC
Chambersburg PA
CBHW050353110426

42812CB00008B/2449